Alice Wright Douse died on July 12, 2016 at the age of 86. She lived a beautiful life as a woman of tremendous faith with a loving character, spirit of generosity, and a heart for servant leadership. Her legacy continues to live on in her family, church, the community and in the work she loved – education. The **Marion J. and Alice W. Douse Community Center** on the campus of Anderson Chapel AME Church in Killeen, Texas was dedicated in November 2015. Soon after, in April 2016, the School Board of the Killeen Independent School District (KISD) voted unanimously to name the thirty-fourth school of the district after Mrs. Douse, the first African American female principal in KISD. The school will be a premier learning environment for up to 1,000 students and opens August 28, 2017 for the inaugural 2017-2018 school year. **Alice W. Douse Elementary School** is the first school in KISD to be named after an African-American.

TAPESTRY

A Collection of Historical Experiences,
Memorable Achievements and Honorable Service
by African-American Families about their
Community Building in a Central Texas city
that now celebrates its Diversity

A collection of memories compiled by the
Community Building and Builders Task Force

Alice Wright Douse

PRESS

Acknowledgements

—ໝ—

Alice Douse

This book was made possible by the support and participation of residents of Killeen and neighboring cities. Thank you! I thank God for His guidance throughout the process and for all the people He provided to assist me.

To the Task Force: Melba Olean Davis, Cloerine Brewer, Mabel May Robinson, Wadella Heath, Hazel Daniels, Shirley Wilson, Thelma Jackson, the late Katie Gibson, Rev. Bertie Sworn, Bobbye Wade and Tommie Jackson, special thanks to each of you, the *Community Builders and Building Task Force*, for valuing the importance of collecting and preserving the history of African America families, their service and accomplishments.

To the participating families, individuals, and churches, I am especially grateful for your participation and the journals you submitted, because your journals collectively tell the history of experiences and events that are shared in this book.

Thank you editorial and publishing departments for your essential guidance, encouragement and patience in the completion of this book. My appreciation to Dainelle Riley of Daydreamer Design for capturing my vision and creating a beautiful cover design.

My wholehearted thanks and appreciation to LaQuita Clark, Lois Fields, Elijah King and two other helpful friends for your willingness to give a greater measure of support to the completion of this book. How grateful I am to you for your extra effort of support to insure the success of this book.

My sincere thanks to Betsy Hilliard, Pat Shannon, John Odom, Jr., the Saegert Family and the late Mildred Shine and Tommy J. Mills, Sr. for the very useful, enlightening and enriching information received from each of you I am thankful and greatly indebted to my family. My sister, Claudy Strong, spent many hours reading and editing copies of journals; my daughters: Cathy, Mtisha, Glenda and Carla, also granddaughters: Yvette and Lea gave assistance in many ways. To my husband, Marion J. Douse, whose love and generous support and encouragement made it possible for me to spend countless hours working on this project, *I Thank God for you.*

Now, to my friends who gave encouragement, I extend my sincere appreciation to you. A final thank you to all community builders whose journals are not recorded in this book. Your invaluable contributions of honorable service and achievements have led to a progressive and diverse community in which we live.

Dedication

—៣—

~To the Trailblazers for courageously persevering in faith
and laying the early foundation for establishing a
community for African Americans in Killeen, Texas.

~To the Youth who experienced the challenges of an emerging
community and met them with courage, dignity and respect; then
developed into responsible and productive citizens
who now embrace opportunities that enrich the
communities in which they reside.

Preface

—⁓⁓—

⁓⁓*

It should be noted that throughout this collection of journals, a variety of terms were used by the families to define themselves as people of African descent. The terms included colored, Negro, Black, African-American and people of color. The usage sometimes depended on the decade or particular period in history, as well as, the personal preferences and experiences of each family.

Three events served as the inspiration for this book. *The first* was the encouragement I received at a Black History program that was sponsored by students of Manor Middle School and their teacher Eltra Youngblood. The encouragement was in response to a reading I presented entitled "Did you know?" *The second event* was a gathering in my home of a group of residents or former residents of the Marlboro Heights and Simmonsville communities to talk about our family history in Killeen. Melba Olean Davis, Mabel May Robinson, Wadella Heath, Bertie Sworn and Katie Gibson attended. Jimmy Ferguson, a Killeen Daily Herald staff writer, interviewed the group and wrote a newspaper article about the project. *The third event* was the gathering of this same group with me at Marlboro Elementary School Library where we continued recalling in greater detail our experiences, accomplishments, sacrifices and contributions of community service since arriving to Killeen and

Fort Hood. Bobbye Wade and Cloerine Brewer who were task force members were also in attendance. There we talked about "old times" and spent a lot of time reminiscing about the early days and how things had changed. We remembered the music of that period that was no longer being played, identified places that no longer existed, recalled our difficult experiences and our happy times. We also discussed the cooperative efforts of families as they settled earlier in Simmonsville and later in Marlboro Heights; and how they were focused on developing a self-sufficient, self-sustaining and self-reliant community for African Americans. By the close of the gathering the group agreed that we should capture as much history of our positive contributions to the community as possible through a community-wide project and publish that history for the preservation of our heritage in Killeen. After the group's acceptance of the suggested plan for the project, this same group of women, including Tommie Jackson, Shirley Wilson and Hazel Daniels agreed to serve as the *"Community Building and Builders Task Force."* Thelma Jackson, Lois Fields and Elijah King also assisted the group with photos.

Several weeks later, the Marlboro Heights and Simmonsville residents filled Marlboro Elementary School cafeteria to hear about the proposed project of capturing African American history through family journals that they would provide. The response from the residents was very positive. The proposal also received commitments from residents to participate. Those participating were given an information packet with instructions and suggestions for getting started with their journaling and the project was considered "launched". Participating residents were also instructed to contact the chairperson for assistance or for additional information. An announcement was published in the local newspaper that invited others to participate. In addition to Killeen residents, the residents from surrounding towns of Harker Heights, Copperas Cove, Belton and Fort Hood, Texas also participated in the project. After the submission and review of all journals the name *TAPESTRY* was selected as the title.

TAPESTRY, African-American History woven throughout the years was developed using the input of many families. We believed that by using family journals to collect the memories of events and family experiences we would gather much of the history we were seeking. This collection of journals relates the experiences and accomplishments of individuals and families and includes their contributions of service and citizen responsibility given toward the progress of this community and city. The book title, *TAPESTRY*, suggests the idea used to collect and develop this history. We were reminded that we can take the memories of events and our experiences to learn of our history because our lives are like sheets of fabric intricately woven with the blending of a rich variety of interesting and memorable events that can produce a vivid and informative history. *TAPESTRY* as a title also reminds us that just as our weaving with many threads in different colors and textures can form an image designed to tell a story when we create tapestry art work; our experiences are uniquely designed and are intertwined with interesting successes and challenges that can form images which create a historical tapestry of our lives. Therefore, it is our expectation that after the reader has read the variety of stories that were in the collection of family journals; collectively, this will produce for the readers a broader, richer and truer picture of the changing phases of African-American life and history in this community.

    TAPESTRY will hold your interest while giving enlightenment about the history and resilience of a group of people who overcame obstacles. You will recognize reoccurring historical and human interest themes that appear in some of the journals regarding housing, employment and personal life experiences. As we envisioned, there exists variety in perspectives within the collection of journals. Some journals show variety in the topics that families chose to talk about. Others reveal the challenges families encountered; and still others show the approaches of families in seizing the available opportunities that were presented to them. In addition some journals confirm that as early as the 1950s there have been African-American residents in the community that were well qualified to provide leadership and hold professional, as well as, civic positions within the city.

The Task Force Pursues Questions of Interest

Killeen, Texas now a very fast growing and diverse city had no African American residents prior to the establishment of Camp Hood. Therefore the task force first sought to determine at what point African Americas became residents of the city. There were three questions of many explored that garnered interest as the "history project" was launched. These were: (1) Who were the first African American residents to settle in the Killeen area? (2) What were their contributions to community building? (3) What contributions did African Americans make who arrived later to the progress of the city? Three sources brought information to the Community Building and Builders Task Force upon which our search was able to build. In a previous writing related to the history of Killeen the author, Gra'Delle Duncan wrote, "The first black ever to work in Killeen is believed to have been employed by T. O. Raney at his garage during the early part of the construction of Camp Hood. As there was no place for him to live, Raney fixed up a cot along with other facilities at the garage and brought his meals to him. He was locked in at night for his protection, but this turned out to be unnecessary"[1]

The second source came early during our launching of this project as the task force was researching to learn about Killeen's earliest African American residents. It was then that Mildred Shine, a native of Killeen, wrote to me (the *Community Builders Task Force* chairperson) and contributed information that enlightened us further about early African American residents in Killeen. She wrote: "Dear Alice, a little bit of information for your book as I promised. Jim Solomon and his wife, Alice, lived in a small house in the rear of Mr. and Mrs. T. O. Raney's house at the 1200 block of Gray Street. Mr. Raney owned a Texaco Station on the Southwest corner of 4th Street and Avenue D. Jim worked there in the back, mounting tires, fixing flats, changing oil, etc. In 1946, when Lewis, my husband (deceased as you know) was discharged from the Army, he and his brother bought into (and later outright) the business. We moved on Gray Street also in 1946. Alice's small son, Cecil Ray,

---

[1] Gra'Delle Duncan, Killeen Tale of Two Cities, 1st, edition. (Eakin Publications, Inc., Austin, Texas 1984), p.97.

was not school age. She did housework for the neighbors and me until they moved. Their hometown was either Bartlett or Rosebud. However, Jim continued to work at the Texaco Service Station for several years with Richard Maze."[2]

Our third source of information came from a task force member, Melba Olean Stacy Davis. Her journal is included in this book. Within her story the task force learned that African American families had lived near the railroad at a place called the "Gin" in the vicinity of the present Chamber of Commerce building. One of the tenants was Melba's relative, Richard Maze, who was the head of his household there. He moved to Killeen in 1946. Melba Olean had also lived at the "Gin" in downtown Killeen with her sister, Osia, and brother-in-law, Richard Maze. As the task force chairperson, I visited with the late Tommy J. Mills and the E. A. Saegert family and learned about the Killeen Gins. Literature from the Saegert family identified the specific Gin that was on Second Street, just south of the railroad in the vicinity of the Chamber of Commerce, as the "Rock Gin".[3] The task force co-chair, Wadella Heath, and I visited the Killeen Daily Herald and Bell County Courthouse archives in search of information to use in this project. Our findings were very limited. In view of the information that we have obtained it appears that Jim Solomon's family, Richard Maze's family, Oratha (Uncle Fuzzy) Flakes' family also Sam and Olean Stacy's family were among Killeen's earliest black residents that we have knowledge of at this time.

KILLEEN, TEXAS

The setting for this book is Killeen, Texas. "The city of Killeen was established May 15, 1882, with the arrival of the first train to this agricultural area. It was named for one of the railroad officials, Frank P. Killeen. The original town loosely included the area between Rancier Avenue on the north, College Street on the west, Hallmark on the south and Eighth Street on the east. However, from Business Highway 190 south to Hallmark comprised "out blocks,"

---

[2]   Mildred Shine, "Letter", Killeen, Texas

[3]   E.A. Saegert, "Saegert Gin Purchase, Operation, and Fire." Killeen, Texas.

not included in the Plat for the original town."[4] Killeen is located in southwest Bell County and is now among the fast growing cities in Texas. Its neighbors to the west are Fort Hood (the largest Army post in the free world) and Copperas Cove. Its neighbors to the east are Harker Heights and Nolanville. Simmonsville and Marlboro Heights are two communities within Killeen that were designated during the forties through early sixties as the only neighborhoods where African Americans could live. The early residents of these two neighborhoods in Killeen established churches, and at the beginning of 1954 their children attended the neighborhood school in Marlboro Heights. Killeen's growth began in 1942 with the establishment of Camp Hood and has continued for over seventy years. Camp Hood also changed the city's racial, religious and ethnic composition. It was formerly a town with no African American residents before 1942; but by early 1943 a few African Americans had begun working and living in the Killeen area. Camp Hood was re-commissioned Fort Hood in 1950 and the neighborly locations of the Fort Hood and Killeen communities resulted in a unique and supportive relationship over the years. This contributed greatly to Killeen's growth and development. The population increased from 1,300 in 1949 to 7,045 in 1950. By 1955, Killeen had an estimated 21,076 residents; 1960—23,377; 1970—35,507; 1980—49,307 and 1990—63,535 residents.[5] In 2000, visitors to Killeen experienced a cosmopolitan or metropolitan city with a population of 86,911. The population in the 2010 Census reached 127,921, with the African-Americans' count alone at 43,610, or 34.09%, and Whites at 57,736, or 77.06 %.[6]

Killeen is now one of the more diversely populated cities in the state of Texas. A unique relationship still exists between Killeen and Fort Hood. The Killeen's business community provides employment opportunities to military dependents and Fort Hood provides employment opportunities to many of the city's civilian residents.

---

[4] Gra'Delle Duncan, Killeen Tale of Two Cities, p.3.

[5] John Leffler, KILLEEN, TX, *"Handbook of Texas Online"*, http://www.tshaonline.org/handbook/online/articles/hdk01

[6] Census Viewer, "Population of Killeen, Texas" http://censusviewer.com/city/TX/Killeen/2010

Military personnel, both active and retired, are homeowners in the Killeen area and in surrounding communities. The city's school district provides the education for military and civilian dependents of Fort Hood, Killeen, Harker Heights and Nolanville residents. Active military personnel and their dependents reside in the city of Killeen, as well as, on the military post. The Killeen area has become a desirable place for families to reside in Central Texas. In 1967, Central Texas College (now named Central Texas University) opened. In 2010, Tarleton State University (now named Texas A & M University – Central Texas) opened. These two institutions provide opportunities for military and civilian residents to receive a college education.

Table of Contents

—ᗯ—

CHAPTER 1

1940-1949:
Camp Hood Ushered in
Diversity for Killeen

—m—

A frican American families became Killeen's newest residents and community builders in this decade. Life experiences that were remembered about the 1940s are shared in this chapter. They were among the early trailblazers who would become the foundation for the establishment of a community" in a city where no African Americans had resided before. A few families first resided in downtown Killeen at a place called "The Gin." Melba Olean Stacy Davis wrote about these first African American residents of Killeen and about other locations where families resided during these early days in her journal. As you read through this collection of journals you will learn about the families who formed the foundation of Killeen's first African American community. You will also learn about their families' experiences, challenges, achievements and contributions as community builders. Some of them remained engaged in community building during future decades. These families demonstrated courage, perseverance and faith as they ventured out in search for a better life and became trailblazers in establishing a community that became the early foundation for African American residents in Killeen. They showed a determination to meet the challenges with which they encountered. They recognized that the opening of Camp Hood would bring other families to the city. They also viewed this time as an opportunity for community building, and their actions ultimately contributed to the development of one of the more uniquely diverse cities in the State of Texas. Meet some of the "Trailblazers" and learn more about them.

Richard T. and Osia O. Maze
A Shared Gift of Service
Richard Wayne Maze and the Task Force

Richard and Osia Maze were among the earliest African American residents in Killeen. Richard, a native of Rockdale, Texas moved to Killeen in 1946. He was employed by Shine Brothers Texaco and Big Chief Company for many years. Prior to this employment he worked for the former owner of the station T. O. Raney. Richard stayed in the employment of Shine Brothers for thirty-three years until his retirement in 1983. He was married to the former Osia Ola Turner a native of Rosebud Texas. They were the parents of eight children. Richard and Osia's involvement in the life of the Simmonsville and Marlboro Heights communities spanned over many years and in many areas. They were among the first group of African Americans to live for a short time in downtown Killeen in the vicinity of the railroad tracks known as the "Gin". Later they moved to the Levy Farm and finally they were among the first homeowners in the Marlboro Heights community. They provided leadership in church, school, with youth and community activities. Richard, while working as an auto mechanic for many years still had time to render service in the Marlboro Heights and Simmonsville communities. His service in the Simmonsville Baptist Church made him highly worthy to wear the title of deacon. He has been credited with holding the church together during a time when they had no pastor. He consistently demonstrated the attributes of dependability, responsibility and sincerity in dealing with others. Osia Maze was gifted in many areas.

She was a community leader in various community organizations. Speaking, teaching, managing, supervising and organizing were gifts she possessed and used in her church ministries and her community activities. Prior to 1962, Boy Scout and Girl Scout troops existed as a community activity. Scouting provided the youth with useful experiences and recreational activities. Osia Maze, Mazelle Beatty McDonald and Jeanne V. Searles were the Girl Scout troop leaders in the 1950s. Former Girl Scouts, even once adults, remember the fun they had with one of their cooking activities at Osia Maze's house. The youth of the sixties and seventies also remember the teen activities that were planned and supervised by Osia and Richard Maze, Willie Vanarsdale and others at the Marlboro Community Youth Center. These adults planned together with other community parents. They coordinated and were overseers of the youth activities in the community. The youth in their conversations speak affectionately about Mrs. Maze and the manner in which the Center was operated. Osia's involvement and her leadership in community organizations is very much a part of her contribution to community building. One of the former youth, Elise O'Neal Spears, commented in her memories of growing up in Marlboro Heights that "No history of Marlboro Heights would be complete without the mention of Mrs. Osia Maze."

Richard Wayne, Sammie and Rev. Charles Edward Maze, the sons of Richard and Osia Maze, participated in the "history project" and shared some memories of their growing up in Marlboro Heights for the family journal. They pursued successful careers after high school, to include college and the military. They are now community builders. Richard Wayne is educated in Criminal Justice. He became the first "on-campus" Juvenile Probation Officer in the 20th-82nd Judicial District Juvenile Probation Department. He is now a public school educator who contributes to the positive development of the youth of this community. Sammie, a Veterans Administration Equal Opportunity Investigator, remembers the Marlboro Heights Community as a place where "neighbors helped one another; parents expected children to respect adults; and elementary school teachers required you to give your best effort at school each day". Rev. Charles Edward Maze, now pastor of Mount Zion Missionary

Baptist Church in Temple, Texas is a faithful and very strong servant for the Lord. As a pastor and spiritual leader, he has had many opportunities to impact the lives of the youth and adults in the church and in the community. He remembers that "occasions such as church celebrations, weddings, and community fellowship activities were outings and times that would bring the community together."

Melba Olean Stacy and Roscoe Davis
My Early Life and Later Experiences in Killeen
Melba Olean Davis

My first visit to Killeen was in 1947. I lived in Rosebud, Texas at that time. I came to Killeen to visit my sister and brother-in-law, Osia and Richard Maze. My Aunt Othella and Uncle Fuzzy were also living here at that time. They all lived at a place called the "Gin." My brother-in-law and uncle worked as automobile mechanics, and my aunt cooked in a restaurant. This first visit was for one weekend. My family's next visit was a year later, December 1948. I moved to Killeen looking for work. Although I had no military ties, I knew that working in the Killeen area would be better than working in the small town of Rosebud due to Killeen's location to Ft. Hood which was known then as Camp Hood. I was a divorced mother with two daughters to support. I met, fell in love and married Sam Stacy who is now deceased. Sam was already working as a service station mechanic and I worked as a maid for 50¢ cents an hour. The only jobs in Killeen at that time for Blacks were service station attendants, automobile mechanics, café cooks, porters and shoe shiners. Sam and Uncle Fuzzy were two of the first few black men to work in Killeen, Texas. Uncle Fuzzy moved from Hoffman, Oklahoma to visit friends in Belton, Texas. He and Sam Stacy decided to come to Killeen near Fort Hood to look for a job and as early as 1943. They were hired at the same service station.

There were other black men who lived and worked in Killeen in the late forties and early fifties. Uncle Fuzzy and Sam Stacy worked as service station attendants. Homer Lee (Blue) Knights was the first black man to hold a job as a porter at the First National Bank; Connie Campbell, Joe Napier (Uncle Joe), Tony Green and Allen Tisdell, Jr. were barber shop attendants, shoe shiners and performed clean up duties. Leroy Walker lived and worked at the Yellow Cab Company. These men worked in Killeen in various capacities all in low paying jobs, but they too were contributing their service with courage to the building of the community. There were other men who lived and worked at Camp Hood. Nathaniel Anderson, a civilian, began working at Camp Hood in late 1942 or early 1943. George Wilson and Jather Seawood troop trained to Camp Hood in 1942. They experienced life as soldiers camped out in north Camp Hood.

My sister and brother-in-law had lived in this place called the "Gin" a year before I moved here. My family moved in with them when we first arrived in Killeen. We occupied a two-room and kitchen shack located near the railroad tracks and not far from the area that now houses the Killeen Chamber of Commerce. The housing and living conditions for Blacks in Killeen at that time were very poor. There were about ten families who occupied these shacks until the city condemned them. My husband's employer, Jack Levy, sent us out to the Lone Star Community (now known as Simmonsville) to talk to William "Bill" Simmons about a place to live. He provided us shelter in a small trailer. The next day he began setting up a boxcar style housing area where Blacks could live. However, many families had moved back to their hometowns and carpooled to get to their jobs in Killeen. Later Uncle Fuzzy rented a three bedroom house from Mr. Farmer whose residence was in Austin, Texas. All four families, who were relatives, moved in the house. The house was located on the corner of Eighth Street and Business 190. It was in the location where the Der Weinerschnitzel building, an "A" shaped building still exists.

When my niece, Brenda Joyce Williams started school, the Killeen schools were not integrated. Blacks had to go to school in Belton. My brother-in-law's employer told us about the school on Camp Hood. The teacher at that time was Mrs. Vera Scott

Wabbington from Belton. She was one of the first black teachers at Fort Hood and in Killeen. However, the school on Post was for the dependents of black military families. Therefore the girls had to attend school in Belton. They rode the city bus to and from school. My sister paid for the rides and at the end of the school year she was reimbursed the money she paid. Mr. Farmer sold his house and once again we had to move. We moved to an area owned by Jack D. Levy and Tom Levy. The houses were located on what was known as the Levy Farm. By then, my sister Osia; brother-in-law Richard Maze; my Uncle Fuzzy and Auntie Othello Flake had already moved to the Levy Farm. Sam, my two daughters and I lived in the rural area of Jack and Tom's Farm until the small children reached school age, then we moved back to Simmonsville to be close to school.

While living in Simmonsville a Baptist preacher, Rev. A. R. D. Hubbard, was sent to oversee the need for a church. He stayed a while and left. This was after other preachers had come to start a church but without success. My father was a preacher and because we were from a religious family, Osia and I along with a few other Blacks met and we organized the first black church in the area. The original name given the church was not Simmonsville Baptist Church. It was after the group met with Bill Simmons and he donated the land on which to build a church that he asked that the church be named for his family. His request was not granted immediately. Reverend Hubbard returned to Killeen a second time to oversee the church. This time after Rev. Hubbard's encouragement, Bill Simmons' request was granted and the church was named Simmonsville Baptist Church. Simmonsville Baptist Church is the oldest church organized as a place of worship by Blacks and for Blacks at that time in Killeen. The first pastor of Simmonsville Baptist Church was Reverend John Wiley Bosier. His daughter, Sarah Sewell, a former resident of the Marlboro Heights community, tells about her father in her journal. During the observance of the 2009 church anniversary I, Olean Davis, was recognized as the only surviving charter member of the church.

In 1954 changes began taking place. The rental duplexes along Stetson, Terrance Avenue and some parts of Lewis and Marlboro Drive in Marlboro Heights did not meet the housing needs of the community's growth. Therefore houses for sale were built for black families in the area. The requirement for starting the building project was that 10 families had to pay a $50 deposit on a house and the project would begin. When the first ten families paid the $50 deposit the project began. There were *more* than ten families who paid deposits to purchase a house. Some of the first black home owners in the Marlboro Heights Community were:

Mattie Lee Buckner	Dock, Jr. and Thelma Jackson
D. S. and Gertrude Freeman	Willie and Georgia Miller
Richard and Osia Maze	Herman and Janice Henry
Leon and Ruth O'Neal	Homer Lee and Willie M. Knight
Milton and Julia Williams	George and Annie Wilson
Jack and Essie Johnson	Mr. and Mrs. Horace Presley
Godfrey and Nonie Langrum	Mr. and Mrs. Yeager
SGT and Mrs. A.B. Lee	Lt. and Mrs. Jones

As the community developed, the properties of the early land and home owners were located on Terrace Drive, Lewis Drive and Highland Avenue. The duplexes along Stetson, Terrace Drive, at the west end of Marlboro and Lewis Drives were rental properties. Hillside Drive was developed later. My sister and brother-in-law's mortgage was seventy-eight dollars a month. My family moved in the new house along with Richard and Osia. I married and in 1968 my husband and I purchased our own house. At that time, we had to pay a deposit of $125 down and our house note was ninety-eight dollars a month.

It was also in 1954 that my children and Osia's children enrolled in Marlboro School which later became Marlboro Elementary. It was the first school in Killeen in which Blacks could enroll. It was located on Parkhill Drive in Marlboro Heights and now the street has been renamed Rev. R. A. Abercrombie Drive in honor of the first pastor of the Marlboro Missionary Baptist Church. Dock Jackson, Jr., was the principal of Marlboro School. He is recognized as the Killeen Independent School District's first black principal. In 2008, the school district re-dedicated Marlboro Elementary School as the Dock Jackson, Jr. Professional Learning Center in recognition of his service to the school district. My seven children and my sister's six children later attended Nolan Junior High School and graduated from Killeen High School.

In 2004, I shared the oral history of the families of Richard and Osia Maze: Uncle Fuzzy, Aunt Othella Flake, and my own family's early life in Killeen in a lecture session at the "Center for African-American Studies and Research" located at Central Texas College. In 2012, I participated in a video production by the City of Killeen where I shared a part of my story as one of the very early black residents of the city. These families that I write about and have talked about were among the earliest Blacks to settle in the Killeen area many years ago.

I have seen many positive changes take place in this city. I completed my high school education and attended college. After twenty years of service with the Killeen School District, I retired as a certified cafeteria manager of one of its elementary school cafeterias having earned wages which far exceeded the 50 cents per hour that I earned when I first came to Killeen. The growth of the city is another positive change, but with it came a negative. The increase in crime has become a threat to peaceful living in Killeen. The reduction of segregation practices and the inclusion of African-Americans in the life of the community are other positive changes. God has richly blessed me. I feel extremely blessed to be a part of Killeen's history.

Vera Scott Wabbington
Mother, Educator, Encourager
Vera Wabbington

I am a native Texan who moved to Killeen in the summer of 1944 to do some student work at Fort Hood and for a while had to live in the civilian barracks on Post. I was employed as a clerk at the Post Exchange and also worked at the Quartermaster Laundry. In April 1951 I joined Iona Davis, and then Cherry, as a teacher at the Fort Hood School for Negroes which was housed in the barracks on the post. It was here that I taught fourth, fifth and sixth grades, while my colleague Vera Lankford taught first, second and third grades.

In 1954, Killeen Independent School District opened Marlboro School and the Fort Hood School for Negroes was closed. It was during this time as students were transitioned to the new school that history was made. Vera Lankford and I were the first black teachers hired by the Killeen Independent School District as classroom teachers and we taught grades 1-8 at Marlboro School in Marlboro Heights. The parents in the community were extremely supportive of the new school. Younger children who previously traveled to the city of Belton, Texas to attend school were no longer burdened with that challenge. The school became an essential convenience because it was a substantial part of the community life for students and their families. I resided in the Belton area from 1944-1958. A few years after getting married I moved to the Midwest.

Because I understand the importance of education and of the importance of effectively delivered instruction to students, I continued my educational journey and earned a Master's Degree in Education from Roosevelt University in Chicago, Illinois. I have more than fifty years of experience in the field of education, and it has given me profound satisfaction and an immeasurable sense of accomplishment. In 1991, the National Association of Black School Educators (NABSE) honored me as Teacher of the Year. The commendation continued in 1992, as I was recognized for Educational Achievement from the NAACP and I was also the recipient of the "Who's Who in American Education Award."

I continued to refine my teaching skills in Gary, Indiana where my compassion for others was evident. Reaching out to those in need was always of paramount importance to me. I cherish and value my family, as well as my many close friendships. This made leaving Gary after twenty-six years more difficult. I was greatly impacted and saddened by the sudden death of two very close friends and co-workers. However, I regained my strength and held steady in my faith to persevere.

It is said of me that my strength and perseverance are reflected in my ability to face difficult life situations and maintain a spirit that is not only hopeful and trusting, but also positive. Having overcome obstacles too numerous to mention I still encourage others and remain an inspiration. My immediate family includes my only son, Jack Wabbington, Jr., who has autism. We reside in Fort Worth, Texas. Still living life to the fullest, I love, I laugh and live.

Maurice and Lester Hamilton
The Wisdom of my Parents:
"Dad as a Visionary and Mom as a Faithful Missionary"
Ethel Hamilton Brown

I am the second born, but the first girl in the union of Maurice and Lester Hamilton. Dad moved to the Killeen area in 1949. Mom moved here in 1951. I had already moved from home in Llano, Texas to Cleveland, Ohio where I resided for twenty-six years. On my vacations, I came to Killeen to visit my family. At that time, not having lived here, my dad and I would sometimes drive around the city and he would point out various areas and talk about the changes made. One conversation that really comes to mind is the day that dad told me about the first time he came to Killeen. The story goes something like this, "Sis (my nickname from dad), when I came to Killeen there was only a post office and service station and, of course, Camp Hood. There were racial signs posted expressing how long a black person should stay in the area. On the other side of the coin, a few years later a realtor drove me up to what is now known as Business 190 and pointed out to me that he would sell me as many acres of land as I wanted for $25.00 per acre. At that time what is now called Marlboro Heights was nothing but wilderness. I thought, "What would I want with this wilderness?" I came to my senses when the value of that property increased and that is when I became a land owner. I am saying this to you because I didn't have a vision then, but since then I have been an aware person and act on projects more readily now." He added, "that's why I always tell you kids to have a goal or target to accomplish and don't stop at nothing less". My dad was owner and operator of one of the earliest black businesses in the Killeen Area. Many people in Killeen will remember Maurice Bar-B-Q. Its first location was in Killeen. He later moved the business to Harker Heights where it is still operated under the name of Maurice Bar-B-Q.

My mom was a housewife and an avid churchgoer and church worker. Both mom and dad were members of Anderson Chapel AME Church. They joined when Anderson Chapel worshiped in the small white church building on Jefferies Avenue. My mom was recognized by the church for her mission work and her faithfulness to the Lord's work. Anderson Chapel AME Church's Missionary Society was renamed in her honor along with another faithful missionary worker of the church, Mary Manjang, as "The Hamilton-Manjang Missionary Society." Anderson Chapel's two mission houses were also named the "Hamilton-Manjang Mission House I" and the "Hamilton-Manjang Mission House II." This group of mission workers at Anderson Chapel continues to faithfully engage in outreach services in the community and in the church. Dad and Mom are both deceased, but we feel that they have both left a legacy to this community. They will forever remain in the hearts of our family.

Maurice and Lester Hamilton
My Dad's early developing
Work Ethics Yielded Rewarding Success
Adalee Hamilton Snell

Maurice Hamilton, the first black businessman in Killeen, was my father. He was born February 3, 1910 in Cedar Valley, located between Austin and Dripping Springs in Texas Hill County. He was the only child of Mrs. Ethel Hamilton. Maurice got his first real taste of work at age five on a ranch in Ozona. He tried his hand at riding a cutting horse and helping herd cattle. He moved to Llano, Texas in 1918 where he met the girl who would become his wife. Her name was Lester Ward. She was nine years old and he was eight. In 1925 Maurice and Lester got married and they had a family of ten children. There were four boys: Maurice Jr.; twins Ronald K. and

29

Donald K. and Roy Allen; six of the children were girls: Ethel M. Hamilton Brown, Thelma L. Hamilton Williams, Adalee Hamilton Snell, Dorothy Hamilton Leonard, Martha J. Hamilton Lockely and Cludett E. Hamilton Johnson.

My dad had a strong and enduring work ethic. Even in the later years of his life he was able to work long hours with a busy schedule and continue to give service with a smile. He began barbecuing in the 1940s with help from his customers. In 1946 he moved to Llano, Texas. He came to Killeen in 1949 to find a place to move his family. Then in 1951 he moved his family to Killeen, Texas. My dad's first business in Killeen was on Business 190 (now known as Veteran Memorial Boulevard) just across the bridge in the area which was then known as the rodeo ground. Then the business burned down in 1968. He then moved the business to Roby's, a restaurant also just off of Business Hwy 190. This building housed Maurice Bar-B-Q and Restaurant. Maurice later moved the business to Harker Heights, Texas, where it is currently located. My sister Thelma, my brother Roy and his wife Della were the family members who worked along with Dad in the business for many years. Since my dad's death, Roy and Della along with family members continue to operate Maurice Real Pit Bar-B-Q. The work ethics of my dad—which he acquired at an early age rewarded him with success. Our dad, Maurice Hamilton, and mother, Lester Hamilton, are deceased now. Their contributions of service in the church and in business were helpful to families in the community.

Robert B. and Bernice Watson
Looking Back on the Way it was Then
Sgt. (Ret) Robert B. Watson

My wife, Bernice, and I reside in the Sunnyside Community of Brookshire, Texas. I recall my Killeen/Fort Hood experiences. "I first came to Fort Hood while working as an ROTC instructor at Prairie View A and M College when we were required to complete an assignment on the Rifle Range. We could fulfill this requirement in either San Antonio or Killeen. Therefore, we were sent to Fort Hood on a one-day assignment. My second assignment to Fort Hood was in 1949 and I was assigned to the 73rd Combat Engineers Battalion, which was a black troop. I lived in the barracks; but my wife lived in Waco, Texas and worked at the Veterans Administration (VA). I left Ft. Hood for Korea in 1950 with an assignment again to a Black troop and returned in 1951. Next I received orders to Fort Sill, Oklahoma where I attended Intelligence School and successfully completed my schooling. Prior to leaving for Intelligence School I submitted my application to return to Prairie View A and M College and when I returned to my unit at Fort Hood my orders assignment was for my return to Prairie View A and M College as I requested. But I kept returning to Fort Hood. In fact I had two more tours to Fort Hood. I was there in 1952 and again in 1956. We moved to the Marlboro Heights Community and resided on Terrace Drive for approximately six months. Leon O'Neal and his wife Ruth who were friends of ours, found the house for us. From Marlboro Heights, my family moved into housing quarters at Fort Hood. My wife Bernice then worked at Hillandale Hospital in Killeen.

"Segregation was a way of life at Fort Hood until 1954. That was nothing new to me. I had lived with it all of my life. If you drove down Headquarters Avenue on Post and turned left on 161st Street, you were in a black neighborhood. All of the troops were black. They had their separate chapel, service club, swimming pool and PX in this neighborhood. They had their bus rules. Downtown Killeen was off limits for the black troops even though there was no place for the troops to go and nothing to do in Killeen. However, we did have a better place to go on Post. We had the Zebra Lounge. It was the one colored club for us until about 1954 when changes on the Post began. It was then when the main club on Fort Hood was opened to everyone. However, they also had separate Enlisted Men Club for E-1 to E-4 and a separate NCO Club for E-5 to E-9. These also existed after this change. The bowling alley and the main commissary were the two places that were never separate. They were open to everyone as long as I can remember. I purchased a car so that I did not have to sit in the back of the bus. There has been a theory relating that Fort Hood literally integrated its troops overnight. If so, the idea of integrating the troops was a positive decision.

31

"Community building had begun when I returned in 1956. It began with the development of the Marlboro Heights Community and among the neighbors who lived there. It was a friendly place to live. The community was also a safe place for families to be. Therefore my family also became involved in community building as we resided in Marlboro Heights. My contribution was through my military service; my wife's contribution was through her work in the community; and together our contribution was by being responsible tenants in the neighborhood and law-abiding citizens in the city."

CHAPTER 2

1950-1959:
Four Quality of Life Decisions

—ɯ—

C amp Hood was re-commissioned as Fort Hood in 1950 and became a permanent post. The first church, Simmonsville Baptist Church, for African Americans was established in this decade. It is now the oldest church established by African Americans in Killeen and is still viable in the community. The influx of soldiers and their families to Fort Hood continued to spark growth in the area. The new arrivals in this decade created a need for housing, especially for African American families. In fact, housing for these new residents was very limited or non-existent before the Marlboro Heights Community was developed. Families met the challenges they encountered in housing. They began helping others by sharing their living quarters with other families until housing could be found. They practiced the principles of being a good neighbor. The new arrivals of the fifties brought with them core values of faith, compassion, respect and a responsible work ethic. These new residents had a belief in family, education, and the practice of positive and loyal citizenship. It was a time when families assumed leadership roles within the Marlboro Heights Community to create a neighborly, caring and respectful neighborhood that developed into a self-sufficient and self-sustaining, self-reliant community. Daily living experiences for this African American community were impacted by four quality-of-life decisions during this decade: (1) the creation of the

Marlboro Heights subdivision, a community of livable yet simple housing; (2) the establishment of two community churches; (3) the opening of a neighborhood school; and (4) the integration of African American students into the previously all-white high school. Fort Hood also got its first top grade African American Sergeant Major, Willie Gibson, in this decade. Retiree Willie Gibson later became Killeen's first African American city council member. During later decades many of these early arriving residents had the opportunity to contribute in significant ways to the larger community of Killeen.

Zevery and the Reverend Lizzie Harge
Founders in Masonry and Church Ministry
Zevery Harge and the Task Force

My wife Lizzie Harge and I are longtime residents of the Simmonsville Community in Killeen, Texas. I am a commercial and portrait photographer and a 1948 graduate of the Southwest School of Photography. I served as the official U.S. Army Photographer for several years at Ft. Hood, Texas. I began my civil service career in 1951, and after more than thirty years of dedicated service, I retired from Civil Service in 1985. After retirement I worked on the military post for two contract agents as a Department of Defense Photographer until 1995, making my total combined service at Ft. Hood, Texas, more than forty years of sharing my profession and service. I captured historical moments and events in the life of organizations and also of individuals in the Ft. Hood/ Killeen Community. We are the parents of three daughters: Joliett Harge, Patricia Williams and Carla Fields.

I also contributed to the progress of the community in other ways. My work in Masonry is known to many in the community. My involvement in Masonry has resulted in a family of Masonic organizations serving this community and surrounding communities. I am a:

- Co-Founder and charter member of the New Light Lodge No. 242 F and A.M. Prince Hall Masons, the first Prince Hall Lodge organized in Killeen.
- Co-Founder and charter member of the Starlette Chapter No. 455 O.E.S., PHA.
- Co-Founder and charter member of the Central Texas Consistory No. 306 AASR/PHA 32 Degree Masons.
- Co-Founder and charter member of the Commanders of the Rite 33 Degree Masons, AASR/PHA.

Reverend Liz Harge is the founding pastor of the St. John Faith Outreach Baptist Church in Killeen. She served as pastor of St. John for more than twenty-eight years. Her first church was started in our home in the Simmonsville Community. In 1985 Rev. Harge and her congregation were inspired to build a new church in the same community which still serves as their present place of worship. She was an inspiration for many pastors, evangelists and other laborers of the gospel throughout the state. She contributed to community building as a pastor, spiritual leader and as a mentor to preachers. Prior to answering the "call to ministry," she was owner and operator of Lizzie's Beauty Salon, which was also located in our home in the Simmonsville community. She was well known for her service to the community as one of the early cosmetologists who contributed to the entrepreneurial base in the Simmonsville and Marlboro Heights communities for many years. In 2007 due to illness, she felt it was necessary to retire. Reverend Charles Kennard was installed as pastor of St. John Faith Outreach Baptist Church in December 2007. We believe that we left a legacy to the community through our community involvement that impacted community life.

Greene G. and Gladys Locke
Early Community Builders
Rev. Velma Hayden

Greene Locke was a native of Valley Mills, Texas, and moved to Killeen in the late 40s or early 50s. He holds the distinction of being Killeen's first African American Reserve Policeman during the 1960s. His presence in the Marlboro Heights community helped the residents feel safe during the early days. Families were sleeping with windows and doors opened, and sitting in their yards at night and he patrolled the community every evening. He was a World War II Veteran and Post Commander of the Veterans of Foreign Wars, Post 9191. He served as a board member of the EEOC on Fort Hood and was knowledgeable in getting projects accomplished as a community builder. He was also a "Master Woodwork Craftsman," and utilized these skills when assisting with renovation projects at Simmonsville Baptist Church and Anderson Chapel AME Church during the early days of their existence. Greene later joined Anderson Chapel AME Church and served on its Board of Trustees. He worked as a supervisor at Fort Hood until his retirement from civil service. He was also an asset to the community in other areas. His involvement in community building included:

- Co-Founder and Charter Member of the New Light Lodge No. 242 F. and A.M. Prince Hall Affiliated Masonic Lodge organized in Killeen.
- One of the three co-founders of the Central Texas Consistory No. 306 AASR-PH;
- A Grand Inspector General; Commander of the Rites 33 Degree Mason; and member of the United Supreme Council in Washington, D.C.

Gladys Locke, his wife, was an early resident of the Simmonsville Community and a part of the group of early planners and organizer of Simmonsville Baptist Church. For many years she was a member of Simmonsville Baptist Church and worked in the church ministries there. In later years she joined her husband, Greene, as a member of Anderson Chapel African Methodist Episcopal Church. Gladys initiated a building project to add a fellowship hall to Anderson Chapel's original structure. A team including Merdine Talley, Thelma Hamilton Williams and her daughter, Doris Locke, along with the membership assisted her in accomplishing this project. It was dedicated to the Lord in memory of her service. When the old church building was torn down, a garden was created and dedicated to Glady's memory as the replacement memorial. Her community building involvement also included service as a member of the Ladies Auxiliary of the VFW Post 9191, the PTA and the church. Greene and Gladys are now deceased; however, they were dedicated community builders.

Joseph L. and Jennie V. Searles Family
Community Involvement that Counts
Joseph "Joe" Searles, III

My mother Jennie V. Searles and I accompanied my father, SFC Joe L. Searles, to Fort Hood, Texas, in 1951. We are natives of Asheville, North Carolina and Washington, D.C. Our first residence was in the barracks that accommodated most military personnel and dependents near what was then called 72nd Street. In 1953, we moved to 704 Central Avenue in Walker Village. This was a brand new Capehart development in honor of Senator Capehart, a member of the U.S. Senate and chairman of the Armed Service Committee. General Dwight Eisenhower, a Republican, was President of the United States. The Governor of Texas was Allen Shivers, a Democrat. Regardless of political parties, Central Texas in the early 1950s was deeply rooted in a very segregated system. Blacks worked in low paying jobs, and were not admitted to movies, restaurants or some clothing stores. They were only allowed then to manifest their basic business at the gas station. Earlier in the forties, Jackie Robinson, an officer at Fort Hood had to catch the bus outside of the city of Killeen. We spent about ten years at Fort Hood before my family left the Killeen area in 1962. I returned to Killeen during the 1960s and again in 2007. Each time I have been overwhelmed by the social and economic advances that Blacks in Killeen and the city of Killeen have made. This kind of progress is encouraging. The size of the city of Killeen is overwhelming, with four high schools larger than the one from which I graduated. The segregated practices of the early years were changing in the 1960s and had changed a great deal more by 2007. Diversity was evident in many areas and aspects of the community; residents' participation in the larger community was more inclusive; residential choices were open; marketing and business pursuits showed growth, and diversity in employment opportunities provided sources of services that residents could be engage in.

My father was Provost Marshall Sergeant for Fort Hood. Our family life at Fort Hood was memorable. My mother initially worked at a child care facility and I had a series of various jobs on the Post from setting pins at the bowling alley to working at some of the canteens there. To make money we cleaned theaters on the Post as a family, specifically Theaters Number One and Two which were adjacent to each other. Occasionally, I had to clean them by myself when my parents had to go to Masonic and Eastern Star meetings. We also cleaned quarters as a family when people transferred.

In 1955, my mother, Jennie V. Searles, was managing the Fort Hood nursery for children who were military dependents and was offered the job of Girl Scout Leader on Fort Hood. By this time the high school in Killeen had integrated and my mother was the only black person running an integrated Girl Scout Camp in Texas. My father was a 33rd Degree Masons and my mother an Eastern Star. They both were very active in the community. He became Deputy Grand Master of Sunset Lodge of the Masons. We attended church on the Post and at Marlboro Heights Baptist Church. I was elected president of the Protestant Youth Fellowship, an organization of some two to three hundred young people at Fort Hood that was sponsored by an auxiliary organization called "The Dad's Club" on Fort Hood. The organization was started by the Post Commanding General

Doan that preceded General Biddle. The Dad's Club mandate was to support youth endeavors such as Boy Scouts, Cub Scouts, Little League, youth football and summer camps for children like Camp Moonraker on the Post. I was the first black member of the Cub Scouts and Boy Scouts Troops Pack Troop 111 and the first black to attend summer camp at Camp Moonraker. I also attended the Boy Scout Jamboree in California in 1954.

On the social side, if you were not military and had children, there were no educational opportunities for Blacks in Killeen before 1954. You had to go to school in Belton or Temple. If you were military or worked for military on Fort Hood there were segregated facilities for education. I personally attended a segregated elementary school operated on Fort Hood. I was in third grade. The school was a barracks, and went from first to sixth grade. It had two black teachers, Miss Lankford and Miss Scott, who taught about thirty-five to forty students from first to sixth grade. As an aside, Miss Scott acted as coach for the boys track and a few games of basketball. This existed until the new school was built in Marlboro Heights for black students in Killeen, Fort Hood and Simmonsville in grades one through ten. By the time I left high school in 1959 and went away to college, I know my parents began to work more in the Marlboro Heights community. One of the things they undertook to do was to acquire a barracks from the Army for $1.00 so they could start a youth center in Marlboro Heights. I know for a fact that their philanthropy was considerable in the community of Marlboro Heights. Even though my father is gone, and my mother does not remember the details, when I returned from college they spoke so highly about what they had done and what they were doing in Marlboro Heights. Apparently their dedication and commitment was one of the joys of their lives at that time.

My parents left the Fort Hood/Killeen area when my father was transferred to Fort Wainwright in Fairbanks, Alaska. SFC Joseph L. and Jennie V. Searles were committed and dedicated community builders in the Killeen/Fort Hood areas. Their participation and leadership in community organizations and their involvement with the community youth enhanced the quality of life for the community and for black youth during the decades of the fifties, sixties and thereafter. Like so many other community builders their contribution to the Killeen/Fort Hood area and specifically to the Marlboro Heights community showed their commitment.

Joseph "Joe" Searles, III
"An Achiever Making a Difference"
Joseph L. Searles III

I attended Marlboro School in Marlboro Heights through eighth grade. Mr. Dock Jackson was my principal and teacher. By the time I was eleven years old I started to work construction at $1.00 an hour. Since I was five feet nine and weighed one hundred fifty pounds I worked alongside black men of various ages from 20 to 60 years old. In 1956, I enrolled at Killeen High School along with 13 other black students who were high school freshmen, sophomores and juniors. We were the first black students to integrate the formerly all-white high school. Prior to the decision of the Killeen School District Board of Trustees to integrate the black high school students into Killeen High School, black high school age students were bused to a school in Belton, Texas.

I joined the varsity team as a sophomore and starting my junior year I was a star back on the Killeen Kangaroos Football Team. By the time of my graduation in 1959 I had set many records on the football fields where we played. Sports writers of the daily newspaper wrote about this period of my school days shedding insight of the challenges of the times and the courage and perseverance required of me. Some of their comments can be found in the Killeen Daily Herald Newspaper articles: *"Young Joe is recalled with Delight and Gratitude"* and *"Breaking Barriers."* I was the first black player on Killeen High School's varsity football team. My response to the comments in these newspaper articles is that those years instilled in me a lot of confidence. It gave me a desire to win over all obstacles, no matter what. The team played a lot of home games that first year. I believed that integration was tougher in some ways on my black schoolmates who may have believed that I received better treatment because I played sports but this was not the case.

After high school and college, I continued to achieve and receive recognition for my accomplishments beyond my athletic career. I attended Kansas State University and George Washington University Law School. I was selected by the President of Kansas State University to serve as chairman of its prestigious Diversity Advisory Council and as vice-chairman of the President's Entrepreneurial Round Table, comprised of distinguished Kansas State Alumni and businesspersons. I also continue to be a distinguished lecturer at the University. I serve as President of the New York/New Jersey Chapter of the National Football League Player Association, and I am an elected member of its National Steering Committee for this union of retired professional football players.

My achievements and service include experiences and recognition as:

- A former investment and commercial banker highly recognized for my experience in finance/asset development and urban revitalization.
- One of the early urban development specialists credited with using mainstream strategies to dynamically transform the size and quality of minority business ventures.
- Having established a distinguished career that includes serving two gubernatorial appointments as Chairman and Director of the State of New York Mortgage Agency where I

was responsible for municipal housing issues totaling more than $600 million dollars.

- Having attained national and international prominence as the first black member and floor-broker on the New York Stock Exchange.
- Having served as a vice president of the Public Finance Department at Manufacturers Hanover Trust Company, now J.P. Morgan Chase.
- Having worked with the Federal Government and numerous state municipal agencies in housing, economic development, and urban affairs.
- Treasurer of the New York Urban League and also a member of its current Board of Directors.
- Having served as Chief Real Estate Officer/Consultant at Harlem Commonwealth Council (HCC), one of the leading community development corporations in the nation, engaged in retail and commercial development in Harlem.
- Having held senior management positions at Bedford Stuyvesant Restoration Corporation and the Center for Advocacy Research and Planning (CARP), both non-profit agencies.
- The first Chairman of the 125th Street Business Improvement District (BID) in Harlem, Black America's premier business arena.
- Having served as a member of the development team for "Harlem USA," and currently is a partner in the $141,000,000.00 retail/entertainment Project in Washington, D.C. called "D.C. USA."
- Being considered a leading expert on urban retailing.

On my return visit to Killeen in 2007 as the guest of Fairway Middle School in the Killeen Independent School District, I was also fortunate to meet the gentleman of color who became the first black Mayor of Killeen, Mayor Timothy Hancock.

Dalton and Ida Marie Breaux
Family, Country, Community
SGT Major (Ret.) Dalton Breaux

I am Dalton Breaux, the son of Mr. and Mrs. Valarien Breaux, of Lafayette, Louisiana and a 1943 graduate of Paul Breaux High School in Lafayette, Louisiana. My wife is the former Ida Marie Benoit. We are the parents of three adult children Gwendolyn, Gloria and Dalton all of whom were Killeen High School graduates. I entered the Army in 1943 and completed combat training with the 372nd Infantry Regiment while serving in Honolulu, Hawaii, Island of Oahu. My military career has provided me with opportunities for service in many places and under many different circumstances. My military career chronicles a twenty-six year period of achievements, leadership, commitment and recognition for the successful service that defined me as a soldier. I served my country in World Wars I and II. I am also a veteran of the Korean conflict. My assignment to the 1st Armored Division's 73rd Armor Field Artillery at Fort Hood, Texas began April 1951 which was about a month after the unit's activation in March 1951. By 1964, I held the record of having served with Btry A 1st BN 73rd Field ARTY, 1st Armored Division, 73rd Armored Field Artillery Battalion at Fort Hood, Texas, longer than any other member in the unit.

In addition to being a 1952 honor graduate from the Fort Hood Non Commissioned Officers (NCO) Academy I have received many commendations and awards for academic achievement and for the performance of my duties throughout my military career. I retired from the 2nd Armored Division during a ceremony held at Division Headquarters on October 31, 1969 with a military career that was successful and varied in experiences. After retirement I started a new, but related, career that spanned nineteen years (1969-1988) in employment with the Killeen Independent School District as the Junior Reserve Officers Training Corp (JROTC) instructor at Killeen High School. The JROTC program began at Killeen High School in the 1967-1968 school term. There were also opportunities for the girls in the JROTC Cadet Program. The Wallaby Debs constituted the female contingent of the KHS JROTC. The Killeen High School JROTC made history when it established its first all-female color guard.

An important part of the Breaux family's life in the community is our active participation in the ministries and activities of our church, St. Joseph Catholic Church in Killeen. I am a member of the Knights of Columbus 4th degree Assembly of Council 4724 in Killeen, Texas. Since 1963 I have served in various capacities. Honors of recognition have been bestowed upon me acknowledging my commitment to the principles of the Order.

Through the *TAPESTRY* task force research they learned that during the 1970s when there had been no African American employed in a management position in Killeen, especially for a major department store that my wife, Ida Marie Breaux, distinguished herself as the first African American to serve in management at Woolworth in Killeen, Texas. Woolworth was one of Killeen's major department stores that opened in the seventies at Killeen's first shopping center, Mid-Town Mall. The mall was located on Business 190 (now Veterans Memorial Boulevard). My wife, Ida Breaux, was also active in community involvement activities in Killeen. In 1973, she served on the steering committee of an important education and community project with the Killeen Independent School District and other community representatives to plan a Vocational Conference which Killeen would host. This project's committee participants included: vocational administrators Sandy Hooper and Janie Sullivan; teacher Jacquie Patterson; Assistant Superintendent Herbert Groth; Ida Breaux of Woolworth Department Store and Charles Hollinger, both representing business. Community representatives Dick Wilson, Louis Shine, Gerald Skidmore, and other representatives from various sectors of the community also served on this committee.

Our contributions to the community extend beyond our experience with the military, with business and with the school/community project just described. We have communications that indicated that as long time residents in the Killeen area we have responded to issues of concerns that are important to the welfare of all citizens. We have been involved in community, county, state and national matters. For example, Ida's service as a juror in a Federal case was recognized by the United States Attorney Ronald F. Ederer of the U.S. Department of Justice. Our advocacy activities are also documented in letters, certificates and newspaper articles collected over the years–Letters from the United States Senator of Texas Phil Gramm, the United State Senator, Lloyd Bentsen and Congressman Chet Edwards of the United States House of Representative (later elected United States Senator). We participate in surveys on issues such as education, healthcare, national defense, etc. We continue to demonstrate an interest in better government, and we work for positive outcomes that will benefit the lives of the citizens. We are community builders. Our adult children are also community builders – Gwen Ann Breaux serves as a professional development training consultant; Gloria Marie Breaux McNeal serves in leadership positions and on Advisory Boards; Dalton V. Breaux, a Gulf War veteran and U.S. Army retiree is an educator positively touching the lives of many youth in the community. In 1990, Gloria was appointed Director of Auxiliary Personnel in the Killeen Independent School District's and was the first African American to serve in this position. As a family we are giving back to the communities in which we reside. The involvement of the Breaux family has been varied. Whether it was in regards to the military, education, business, politics, religion or today's social concerns we have made valuable contributions to the life of the community. Yes, we are community builders.

Charles D., Sr. and Geneva Smith
"Marlboro Heights: A Good Neighborhood"
Geneva Smith

My husband Charles D. Smith, Sr. and I are natives of Georgia. His hometown is Moultrie, Georgia and my hometown is Fitzgerald. We are the parents of four sons: Charles Jr., Harry, Dennis and Vernon Smith; and four daughters: Julia M. Smith Price, Gladys Smith Nealous, Catherine M. Smith and Cynthia M. Smith Fryre. Charles

Sr. first moved to the Killeen/Fort Hood Area in 1950. When we arrived in Killeen, there were just a few stores downtown in which to shop. Charles, Sr. was transferred to Ft. Sill, Oklahoma and later spent a tour in Germany. The family accompanied him to Germany and we spent a great deal of time traveling during our stay. On November 8, 1962 we returned from Germany and moved into the Marlboro Heights Community. I have always believed that Marlboro Heights is a good neighborhood and that we also have good neighbors. We worked together in making our neighborhood a nice and safe place to live. My family enjoyed a good life here. Our house was a place where the other boys in our neighborhood liked to gather.

While the children were growing up I mostly worked at night. Our children felt safe at home and at school. There were times during hot weather when we slept with windows up, doors opened with only screen doors locked. Our children attended Marlboro Elementary School growing up and enjoyed the school activities. The principal and teachers at Marlboro Elementary took good care of our children. All of the Smith children, including the grands and great-grands, are graduates of Killeen High School. Our oldest son, Charles Jr., graduated in 1965 the first year that Killeen High School opened on 38th Street. Our children are adults now. Some have moved away and have their own families. Charles Sr.'s work was the Army, and he retired with an honorable discharge. I joined and worship at Anderson Chapel AME Church. We are responsible homeowners and community builders in Marlboro Heights.

Joseph, Sr. and Mercedes Polk
Love of Family, Country and Teaching
Mercedes Polk

Joseph Warren Polk, Sr. and I are both natives of New Iberia, Louisiana. Joseph Sr. graduated from high school in 1947 as valedictorian of his senior class and later that year joined the Army to provide a better life for his family. Joseph's career in the Army and teaching were his passions. He taught young men to defend themselves and their country. His motto: "I am a soldier." That is how he lived. He fought in the Korean Conflict and received a Purple Heart. The family moved to the Killeen-Fort Hood area in 1952. This assignment to Fort Hood was his last changes of duty stations. We lived in Simmonsville for one year. When we first arrived in the area what is now Marlboro Heights looked like a wilderness at that time. From Simmonsville we moved to Fort Hood where we lived for eight years.

In 1964, our family moved to Marlboro Heights, and our children attended Marlboro Elementary School. We enjoyed our neighborhood and we felt safe. We had no air in the house and we could leave the back door open to get a cool breeze through the house. The parents in the community supported the school in its activities and with its school rules. The principal and teachers looked out for the students and showed lots of care for them. All of our children enjoyed attending school at Marlboro Elementary. When the children went to junior high school, Mother Muriel Bell was a great help to me. She was a nurse's aide at the school and she chastised the students just like a principal of the school would do.

We are parents to two sons: Joseph Warren Polk, Jr. and William Henry "Simon" Polk; and one daughter, Loretta Polk Mitchell. They are all Killeen High School graduates. When William was in second grade I started working at Fort Hood as a Non-Appropriated Funds employee. I took my job seriously and remained in that employment for twenty-four years. Joseph Sr. suffered from his battle wounds without complaining for over forty years. He fought with honor for his country. As a military family we spent quite a bit of time traveling and we enjoyed the many places that we visited. All of the children are adults now. They have families of their own. My husband and our son William "Simon," are deceased now. The neighborhood has changed somewhat, but I still live in our home in Marlboro Heights. I continue to help make our neighborhood a good place to live. Our family's church membership is at God's Holy Tabernacle Church of God in Christ in the Simmonsville Community of Killeen. However, Killeen is the community my family helped to build by being loyal and responsible citizens and by serving our country with honor.

47

Napoleon and Gwendolyn May
Serving Country Community and Family
Mabel Laverne Robinson

Napoleon and Gwendolyn May are my parents. They are both natives of the state of Arkansas. Our family includes my parents and five siblings, my brother Johnny; and my sisters Carolyn Lorraine, Vickie Lynn, Patricia Sue; and me, Mabel Laverne. We are all adults now with families of our own and it feels good to be able to give back to the communities in which we are residing. Our father served in the military and when he received orders for a new assignment he would take the family with him to other military installations. The family arrived at Fort Hood on May 11, 1952. The family later moved to Walker Village which is one of the housing neighborhoods on Fort Hood. We lived in barracks that had been converted into quarters. I was six years old and ready to enroll in school. There were just a few black people here then. The family later moved to Marlboro Heights and we lived in Marlboro Trailer Park. A large tent which was the "Servicemen Church" was also in this trailer park. We would sometimes listen to the quartets when they were practicing their songs. My father was stationed at Fort Hood more than one time. When we returned to Killeen from one of his tours of duty, my parents purchased a house on Jefferies Avenue in Marlboro Heights. My siblings and I grew up there. Our father at one time was co-owner in a business with Willie Miller, Leon O'Neal, Sr., Milton Williams and Willie Gibson, all of whom were residents of Marlboro Heights. They operated an automatic car wash in Killeen. He received an honorable discharge from the U.S. Army in 1962. He was also retired from civil service having served at the Department of Defense (DOD) and the U.S. Post Office. My father served a number of years with the Killeen Housing Authority in Killeen and was an active member of the local NAACP. Our parents became faithful members of Marlboro Missionary Baptist Church.

Dad also became a deacon in the church and they served in many of the ministries. Our father is now deceased and our mother still resides in the home. Our parents were loyal, law abiding and greatly valued community builders. Their contribution to a better community was through service to the country, to the community and in the home with family.

Jather and Birdie Seawood
Fort Hood First Black Troops Advance Party Trailblazer
Jather Seawood

My military career kept me returning to Fort Hood and the Central Texas communities. I am originally from Arkadelphia, Arkansas where I was reared and educated. Then I attended college in Chicago, Illinois. My wife Birdie was reared and educated in Chicago. I served twenty-four years in the Army. I was assigned to Fort Hood in 1952 as a part of the "All Black Unit" 25AIB from Fort Bragg, North Carolina, advance party. There was also a second "All Black Tank Battalion Unit" that was a part of the advance party to arrive at Fort Hood when we did. Our unit, the 25AIB, "troop trained" to Temple, Texas. The Tank Battalion's buses picked us up in Temple and took both Tank Battalion advance parties out to North Fort Hood to "Tent City." There were no barracks out there. Our two "All Black Units" were the first black troops over there and they opened a little house in Gatesville for our entertainment hall. There was a ribbon cutting ceremony for the opening of the little house and I cut the ribbon. It was a two-room house and was the only place we could go for entertainment. We had a separate NCO Club in 1952, separate laundry and separate church. We were not allowed, day or night in downtown Killeen. There were no women there, only men. We created our own entertainment. There were very few trees on Post and the weather was very hot. I left Fort Hood for a tour of duty and returned in 1958.

The Marlboro Heights community was specifically being developed to be a community for Blacks and houses were built for rent and for sale. In April 1961, we purchased a house in Marlboro Heights and my wife Birdie, two children and I moved there. There was no other place where black families could live except the Lone Star Community (Simmonsville) across the Business 190 Highway before Marlboro Heights was planned. There were black families who had ties with on-site employment at surrounding ranches in the area and lived in housing on those sites. My wife and I became involved in the community. We were both members of Marlboro Heights Missionary Baptist Church until May 31, 1994 when we became charter members of the newly established Greater Peace Missionary Baptist Church and served on several ministries. Birdie and I are also members of the Masonic Family. I served as a Worshipful Master of New Light Lodge #242 for over thirty years; District Deputy Grand Master of District #24; member of Central Texas Consistory #306; Harge's Commander of Rite; Nubia Temple #191; 33 Degree Grand Inspector General and a member of the Veterans of Foreign Wars, Post 9191. After my last tour of duty from 1962-1965 I remained at Fort Hood until my retirement on December 31, 1969. After retirement from the Army, I served as the city of Killeen golf course superintendent and retired after fifteen years of service. I also worked for the Killeen Independent School District. We are committed and dedicated community builders.

Reverend Dr. John C. and Mabel L. Robinson
A Family in Ministry
Mabel L. Robinson

Reverend Dr. John C. Robinson and I, the former Mabel Laverne May, fulfilled a mission of great significance to the spiritual life of our city and the surrounding communities. We are community builders as church founders. I first came to Killeen in 1952 when my father received military orders assigned to Fort Hood. I was six years old. We lived on Post for a time. Joe Searles and I attended the same school on Post and he sometimes escorted me to school. The school was a barrack-like building at Fort Hood. Blacks and Whites attended separate schools both on Post and in the city. Miss Vera Lankford was my teacher. She later married and became Mrs. Nelson. The other teacher was Miss Vera Scott. Later we moved to Marlboro Heights. Because I lived on the Post for a time and then moved to Marlboro Heights, I attended school at Fort Hood and later at Marlboro School in Killeen. Mrs. Vera Lankford Nelson was my teacher again. Professor Jackson was my teacher in the upper grades.

My father was stationed at Fort Hood several times and when we returned to Killeen from one of his tours of duty my parents purchased a house on Jefferies Avenue in Marlboro Heights where we grew up. I was a junior in high school then. However, I was not one of the students that went to Belton for my schooling. Killeen High School was our only high school at that time and it was in the building that became Fairway Junior High School. I graduated from Killeen High School in 1964. In fact, all of my siblings: Johnny, Carolyn, Vickie, and Patricia, graduated from there too. In 1956, Joe Searles and thirteen other Marlboro School high school students were integrated into the all-white Killeen High School. Joe Searles also became the first black football player at Killeen High School.

I met my husband John C. Robinson while he was stationed in the military at Fort Hood. We were married on February 20, 1966. After marriage, our first home was in Marlboro Heights. Our marriage was blessed with three children: Tammy, Christopher and Melissa. We now have grandchildren and a great-grandchild. My family is gifted. Our family members are natives of Arkansas, Alabama, New York and Maryland. John became a civil service employee at Ft. Hood for a while after leaving the Army. He left to work for the federal government as a federal agent and joined the Department of Interior Fish and Wildlife Services as a Special Agent. He also worked for the U.S. Government Department of the Treasury as a Secret Service Agent. My husband's education experience is in law enforcement and he has also earned a degree in theology. We lived in other states and countries such as Washington and Europe from 1968-1982.

During this period we traveled as a family to Israel, Turkey, Cyprus, Egypt, France, Italy and Greece. We also visited Canada, Alaska, Hawaii, Spain, many islands in the Caribbean. Actually, we were in Greece on 9/11 which was a sobering experience. I have lived in Europe as a child and as a wife.

In 1982, the family returned to Killeen to start and pastor a church. When we returned the city had grown and there were many more minorities here. My husband and I founded the "First Church of God in Christ" in October 1982. We started out in our home. Our first church building was on the corner of Rancier and Massey Street in Killeen. Our new church is located at 5201 Westcliff Road in northeast Killeen. Rev. John C. Robinson is also Superintendent of the Greater Killeen District Churches of God in Christ. I serve as President of Texas Northeast Pastor and Ministers' Wives Circle (State). I teach Bible classes, Sunday school and serve as President of the Department of Women at my local church. Our having founded and started a church beginning in the home; later meeting in the schools; and now in our second church building on Westcliff Road has been a family and church accomplishment for which we are grateful to our Lord. We returned to Killeen ready to fulfill a new mission and it is a significant contribution to the community.

At one point in my life I had a personal obstacle to overcome, but it is no longer an obstacle. It was accepting the fact that I am a pastor's wife. Agreeing to say yes to the Lord was not easy, but once I stopped fighting it—well it's been an awesome journey. There are many important and valuable experiences, needs and choices we have in our lives: family, education, etc., but most important for our family is having a right relationship with our God and how we live our lives. God loves us; He cares for us; He will be there for us. It was an especially sad time for my family when we lost my sister, Vickie, in 1989 at the age of thirty-five. During that time I learned that God can take you through unbearable times. I aspired to be a doctor as a child, but now I am a teacher of children, women and men. Prior to 1968 my education experience was in business, and now I have also earned a degree in theology.

Our son Christopher is in the military, stationed in New York. Our daughters live in Bedford. Tammy is the admissions coordinator at ATI Training School. Melissa is employed at the Independent Corporate Sales Central Training Center. All three are giving back to the community. We continue to be community builders and spiritual leaders in the community.

Leon H. and Ruth Christina Hodge O'Neal
Lasting Memorable Footprints
Leon H. O'Neal II

Our father, Leon Herbert O'Neal, Sr. is a native of Georgia. Before his induction into the Army he had attended Clark University in Atlanta, Georgia and had taught for four years in the elementary grades. In January 1942, he was drafted into the Army at Fort Benning, Georgia; the month after the United States declared war in World War II. The Army sent him to Camp Walters near Mineral Wells, Texas. After working for a few weeks in a headquarters company, he was promoted to sergeant first class because of his ability to type and maintain the company morning report. Ruth Christina Hodge, our mother, is a native Texan from San Antonio, Texas. She was a graduate of Spelman College in Atlanta, Georgia. These former teacher co-workers married on November 15, 1942.

When our parents arrived in Killeen, Texas in 1953 as a military family because of Dad's orders to Fort Hood, Texas our arrival to this area was quite an experience for the family. Inadequate housing and discrimination were conditions that existed at that time. The family settled in the Marlboro Heights community with their four children: Phyllis Jane, Ruth Elise, Charles Reuben and me. Community building through contributions of personal service and involvement kept the O'Neal family engaged in school, church, community and civic activities. Our father was primarily engaged in his military responsibilities, but took time to also become involved in activities in the community. The family was active with the Boy Scouts, and our mother served as den mother for the scouts. Our parents also worked with the first Teen Club in the Marlboro Heights Community. Mother served in PTA on the membership committee and as the Marlboro School PTA President. She was a charter member of the Marlboro Heights Missionary Baptist Church, a Sunday school and Bible study teacher; a dedicated educator and an advocate for children. She was an encourager to others. She taught at the Marlboro Elementary School for many years until its 1969 closing which resulted from the action and orders of the Federal Department of Health, Education, and Welfare (HEW). Marlboro Elementary School then had been determined a segregated school within the Killeen Independent School District. When Marlboro Elementary school closed at the end of the 1968 school term, its students, faculty and staff were assigned to other campuses in the district for the next school term. Our mother was transferred to a teaching assignment at Meadows Elementary School on the Ft. Hood installation.

Community service for our mother was always important. While teaching at Meadows Elementary School, she and two other members of Delta Sigma Theta Sorority, Inc., initiated plans for the establishment of a local graduate chapter in the Killeen area. Through the efforts of these three Deltas—Ruth O'Neal, Louise McGhee and Julia Williams—and ten other Deltas that included my sister Elise, the Killeen Alumnae Chapter of the Delta Sigma Theta Sorority, Inc. was chartered in February, 1974. Delta Sigma Theta Sorority is a public service organization of college educated women committed to rendering service in the community. As a Christian, a mother, a teacher, a Delta and community person, our mother was involved in volunteer service. She continued to teach at Meadows Elementary School until her retirement of twenty-one years of service teaching the youth in our elementary schools. She was a member of the Killeen Chapter of Texas Retired Teachers Association and the Killeen Heritage Association. In 1986 she served on the Bell County Sesquicentennial Committee and the Killeen City Council recognized her participation with an award. Our mother, Ruth C. O'Neal left lasting footprints in the sands of time in her home, the school, the Marlboro Heights community, the city of Killeen and Bell County, Texas.

As a resident in the Marlboro Heights community, our father, Leon Herbert O'Neal Sr. demonstrated a business interest in his community involvement. My sister Phyllis, my oldest sister, remembered our father's involvement in the first integrated cafe in Killeen, "The Ebony Grill". It was located on the corner of 2nd Street and Business Highway 190 (now renamed Veterans Memorial Boulevard). In addition, during the 1960s our father, Leon O'Neal, Sr. Joined with Willie Miller, Willie Gibson, Napoleon May and Milton Williams (all of whom were Black residents of the Marlboro Heights Community) and together established an automatic car wash named 8th Street Car Wash. He served twice as Commander of the Veterans of Foreign Wars (VFW) Post 9191. His community involvement included being a charter member and a 32nd Degree Mason of the Masonic New Light Lodge #242 Prince Hall Masons. He participated in the writing of the By-Laws which were accepted by the Grand Lodge without changes. He was also a charter member of the Masonic Central Texas Consistory #306, and Scottish Rite of Killeen. As a resident of Killeen he served as a member of the Board of Adjustment from 1980 until 1983.

Leon H. O'Neal, Sr. retired from active duty in the United State Army at Fort Sill, Oklahoma in June 1967 with twenty-five years of honorable service to this country. He was a veteran of World War II and took part in the Normandy Invasion of Europe in June 1944. He also served in the Korean War. He received many certificates for the manner in which he handled his responsibilities. On July 21, 1967, the Killeen Daily Herald carried this headline: *"Veterans Map Plans for KHS ROTC Program."* Included in the article was a photo of LTC (RET) Cloud Carter, a career army veteran of twenty-two and a half years and our father, SFC (RET) Leon O'Neal a career army veteran of twenty-five years. This article announced that these two veterans of the Army had officially begun the work of setting up the Junior ROTC Cadet Program at Killeen High School. The announcement of the Killeen Independent School District's hiring of SFC (RET) Leon O'Neal as a co-organizer with LTC (Ret) Cloud Carter met with great acceptance and pride by the citizens in the community. Killeen's historical records will show that SFC (Ret) Leon Herbert O'Neal, Sr. was a history-maker in the activation of the JROTC Program. Our father remained with the high school ROTC Program as property custodian until 1972.

His community interest and service was reflected in his involvement in community organization and civic assignments until his death on March 29, 1983. Our parents' legacy lives on through their children. All four siblings became goal setters and achievers in school and in the community. They also attended Marlboro School, their neighborhood school and are Killeen High School graduates. Elise, Leon and Charles achieved a college degree and Phyllis achieved in her chosen field of cosmetology. Each of us can include among our many accomplishments a distinguishing experience of becoming a first achiever in uncharted endeavors for young black youth of the Killeen area at that time.

Phyllis O'Neal Kerley became the first black grocery cashier in Killeen when she worked at Safeway Grocery Store in 1970. Elise O'Neal Spears was the first black student initiated into the National Honor Society at Killeen High School. She is now a wife, mother, grandmother of six, news writer (reporter), volunteer, coordinator and entrepreneur. During an interview as an adult with the book's editor Elise's memories include the community's growth pattern and times of the street openings in the Marlboro Heights Community; her school days activities, especially recess; the community leaders like Osia Maze because of her leadership; the youth activities at school, at church and as a girl scouts. She also remembered that before integration, Marlboro School participated in athletic competition against area schools that required their travel; Also that their Marlboro School Choir participated in the University Interscholastic League (UIL) at Paul Quinn College in Waco, Texas even though the school did not have a music teacher. Now, Elise has become a community builder in the city where she resides.

In January 1961 seventh and eighth grade student from Marlboro School and I integrated Nolan Junior High School. In high school I was also an outstanding student athlete, and become the first black student athlete to sign a Longhorn football scholarship with the University of Texas. Charles R. O'Neal did not forget his roots. He returned to the community on several occasions to make an appeal to the Killeen School District Board of Trustees to give recognition to Killeen's first black principal, Dock Jackson, Jr. He became the first former Marlboro School student to become an advocate in the interest of the community in which he was reared. On Sunday, August 24, 2008, the Killeen Independent School District Board of Trustees re-dedicated Marlboro Elementary School as Dock Jackson, Jr. Professional Learning Center. Charles R. O'Neal, a community builder through his work with the Dallas Black Chamber of Commerce, delivered a tribute honoring his former teacher and the community's first black principal, Dock Jackson, Jr.

Nathaniel and Murtha L. Anderson
Hearts of Courage, Faith, and Love
Mildred Anderson Debose

Our father Nathaniel Anderson was born in Milam County, Texas. He was among the first Blacks to work on Post. He started working at the old hospital in the early 40s, when the post was called Camp Hood. The hospital was located in the area where the Mini Dome or Soldier Dome stood at one time. For many years, he worked in the Officers Open Patient Mess Hall under Colonel Gardner. Because of racial discrimination in Killeen, he had to live on Post in the civilian barracks located in the area where the veterinary clinic stood across from the old commissary on 178th Street. Blacks could not live in Killeen, nor could they go to a grocery store in Killeen. Therefore, our father had an I.D. card to shop in the commissary. His father-in-law, Julius Staten, also lived in the civilian barracks. Mr. Staten was a barber at the Post Exchange (PX), and he cut hair from the early forties until his demise in the early sixties.

Our family which included our father, Nathaniel Anderson, our mother Murtha L. Staten Anderson, and their children lived in Cameron, Texas. This was about sixty miles east of Killeen, and our father would travel home on his off days at work. Then in 1953 he moved the family to Walker Village where we lived for eighteen months. While living in Walker Village my oldest Sister Ardella and I, had to ride the bus to Belton to attend school at T. B. Harris High School. This was Belton's high school for black students. We rode the bus for two years before Ardella and I returned to Cameron so that Adella could graduate from high school in Cameron. The younger children attended school on Fort Hood. A government bus would pick them up and transport them to and from the government quarters and school. After the family received a letter from Colonel McAllister saying that civilians could no longer live in government quarters, we moved to Route 1 on the property of Mildred and Tom Levy. We lived there a number of years as a family until the Lord blessed our father to be able to buy land on Hillside Drive in Marlboro Heights to build a house. Upon moving to Marlboro Heights our father became one of the eighteen charter members of Marlboro Missionary Baptist Church where the Reverend Dr. Roscoe. A. Abercrombie was pastor. He served there faithfully until he accepted the call into the ministry and became the pastor of two churches in Texas. Rev. Nathaniel Anderson served as pastor in the ministry of the Lord faithfully until his demise in the sixties. His widow, our mother Murtha Anderson, still resides at their home in the Marlboro Heights community. Our parents were blessed with twelve children, eleven of whom graduated from Killeen High School. My sister, Ardella, graduated from high school in Cameron, Texas. Some of the children pursued further training after high school. All four of their sons served in the Armed Forces, and one retired from the Air Force.

Our brothers, Oscar and Cecil Anderson, were among the first fourteen black students to integrate the then all-white Killeen High School in 1956. The courage of these fourteen young secondary students who integrated Killeen High School is to be commended. The group included juniors: Cecil Anderson and James Benford; sophomores: Mary Dockery, Marjorie Jarman, Dorothy Johnson and Suzie Lloyd; also freshmen: Oscar Anderson, Prentis Clayton, Patricia Dockery, Sandra Terry, Joseph Searles, Ethel Jo Todd, Brenda Williams and Johnnie Yeager. They opened doors for many students that came after them. There were students that embraced integration of the high school and accepted the friendship of their black student classmates or teammates.

John C. Odom, Jr., Oscar's football teammate and friend of Oscar, wrote and shared with the task force two positive responses he witnessed from Oscar Anderson and Coach H. E. Hepler that impacted his life as a student and in later years when he saw this same type of injustice being practiced. The first positive response was the courage and dignity shown by Oscar when after one of their football games a restaurant manager where the team had stopped to eat attempted to separate him from eating in the main dining area with his teammates. Oscar was neither disrespectful nor did he react in a negative manner. The second positive response was that of Coach H. E. Hepler who quickly responded to the manager and insisted that Oscar eats with the team. When the manager resisted his requests, Coach Hepler resolved the situation by instructing the team to return to the bus; and the team left the restaurant as instructed. Coach Hepler boarded the bus and we drove to another place to eat. Oscar's courage and confidence did not let that incident of prejudice stop his participation in sports nor did it reduce his determination. During the school year, Oscar continued to practice teamwork and played with the kind of confidence and effort that brought honor to the school and to Oscar. The friendship of John and Oscar continued over the school years and at graduation they both signed brief friendship messages in each other's school's Annual as seniors traditionally do.

The family of Nathaniel Anderson is very much a part of the "Black History" in the Killeen area. They were among the trailblazers who dared to show courage and to keep the faith needed to persevere during those earlier years.

George and Annie Wilson
Memories of Growing Up in Killeen, Texas
Shirley Wilson and Susan Renee Hardnick

Our parents George H. Wilson and Annie Richardson Wilson brought our family to Killeen in November of 1954 when I was just four years old. Susan Renee and my siblings are the late Abraham Richardson, James, Mary, Kenneth and Robert Wilson. The first five children came with our parents from Newport News, Virginia where our father had been stationed at Ft. Monroe and had served in the Korean War. Because we were new to the city, Daddy said he felt that he was stuck in an area where he planned to stay no longer than he had to. Mom, who was pregnant with my brother Kenneth, felt that she was in the middle of nowhere. We stayed at the Fort Hood Guest House when we first arrived in Killeen. By Christmas our parents had purchased a home in Marlboro Heights on Parkhill Drive which is now known as Rev. R. A. Abercrombie Drive. My older siblings enrolled at Marlboro School. There were only two houses on the street at that time. Our household goods and our toys for Christmas had been shipped from Virginia but had not arrived. We knew the toys were coming therefore, every time we heard a truck we would run outside to see if it was the truck with our toys. My mother had a green double-burner hotplate that she used to cook our meals. By the time our first Christmas in Texas arrived, we had Christmas dinner but no presents. However, the truck finally arrived in January and we had our celebration at that time.

In 1955, Marlboro Heights Baptist Church was being built. My older brothers, Abraham and James and other older children in the neighborhood were allowed to assist with some construction tasks. While the church was under construction the worship services were held in Marlboro School. The church, the school and the community worked together in harmony and with purpose and played an important role in the development of our community. When the construction was completed my mother united with the church. Our school plays were also held at the church.

In 1956 I began first grade at the Ft. Hood "Under School." The school was located in a barracks building at that time and it cost my parents $3.00 a month for me to attend. A bus from Ft. Hood picked up students in our community and took us to and from school. I attended school at Marlboro School when I began second grade and Mrs. Vera Nelson was my teacher. First, second and third grade students were in one classroom. There was no cafeteria and you either had to go home for lunch or stay in the classroom to eat your meal which was usually a sack lunch. During this time, we purchased our first brand new car, a 1956 Chevrolet station wagon, for $3,000.

Marlboro Heights is located on a hill, and in 1957 there was a big flood. There was so much rain, and we watched from the window as the water ran down the hill. Our mother was working across town and had to wait until the water receded that evening before she could return home. We went to Germany and returned to Killeen in 1961. James and Mary, my brother and sister, enrolled in Nolan Jr. High School which had just opened when we returned. Susan, Kenneth and I enrolled at Marlboro School. Susan remembers a life lesson that her teacher, Mrs. Tommie Jackson stressed when they were not taking their education seriously. It was about our need to be able to read, write and spell well, study harder, be smarter, and that education was one of the keys to our success in life. Susan still shares this lesson with others. We went to Germany again in 1962 and returned in 1964.

For recreation we would go to the swimming pool, skating rink, movies and bowling alley on Ft. Hood. Blacks did not have access to these activities in Killeen nor to the use of these Killeen facilities until very late during the decade. However, Marlboro Heights had a teen club on the corner of Parkhill Drive and Terrace Drive. It was the white building at the intersections of Terrace and Parkhill Drive which is now renamed Rev. R. A. Abercrombie Drive. The building was just referred to as "The Center", Richard Maze, Mrs. Osia Maze and Willie Vanarsdale oversaw the activities. Admission to dances was usually twenty-five or fifty cents. I located an old flyer where we had a Mr. and Miss Teen Contest on August 13, 1965 and admission was fifteen cents. In 2009, the Hill County Community Action Centers began operating in the building that was formerly known as "The Center."

When the construction of houses began in a new housing development adjacent to Marlboro Heights our parents purchased a home in this area known as the Rose Addition. Expansion and changes were taking place in the community. Haynes Elementary School was built on Zephyr Road and our brother Robert attended school there. My father retired from the Army at Ft. Bliss, Texas and later retired from civil service at Ft. Hood, Texas. My siblings and I attended and graduated from Killeen High School. Abraham, my oldest brother, was employed by the J-Hawk Corporation for twenty-seven years, but is now deceased. This Corporation owned Gibson Discount Center and Ideal Furniture Store. James and Kenneth are Vietnam veterans. James retired from the Army. Susan Renee' has been employed with the Federal Government for over twenty-five years. I have also been employed with the Federal Government and with the State of Texas for over twenty-five years. Some of my siblings and I attended Central Texas College in Killeen, Texas. I, Shirley, received a BA degree in Social Work from Paul Quinn College when it was located in Waco, Texas. I also received a Master's Degree in Business Administration from Prairie View A and M University in Prairie View, Texas. My parents, who only wanted to stay in Killeen a short time, still reside here and over the years they contributed to making Killeen a better place in which to live. Our parents have been loyal community builders.

Sarah Sewell's Family
My Father, John Wiley Bosier and My Family
Sarah Sewell

I was born in Smithfield, Texas and reared in Taylor, Texas. In 1953 my husband and I arrived in Killeen during his military assignment. We first lived in Hood Village and later in Walker Village at Fort Hood. We purchased a house and moved to the Marlboro Heights

Community in 1960. We first worshiped at Simmonsville Baptist Church but in 1969 began worshiping at Marlboro Missionary Baptist Church. Our new home in Marlboro Heights was closer to our new church and more convenient for the entire family to attend. I was employed by the Killeen Independent School District (KISD). I worked as a clinic aide, an instructional aide to special needs students and a substitute teacher. In these positions it allowed me to positively affect the lives of many youth in my immediate community and those from other neighborhoods in the city. My last campus assignment with the school district was at Marlboro Elementary School. This school closed at the end of the 1968 school year, but later re-opened integrated after a few years.

My parents, Rev. and Mrs. Bosier, valued education for their children. I completed training in business and cosmetology. My sister was an educational aide that also worked with special needs students. My brother became an attorney. I also value education for our children. Both are Killeen High School graduates. In early 1950 my father, the late Reverend John Wiley Bosier, came to the Killeen area from Taylor, Texas to help build Camp Hood, Texas. He was a Baptist minister. He is considered the church's founder and the first appointed pastor of the Simmonsville Baptist Church. He was born in 1908 in Winchester, Texas, a little town on the other side of Smithfield, Texas, to the late Mr. Young and Mrs. Cindy Bosier. His father, Young Bosier, was a school teacher and his mother, Cindy, was a housewife. My father finished high school in Smithfield, Texas; married Elnora Bosier, my mother, and moved to Taylor, Texas. There they resided with their six children. It was from Taylor, Texas that Rev. Bosier commuted when he was helping to build Camp Hood. At the age of twenty-three my father attended the Baptist Seminary and College in Austin, Texas and graduated as a Baptist minister.

Rev. John Wiley Bosier became the pastor of the Lone Star Community Baptist Church which later was renamed Simmonsville Missionary Baptist Church while also working to build Camp Hood. He reorganized the members and built a church sanctuary. He became a significant contributor to a historical legacy, Simmonsville Missionary Baptist Church, an institution that is still a viable part of this community. The small white-framed church served its member-ship for many years. It is still owned by the church and located in the Simmonsville community. Before the small church was finished, the church held its services in the building on the corner of Business 190 (that has been renamed Veterans Memorial Boulevard) and 38th Street. This building was known as the Cadillac Inn. The owner of the building was willing to let the church have service there. My father's relationship with some of the local ministers in the city provided an opportunity for fellowship.

From its early humble beginning, Simmonsville Missionary Baptist Church has been moved from its original location of the Little White Church on Todd Avenue to a larger and newer bricked structure on 42nd Street. The church has been led by three other pastors after my father left and our family moved to Houston. They were Rev. A. R. D. Hubbard, Rev. Eddie Coppage and its current pastor Rev. Hubert E. Debose, Sr. My father's local ministry also includes being the pastor of the non-denominational church on Zephyr Road in Killeen. This is the small church that is next to the VFW Post 9191. Although my father was a pastor here, he never lived in Killeen. His ministry as a pastor included churches in Taylor and Sweatner, Texas. His last pastoral assignment was in Houston, Texas. He was eighty years old when he died in 1988.

James H. and Vera Lankford Nelson
Service to Country, Community and Education
Vera Nelson

I am a native of Belton, Texas. My relationship to the Killeen and the Fort Hood communities started in the early 50s when I was a teacher in the Fort Hood School System. The schools at Fort Hood were not integrated at that time, and I was one of two African American teachers employed to teach the elementary school age African American students who were dependents of African

American military personnel and were attending school on Fort Hood. I was not married at that time, and students knew me as Miss Lankford. Students knew my co-teacher as Miss Scott. Fort Hood maintained its own school system until 1952 when the Killeen School System and Fort Hood School System consolidated and formed the Killeen Independent School District (KISD). In 1954 when Marlboro School opened, Vera Scott, my co-worker, and I and all of the students who were attending the school on Fort Hood moved to the Marlboro School in the Marlboro Heights Community of Killeen. Black students who lived in the Marlboro and Simmonsville communities and those who lived on sites such as private farms or ranches in the area also attended Marlboro School if they were in grades 1-10. Students in grades 11-12 attended the T. B. Harris High School in Belton, Texas.

When Vera Scott and I arrived at Marlboro School in 1954 we were again the first two faculty members. I taught the students in the lower grades, and she taught the students in the higher grades during our first year. Because of this assignment we also hold the distinction of being the first two African American teachers employed in the Killeen Independent School District. The faculty increased for our second year at Marlboro School when Dock Jackson, Jr. was employed as a teaching principal and coach. At that time I taught students in grades 1-3; Miss Scott taught grades 4-6 and Dock Jackson taught grades seven and above. From 1954–1969, I witnessed and experienced the growth and many changes of Marlboro School. It became Marlboro Elementary School when Nolan Junior High School integrated black students. Kindergarten was added in later years as a grade level. At the end of the 1968 school term under orders of the Federal Department of Health, Education and Welfare (HEW), Marlboro Elementary School was ordered to be closed. This Department identified Marlboro Elementary as a segregated school within the Killeen Independent School District (KISD). Faculty and students were re-assigned due to the closing. I joined the faculty of East Ward Elementary School and remained there until my retirement from KISD in 1990. At that time I had given thirty-eight years of service to the youth of Killeen and Fort Hood.

My husband James Nelson retired from the Army with over twenty years of service. After retirement he became the first African

American Bell County Deputy Sheriff, contributing his service to the county and to his community. He also worked at Fort Hood as a federal service employee, again contributing his service to the military personnel and their families. We are the parents of two adult sons, Michael and Eric. They are both Temple High School graduates. Michael chose a career in law. He now holds the position of Associate District Judge in the Family Court of Bell County in Belton, Texas. Entrepreneurship sparked Eric's interest. As responsible citizens, both of our sons are now giving back to their community in their chosen interests. My husband is deceased, but he has left a legacy of selfless service to his country, to Bell County and to his community. He was also a community builder.

I am pleased to have been a part of the history of Killeen. I am also very proud of my service to the Killeen Independent School District community of students and parents. I have experienced many memorable moments in my teaching career working with children at the Fort Hood School, the Marlboro Elementary School and East Ward Elementary School. The contributions that I have made to the Marlboro Heights community and the students of Ft. Hood and the Killeen Independent School District has been fulfilling for me as an educator. My contribution to community building as a first grade teacher was in areas of teaching good citizenship; providing the foundational skills for learning; encouraging students to believe in their ability to do great things and exposing them to the beauty of the world around them. My last classes of first graders are adults now and as citizens are giving back to the community in which they reside in various ways. I am a proud and grateful community builder who has had the opportunity to serve the community in Killeen and Fort Hood through their children.

Dock, Jr. and Thelma Jackson
A Committed Teaching Team
Thelma Jackson

My husband, Dock Jackson, Jr., was Killeen's first black principal of the Killeen Independent School District. He gave seventeen years of dedicated service as an educator to the Killeen School District. Fourteen of those years of service were in the role of a school administrator in Killeen. He gained the respect of the community; provided leadership in educating the youth and adults; provided leadership as a school administrator and was involved in the civic and community organizations and on municipal agencies and committees. He is deceased, (November 16, 1999), but he left this account of his arrival and experiences in Killeen. Those who knew and worked with him will not forget the service he provided to the Killeen community and to surrounding communities of Rogers, Rosebud, Temple, Fort Hood and Gatesville, Texas. He was a trailblazer and a community builder. This is his account of his arrival and experiences in the Killeen School District: He wrote:

"I earned my Bachelor of Science Degree from Teacher College in Tyler, Texas and my Master's Degree in Education Administration from Texas Southern University in Houston, Texas. I arrived in Killeen from Rosebud, Texas in August 1955 so that I could begin my employment as principal and teacher at Marlboro School. Dr. C. E. Ellison was superintendent of the Killeen Independent School District (KISD) at that time. None of the Killeen schools were integrated upon my arrival. Marlboro School had opened in 1954. During the first school year the school had only two teachers: Vera Lankford and Vera Scott. I was hired in 1955 as a principal/teacher. The 1955 school year began with sixty-five students that had enrolled from the Fort Hood area, Marlboro Heights, Old Simmonsville (the Lone Star Community) and from private ranches and farms where a few students lived. This represented the black student population in Killeen and Fort Hood at that time. Students were bussed from Fort Hood to Marlboro School where first through tenth grade were taught. Miss Nelson taught first through third grades; Miss Scott taught fourth through sixth grades; and I, Principal Dock Jackson, taught seventh through tenth grades and performed the duties of principal. There were no eleventh graders, and one twelfth grader who attended the all black school, T. B. Harris, in Belton, Texas. The School Board paid her bus fare to and from school.

"I was also hired to start an athletic program along with other duties. Therefore, I was called teacher, principal and coach. We had to rotate subjects and grades to get in the number of hours per week. We had basketball and track in our athletic program where we competed against other schools. We had both girls and boys basketball teams. Joe Searles was the first outstanding black athlete coming from Marlboro School and he was an outstanding athlete at Killeen High School. Killeen High School was integrated in 1956. Then all ninth, tenth and eleventh grade students attended Killeen High School. Because of the integration of the high school, Marlboro School held graduation exercises for 8th graders who would be entering Killeen High School the next year. "The junior high school was integrated five years later in January 1961. Seventh and eighth grade students from Marlboro enrolled at Nolan Junior High school. It was then that we became Marlboro Elementary School with grades 1-6. The student population grew; construction took place for additions to the facility; teachers were added and the school had obtained full academic status. Those educational days carried challenging responsibilities for us all. Then in 1968 representatives from the US Department of Health, Education and Welfare Department (HEW) visited the Killeen School District and Marlboro Elementary School's closing was announced. Marlboro Elementary School was identified by the United States Health Education and Welfare Department (HEW) as a segregated school and the Killeen Independent School District (KISD) was cited as operating a dual school system because of this. Marlboro Elementary school closed at the end of the 1968 school term in May 1969 and kept its designated name, "Marlboro," while being used for administrative offices and services. Later it re-opened as an integrated elementary school, but closed again in February 2003 when the entire student body, faculty and staff move to the newly constructed Ira Cross Elementary School. Marlboro School's most current use has been as *Dock Jackson, Jr. Professional Learning Center* where proprofessional development sessions for teachers and school personnel are conducted and tutoring for students is held. It is equipped with a teacher media center, professional library, computers and meeting rooms to accommodate small, medium, large and very large gatherings. This facility is a legacy to the Dock Jackson, Jr. family and to the community.

"I was actively involved in the life of the Marlboro community and of the city of Killeen. The school was one of the central institutions in Marlboro Heights. It was a location for community events and activities. The school facility was used by the Marlboro Baptist Church when it was being organized and many other community events and activities were held by the churches at the school. My personal community involvement included membership as a charter member in the Black Masonic Lodge #242. It was organized at Marlboro School, and I supervised the school provisions of this lodge. I was also in some of the civic and service organizations in Killeen. I was the first Black to belong to the Killeen Rotary International Civic Club. I was also the first Black appointed to the Killeen Housing Authority in January, 1965 and gave ten years of service in this position. The Killeen Daily Herald's article on January 26, 1965, announcing my appointment carried this headline: *"Jackson Named to Housing Panel."* The article read:

> *The Killeen City Council Monday night named the first Negro to serve on the Board of the Killeen Housing Authority. The new appointment is Dock Jackson, Principal at Marlboro Elementary School. He was named to fill the vacancy that would be created March 15th when the term of Toby Boystun expires. Provision had been made when the housing authority was created about 14 years ago for a Negro member to serve on it, but until Monday one had never been named. The city council approved the appointment of Jackson."*

On August 24, 2008, The Killeen Independent School District Board of Trustees rededicated Marlboro Elementary School as Dock Jackson, Jr. Professional Learning Center. Teachers receive training and students are tutored at this center. As educators and community builders, Dock Jackson provided leadership in educating both the youth and adults and was involved in the civic and community organizations. He also provided leadership as a school administrator and served on municipal agencies and committees.

I am Thelma Buhl Jackson and I grew up in Lott-Rosebud, Texas. I received my Bachelor of Science Degree from Paul Quinn College at Waco, Texas, and my Master of Education Degree from Texas Southern University in Houston, Texas. My tenure as a teacher began at Marlboro School. During my tenure in Killeen Independent School District I taught third, fourth, fifth and the sixth grades. I was also a member of the faculty at Sugar Loaf Elementary and Hay Branch Elementary Schools. I retired in 1991 with thirty-four years of service to the youth in this community. My community involvement includes membership in Delta Sigma Theta Sorority, a public service organization of college educated women; Killeen, Texas Retired Teachers Association and a member of Greater Peace Missionary Baptist Church. I am also actively involved in the church ministries to include Mission, Christian Education through the children church and the church Climate Ministry. The late Dock Jackson, Jr. and I are the parents to four adult children: Michael, Tyrone, Vanessa and Adrian. Vanessa and Adrian are graduates of Killeen High School. Michael earned his Bachelor's Degree from Prairie View A and M University in 1972, and is now an Insurance Broker in Houston, Texas. In 1976, Tyrone earned his Bachelor's Degree from Prairie View A and M University, and after graduation served as an officer in the U.S. Navy. After completing his military commitment, Tyrone became an Assistant Principal at the Katy School District. Adrian, our youngest son, is employed in the Appraisal System at Lancaster, Texas. Our sons are using the career each has chosen to give back to their community. Our daughter, Vanessa, resides at home with me in Killeen.

Jamal Adrian Jackson, our grandson, also has some memories of the life of his grandfather, Dock Jackson, Jr. He wrote that his grandfather was born in Rosebud, Texas to the late Mr. and Mrs. Dock Jackson, Sr. and completed his public school training in

Rosebud. He was a young deacon and an active choir member in the Independent Baptist Church. His early public school work began in Rogers, Texas where he was a science teacher, a track and field coach and a basketball coach, and his teams were quite successful. Later in 1955 Grandfather became the first black principal in Killeen, Texas at Marlboro School and remained its principal for fourteen years. During those years the school became Marlboro Elementary School. At one time he was an instructor at Ft. Hood Education Center. He was also an instructor at Gatesville Boys School. He worked as Director of In-School Suspension in Temple, Texas for fourteen years. His love for knowledge and education enabled him to give thirty-eight years of service as a teacher and administrator. During his lifetime Grandfather was one of the persons instrumental in developing a youth center and the Progressive Civic League in the Marlboro Heights Community. He was responsible for securing funds to support the league. He was a member of Omega Psi Phi Fraternity which is a public service fraternity. He helped to secure a number of homes for the needy. Grandfather has left a legacy to the Marlboro Heights Community and to all of the students whose lives he touched and all of the teachers that were his associates. His legacy shall not be forgotten.

Reverend Dr. Roscoe Albert, Sr. and Lucille B. Abercrombie
"Servants of God, Well Done"
Research Team

Reverend Dr. R. A. Abercrombie was a native of Gholson, Texas. He came to Killeen from Waco, Texas in 1955 as the founding pastor of Marlboro Heights Missionary Baptist Church. He inherited a neighborhood of black military and civilian families who were willing to begin building a community patterned after Christian principles. Marlboro Heights was a community planned and developed specifically to provide

71

housing for black families. Reverend Dr. Roscoe Albert Abercrombie, the spiritual and community leader, became the "go to leader," initially for the residents of Marlboro Heights; then later for all minorities; and still later for school boards, city councils, service agencies and community and business leaders of the greater community of Killeen and Fort Hood. He gained the respect of the community's adults and youth and he maintained this earned respect throughout his tenure as pastor of Marlboro Missionary Baptist Church and as a community leader. He and other residents were instrumental in the establishment of a chapter of the NAACP, the VFW and an earlier community organization known as the Progressive Civic League. Prior to Reverend Dr. Abercrombie's call as pastor of Marlboro Church, he served in the U.S. Army during World War II.

After the war, he earned his bachelor's degree from Paul Quinn College in Waco, Texas. On May 1984, the Guadalupe College in Seguin, Texas, conferred upon him the honorary degree of Doctor of Divinity. Reverend Dr. Abercrombie was active in church and in community organizations. He was founder, organizer and President of the first Baptist Ministers' Association of Killeen and Bell County. He was also a life member of the National Association for the Advancement of Colored People, charter member of the Veterans of Foreign Wars Post 9191 in Killeen, Vice Chairman of Bell County Sickle Cell Anemia Association, and life member of Masonic Lodge 620. He gave more than thirty-seven years of service to the Marlboro Heights community and to organizations and agencies of the Killeen and Fort Hood communities. His ministry and leadership have also had an impact on lives of surrounding communities of Central Texas. His service of leadership and mentorship has contributed to the production of many spiritual leaders in this community and abroad. Therefore, he can be considered a Leader of Leaders. His guidance was sought after in many areas of involvement in the life of the black community.

His wife, Lucille Abercrombie, a native of Bay City, Texas was a registered nurse by profession. She received her Registered Nurse Degree from Grady Municipal Hospital School of Nursing in Atlanta, Georgia. Mrs. Abercrombie found employment at the Veterans Administration Hospital in Waco, Texas and remained in this employment for 30 thirty years. She retired after a rewarding career in nursing. She was active in the church and supportive of Dr. Abercrombie's ministry. She served in several ministries at Marlboro Missionary Baptist Church.

In January 1992, Councilwoman Rosa Hereford asked the Council to consider changing the name of Parkhill Drive to R. A. Abercrombie Drive to honor Reverend Dr. Roscoe Albert Abercrombie in recognition of his service in Killeen. In a regular City Council meeting on February 18, 1992, supporters of the name change packed the council chambers, and after listening to the testimony from many supporters the council approved a resolution to name a street to honor Pastor Abercrombie. February 23, 1992 was the date set for the renaming ceremony. A committee co-chaired by Katherine Gordon and Rev. A. R. Speight along with committee members Cloerine Brewer, Jessie Anderson, Adrian Hankins Williams, and Cora Robinson planned the ceremony. City officials, church members, families, residents of Parkhill Drive, Marlboro Heights, the community at-large and friends from Killeen and Fort Hood gathered for the history-making ceremony. It began with the invocation delivered by the Reverend Hubert. E. Debose, Sr., then Alice Douse presented expressions acknowledging the significance of the occasion. She told those assembled that, *"Today, we are all eyewitnesses to history in the making and it is a chapter of history that brings a great deal of pride but with a sense of humility to our honoree and to those who know him. Reverend Dr. Roscoe Albert Abercrombie's influence and guidance helped to shape the emerging community of Marlboro Heights, a small community which later became a vital part of the city of Killeen and this Central Texas Region because of its residents."* She then addressed the Honoree, Rev. Abercrombie: *"The persons assembled here today and many more in the community would like to say to you 'Thank You because you have diligently labored in the vineyard of Killeen and the impact of your labor is being felt here and in surrounding areas of the state and abroad. Therefore, today's event is an acknowledgement to you of deserved honor by the renaming of Parkhill Drive as Rev. R. A. Abercrombie Drive; and that this recognition will be a lasting tribute to a deserving individual for your service, your dedication and your achievement as a leader in this community. As a servant of God and mankind and as a pillar of this community since 1955 you have made a positive difference in this city."* Killeen's Honorable Mayor, Major Blair, Mayor Pro-tem Fred Lathan; City Manager June Lykes and Councilwoman Rosa Hereford participated with their expressions or their presence. The long-awaited moment came in the ceremony when the Honorable Major Blair, Mayor of the city of Killeen, addressed the audience and began the renaming ceremony. He presented the proclamation that proclaimed Sunday, February 23, 1992, Rev. R. A. Abercrombie Day, and stated, *"The street naming is just one honor for a man who has done so much to improve the lives of others in the Killeen area. It is a lasting tribute to a very deserving individual. Reverend Abercrombie has made a lasting impact on his congregation, and the entire city of Killeen, not just Marlboro Heights."*

As Reverend and Mrs. Abercrombie sat together focused on the sign post at the corner of Longview and Parkhill Drive, three of their sons unveiled the new street sign at that corner and the crowd erupted in cheers. The street sign was complete with title and name: ***Rev. R. A. Abercrombie Drive.*** The street is now a landmark for generations to cherish with respect as it extends from Veterans Memorial Boulevard (passing the original site of Marlboro Missionary Baptist Church) to the corner of Zephyr Road.

PROCLAMATION

WHEREAS,	Reverend R. A. Abercrombie has served the Killeen religious community for many years;
WHEREAS,	Reverend R. A. Abercrombie has served as a positive role model within the community;
WHEREAS,	Many citizens of Killeen and members of the Marlboro Heights Baptist Church have petitioned the Killeen City Council to rename a street in Killeen in honor of Reverend Abercrombie;
WHEREAS,	The Killeen City Council on February 18, 1992 passed Ordinance #92-2 renaming Parkhill Drive to Reverend R. A. Abercrombie Drive;
WHEREAS,	The friends of Reverend Abercrombie are gathered on this date to share in the renaming of Reverend R. A. Abercrombie Drive;
NOW, THEREFORE,	I, Major E. Blair, by virtue of the authority vested in me as Mayor of the City of Killeen, do hereby proclaim:

February 22, 1992

as

REVEREND R. A. ABERCROMBIE DAY

In testimony whereof witness my hand and Seal of the City of Killeen this 21st day of February, 1992.

Major E. Blair
MAYOR

Doris J. Johnson
CITY SECRETARY

Reverend Abercrombie graciously acknowledged the honor bestowed upon him by the city when it officially named a street "Rev. R. A. Abercrombie Drive." He viewed the sign bearing his name as symbolic and a reflection of his life and responded, *"I have never had a street named after me before. This is what I have done most of my life, stood at the corner and pointed the way to those who were lost and in a maze. That's been my life, telling people "Go this way" or "Go that way," hoping that someone would come to know Christ in a personal way."*

Reverend Dr. Abercrombie's service extended beyond Killeen. He was secretary/treasurer of the State Evangelical Board of Texas, member of the National Baptist Convention of America, a past moderator of Good Hope Western General Association, coordinator of the State Foreign Mission Board, former treasurer of the Union Baptist

Association, Assistant Pastor and member of the Second Missionary Baptist Church in Waco, Texas, and a member of Phi Beta Sigma Fraternity, Inc. He received many awards and honors during his lifetime. Some were from former Texas Governors: John Connally, Dolph Briscoe and Mark White. He had also received recognition and honor from organizations to include the NAACP, United Negro College Fund, The Good Hope Western General Association, the 1st Cavalry Detachment at Fort Hood and others. The community will long remember the legacy of service and sacrifices of Reverend Dr. Roscoe Albert Abercrombie for the cause of a better community and city in which to live.

Reverends Frederick and Velma Hayden
The Gifts of Ministry
Reverend Velma Hayden

Reverend Frederick Hayden and I were longtime residents of Killeen and the Marlboro Heights community, and we made significant contributions to Central Texas and Killeen. This will give you some insight of our lives as community builders locally and in Central Texas.

Fred was a native of St. Louis, Missouri and he pursued a military career and retired with twenty-five years of service to his country. He was one of the charter members of Anderson Chapel African Methodist Episcopal (AME) Church of Killeen and a faithful layman at both the local and district levels of the AME Church. His service as a trustee and as a steward of Anderson Chapel AME Church in Killeen contributed to the growth and the accomplishment of the church's mission. He accepted the call to preach in 1977 and his ministry included serving as pastor of several churches in the Central Texas Conference of the African Methodist Episcopal Church. This includes Wayman Chapel AME Church in Temple, Robertson Chapel AME Church in McGregor, New Hope AME Church in Austin, Bethel AME Church in Cameron, and St. Stephens AME Church in Bartlett. In

May 1995, Rev. Fred Hayden departed this life for a new home not built by hand.

I have resided, worked and worshiped in the Central Texas cities of Lampasas, Temple, Austin and Killeen over the years. I was a former restaurant entrepreneur in Lampasas, Texas. As the community of Marlboro Heights began to develop and expand, my family was among the early residents in the community. In those early days neither Fred nor I had been called to the ministry. However, we were active in community work which included involvement in the ministries of the church. We were homeowners. I was a licensed cosmetologist and beauty operator. This gave me many opportunities to meet and talk to many people and welcome them to the community. Through my assistance and the hospitality of our family that was extended to newcomers, many were directed to us for finding housing, learning about churches and learning about the community.

Community building became a way of life for me for many years. I was capped a Gray Lady in 1952 at Ft. Hood; served as a Red Cross Volunteer; served on the Board of Directors for the Fort Hood Area Ministry of Christian Concerns; was a Human Resource Consultant and on many occasions personally gave assistance to people and families in need. Community building was not limited to my ministry. I sought higher education opportunities for youth who had limited resources, provided mentoring through positive youth activities, and supported agencies with positive purposes and a cause for accomplishing a better community in which to live. My witness through service in the community churches, in the community organizations and my personal witness to others that I met on different occasions became a seed planted in fertile ground from which a vision grew. My father, Rev. Arthur Anderson, was a preacher for many years and was the pastor of Bethel African Methodist Episcopal Church in Lampasas, Texas. He and my mother played an important role in the organization of an AME church in Killeen, Texas. Prior to 1964 there was no AME Church in the Killeen area. The closest cities for families moving into the Fort Hood Area and surrounding cities with a desire to continue worshiping under the doctrines of the AME Church were Lampasas, Texas, to the west and Belton and

Temple, Texas to the east. However, there were churches of other denominations in Killeen where Blacks were welcomed to worship, and many families of the Marlboro Heights Community became active members of these existing congregations.

I had learned through conversation with residents in the community of their church affiliation prior to moving to Killeen and their desire to have a church closer to attend. I talked with my father and mother about starting a church in Killeen. With their consent to the idea, I began contacting families who were commuting to surrounding AME churches or had previously worshiped in the AME denomination. I coordinated the meeting date, place and time for my father. The meeting was held in our home at 3215 Longview Drive with Rev. Arthur Anderson presiding. It was in this meeting on February 10, 1964 that Anderson Chapel African Methodist Episcopal Church was organized. The charter members are Mary Anderson, Mary Manjang, Eddie Mae Johnson, Willie and Bertie Sworn, Marion J. and Alice Douse, Frederick Hayden and Velma Hayden. The church was named in Rev. Arthur Anderson's honor as the founding pastor of Anderson Chapel African Methodist Episcopal Church.

I accepted the "call" to preach the gospel in 1975 and was appointed by the Presiding Bishop as the pastor of the Liberty Chapel AME Church in Liberty Hill, Texas. My faithfulness to this small congregation made a difference in the life of the Liberty Hill community. However, I also followed my vision to expand opportunities for preaching and teaching. Therefore, I met on December 31, 1976 in my home at 3215 Longview Drive with Thomas Todd, Clifford Carruthers, Charlie Brown, Mattie Buckner, Pearl Perry Braggs and Brother and Sister Leroy Johns in a meeting for the purpose of forming a church in Harker Heights. Then at the close of the meeting I had become the founder and organizer of Adams Chapel AME Church in Harker Heights, Texas. A second meeting with the charter members was held on January 7, 1977 to complete the organization of the church. The first service was held in the New Light Lodge No. 242 Hall on January 16, 1977 and continued there until the church was able to secure a building. On February 15, 1978 three trustees and I signed a promissory note to purchase the building at 125 East Arlo Road, Harker Heights. In addition to being the founder, I served as the pastor of Adams Chapel from 1976-1982. The official name became Adams Chapel AME Church. The church is still located at its original site in Harker Heights, Texas.

While serving as pastor of Adams Chapel AME Church, I became the founder of a second church, Thomas Chapel AME on May 20, 1981. The organizational meeting was held in the home of Mr. and Mrs. Jack Turner at 309 Avenue G in Copperas Cove, Texas. The church was named in honor of the late Presiding Elder F.D. Thomas. A building owned by the 1001 Lodge located at 901 N. Main Street in Copperas Cove, Texas was rented and the first worship service was held on the third Sunday in June of 1981. The charter members included Jack Turner, Betty Turner, Charlie Ware, Beverly Ware, Lorraine Edwards, Eric Edwards and Jennifer Edwards. Rev. Aubrey Pickens was the first pastor of Thomas Chapel AM.E. Church and served in this position until 1984. The church is still located at its original site.

I founded and organized a third church, Ninth Hour AME Church. It was originally located in Copperas Cove but later moved to Killeen and then permanently closed in 1995. Bryant A.M.E. Youth Church was the fourth and last church that I founded and organized in Killeen. It was organized as a training church for youth under the supervision of adults. After four pastoral appointments to this young church, Bryant AME Youth Church also closed.

I was appointed by the presiding Bishop of the African Methodist Episcopal Church to co-pastor with my husband, Rev. Frederick Hayden, at Wayman Chapel AME Church in Temple, Texas. After the passing of Rev. Fred Hayden, I was appointed pastor of Wayman Chapel AME Church for one year and was reappointed for a second year as Wayman Chapel's pastor. In 1995 the Presiding Bishop of the Tenth Episcopal District of the AME Church appointed me the Presiding Elder of the Austin Capital District of the Central Texas Conference where I served nine years.

My technical training and professional education was obtained both stateside and overseas. It includes training at Crescent School of Cosmetology and Austin Texas Beauty College in Austin, Texas; Nixon-Clay Business College and Peoples Business College in

Austin, Texas. My professional preparation was obtained from Tillotson College in Austin, Texas; Paul Quinn College in Waco, Texas; Central Texas College in Killeen, Texas; the University of Texas in Austin, Texas; and Seminary of Southern Baptist in New Orleans, Louisiana. On May 18, 1996, I received my doctorate degree from American International Bible Institute and Seminary. I also received college credit from my tour of Asia Minor which occurred when I accompanied my husband on his military assignment to NATO and witnessed an enjoyable and educational experience of touring Asia. I experienced praying at the tomb of John; visiting the last dwellings of the Holy Virgin; touring five of the seven churches of Asia Minor; worshiping in the only living one, which is Smyrna; visiting the prison where Paul was held; viewing a piece of the Leigh with which Christ was pierced in the side; traveling to the Isle of Patmos and viewing the remnants of the Four Gospels.

My tenure of ministry in the AME Church was served with dedication, compassion, understanding and loyalty. As layman, minister, pastor and presiding elder, I made a significant contribution to expanding opportunities for worship under the doctrines and traditions of the African Methodist Episcopal Church in Central Texas. I am grateful to have had the opportunity to be a community builder, not only locally, but also regionally in Bell County and its neighboring communities.

Shelton and Muriel Elizabeth Bell
Living Life Serving Others
Muriel E. Bell

Shelton and I came to Killeen in 1954 when he was assigned to Fort Hood, Texas. Blacks couldn't live in Killeen; therefore, we lived outside of Fort Hood in Walker Village, a housing area on Central Avenue. When the Army completed New Chaffee Village, we moved on Goff St. on our twenty-fifth anniversary.

I have memories about the early days of the city of Killeen at that time. The town and the schools were segregated. Mixed marriages were neither allowed nor accepted in the city. Sears and Roebuck and Montgomery Wards were in Killeen as catalog order stores. The city had a big furniture store and there was also a Piggly Wiggly Grocery Market. Killeen also had a bus station on Second Street and the bus would run from Killeen to Temple. It stopped anywhere along the highway to pick up people. Killeen's train station was just east of the Killeen Chamber of Commerce's current location. My teenage daughter had to get a permit to take a train in Killeen when she was ready to go to college in San Francisco, California. My mother who came to visit us from California was the first black traveler to get *off* the train in Killeen.

Housing for Blacks was very limited in Killeen. Simmonsville, located on the north side of Highway Business 190 (now Veterans Memorial Boulevard) in the eastern part of Killeen, had mostly sub-standard housing available for Blacks. In 1954, a new housing development, Marlboro Heights was started on the south side of Highway Business 190 with prefabricated-like duplexes built along Stetson Avenue. The availability of more houses began when contractors started additional building along Highland Avenue, Terrace, Marlboro and Lewis Drive, and later on Hillside Drive. The construction pattern progressed to developing Longview and Jefferies Avenue (starting on the north end at Business Hwy 190), then to Parkhill Drive (now known as Rev. R. A. Abercrombie Dr.). The development moved to Taft and June Streets (between Jefferies and Parkhill Drive), and then to Zephyr Road. During the early days Marlboro Heights' west boundary was County Road and Stetson Ave. The south boundary was Zephyr Road. The north boundary was Business Highway 190. The east boundary was Jefferies Avenue. The remaining surrounding areas were open fields and low-lying areas filled with cedar trees or tall grass. The Rose Addition of Marlboro Heights was developed south of Zephyr Road. This housing addition and the houses that were built on Haynes Drive (east of Jefferies Avenue) expanded the east and south boundaries of Marlboro Heights.

Jobs were hard to find for African Americans. I am a native of Chicago, Illinois and had worked civil service before. Therefore, I worked in the laundry in order not to lose my civil service status. I was blessed to get a job at the Post hospital on the OB/Gyn Ward, and I enjoyed the work. In 1959 I resigned in order to join my husband at Brooke Army Hospital, Ft. Sam Houston, Texas, where he was hospitalized for four months.

Dr. McRoberts and Dixie Hamilton owned the Killeen General Hospital. Dr. Paggett was a resident doctor there and he admitted his patients to Killeen General. I did private duty nursing and when one of my patients went to the hospital she asked for me to be her private duty nurse there. When she expired I asked to be employed by the hospital and was told they had never had a colored employee. However, when the new wing was completed for newborns at the hospital, I was hired and became the first African American nurse employed in Killeen's General Hospital, which was located at that time on Rancier and a few blocks from the Fort Hood East Gate.

In 1958 Superintendent E. M. Green organized and became pastor of God's Holy Tabernacle Church of God in Christ in the Simmonsville Community. I was a missionary there. I was actively involved in the life of the communities of Marlboro Heights and Simmonsville. In 1960 Reverend Smith, the pastor of the Servicemen's Independent Methodist Episcopal (IME) Church, bought a barrack building and placed it in back of his house at 806 Jefferies Avenue. In 1961, my family moved from Ft. Hood to 804 Jefferies Avenue. Reverend Smith arranged for bus service for soldiers from the Post to attend worship services. I helped Reverend Smith with the young soldiers. I taught Bible Studies, helped feed them and entertain those that came off the post because the soldiers had no place in Killeen to go on weekends. Because of this involvement, I have many positive memories of the families who have lived here. At one time or another I helped work with Marlboro Heights Missionary Baptist Church members when they were establishing their Missionary Circle, Vacation Bible School and Sunday school. My daughter Janice and I also worked with Anderson Chapel African Methodist Episcopal Church during the Vietnam War while the men of their church were gone from Ft. Hood. I also volunteered for Red Cross on the Post.

There were black businesses in the community. The first black businesses were Maurice's Barbecue, Miller's Community Cleaners, Gibson's Barber Shop, Katie's Beauty Shop in her home, Hortense Wright Guilky Beauty Shop, Lee's Beauty Shop in her home, and Big Jackson Trailer Court. A group of men in the Marlboro Community also opened a car wash together. Day cares were also started in the homes and Jeffey Lockett's early childcare school opened at the Marlboro Center.

Community building became a part of my life in this new community of Marlboro Heights. My involvement included teaming with Wadella Heath and becoming co-organizers of the VFW Post 9191 Ladies Auxiliary. I became the Ladies Auxiliary's first president and served in the position for three years. As a volunteer for the VFW, we visited veterans at the Temple VA Hospital. Ted Cornell was the VFW District Commander then and furnished the cars for our visitations to the Temple VA Hospital. Shelton received a change of station orders and we moved away.

In 1965, my husband, Shelton and I returned to Killeen from California. Shelton retired with twenty-one years of military service. I was reinstated at Darnall Hospital until I retired in 1966. After retiring from civil service, I opened Bell's Religious Supply House at 1409 E. Business Highway 190 and Conder Drive. We had the first Bible bookstore in Killeen. I was a representative for the Thompson Chain Reference Bible. After four years with the Bible bookstore, I closed it and was employed by the Killeen Independent School District as a clinic aide (an assistant to the school nurse) at Manor Jr. High School. My duties were to take care of the daily operation of the clinic because the school nurse serviced several schools and was not there full time. It was also my duty to care for the health needs of the students and sometimes the teachers and other employees. I served in this position for ten years and retired at the end of the 1980 school year.

In 1988, I served as a member of the Central Texas Council of Government for eight years. I served as a liaison with RSVP, a service for the elderly that was available in seven counties. I received many certificates of recognition. I also did seminars on self-esteem in the schools and in Bell County. I also taught church etiquette.

In April 1989, I became a widow but remained in the Marlboro Heights community until April, 1993. Then I moved to Copperas Cove, Texas. However, I stayed in touch with the many families, friends, former Manor students, other youth who grew up in the area who now were young adults with their own families. I also stayed in touch with the churches, civic organizations and social events in the Killeen community. My church membership is at the Christian House of Prayer (CHOP) in Killeen and Copperas Cove, which allowed me opportunities of service to witness as a teacher, a student and doer of the Word.

The Lord blessed me to attend Seminary at "Speak the Word School of Ministry" through CHOP. I graduated with a bachelor's degree in the class of 1996. In the year 2000, I moved from Copperas Cove back to Killeen and I continue to be blessed. I had an opportunity to expand God's ministry beyond my church, beyond the city, beyond the Bible Study Group to the residents of the Veranda Apartments in Killeen where I lived. My God's ministry also expanded to a TV ministry on Killeen's Christian Television Station, KPLE, Channel 31 or Cable 45. At the age of eighty-three I made my television debut on March 19, 2002, hosting a weekly television program, "Ministry of Hope." I talk about whatever the Lord leads me to talk about. My preparation was through fasting and prayer. I wanted to do the weekly program because I love God's people and wanted to share with them my relationship with God.

O'Neal and Cora Wynn
No Pot of Gold, but a Richer Fulfilling Life
O'Neal Wynn

My family and I came to Killeen from Dallas in 1956. At the time of this interview by the task force representative I had lived in Killeen for more than forty years. I talked about my experience when I first came to

Killeen with great details. This is my story told my way. My motivation to come to Fort Hood came from a conversation with my brother-in-law. I was told that I could get rich down here in five years. Therefore, I came here to put up shoe shine parlors all around Killeen, get rich and then go back to Dallas. My first impression of the town was one of awe because I was looking at all of the soldiers who could be potential customers for my shine parlors over a five year span. Housing was scarce in Killeen, but I had purchased a house in the Simmonsville community before coming to Killeen. My wife's mother and father, who lived next to the house we had purchased, were overseeing the local transactions for me until I could move down here. We had just a few neighbors in the area. Our community was not as developed as the new development across the Highway 190, known as Marlboro Heights. We knew that Marlboro Heights was there in 1956, but we stayed right here in Simmonsville and my family began making improvements on our home. There were no indoor toilet facilities, so I went about two miles out to county to see a man who put a water toilet in my house. My family was the first family in the Simmonsville community to have an indoor water toilet installed in our home. We purchased a vacant lot next to our property on which an outdoor toilet existed that was used by anyone in the neighborhood and referred to as a community toilet. After we had installed our water toilet I gave the neighbors a thirty day notice to have water toilets installed because that community toilet will be torn down. After thirty days it was torn down and the ground where it sat was filled and covered with concrete. Afterward, all the home-owner neighbors had water toilets installed in their homes. My family allowed the nearby church to use our home bathroom facilities initially until they had indoor plumbing installed. Improving my community was important to me. I became a community builder.

In 1963 we purchased another home in Marlboro Heights as our new residence. "It was time now to establish my shoe shine business and begin work; however, my first job to start off was part-time, working for the concessionaire owner. He was the one who had the concessionaire and was over all of the barber shops on the post. My job was to clean all the barbershops early in the morning. The owner wanted to pay me but I didn't want to be paid because I wanted to shine shoes at the shops. The owner said, "You are welcome to shine shoes out here, but you won't make any money. Low quarter slippers were fifteen cents a pair to be shined and combat boots were thirty-five cents a pair for shining them." I couldn't charge anybody more than these prices then. Now today, more than fifty years later, the shines are six and seven dollars a pair. That's what I thought I was going to earn when I got here. I thought this town was really bigger than it was. I thought I would have about thirty to forty shoe shine locations when I got through putting them up and this would take care of my family. There were hundreds of shine parlors where I had left in Dallas, but I didn't have any of those shoe shine places. I just worked at my shoe shine stand at the Adolphus Hotel and I knew just how much I made. I also knew how the people were so nice to me. Some would tip me fifty cents, a dollar and some tipped me more. In Killeen one of the bank owners told me that they would let me have the money I needed; but I didn't pursue it because I thought Fort Hood was a temporary post. I had heard rumors about Fort Hood's temporary status. I never thought the post would become as big a deal as it is today.

"My first eight-hour job when I moved to Killeen was working with another concessionaire owner who had all the laundries on the Fort Hood post. How I began working for him can best be described by saying I just went in, took the job and later ran the laundry for him. Getting this job came about in a strange way. The laundry owner hired me and another lady to get the laundry ready for an inspection at Fort Hood. After the inspection was over, he told me that he didn't have anything for me to do. I explained to him that I have a wife and four daughters to take care of and I need to work. The owner's reply was that he was sorry, but he can't pay any more help. Then I told him that I'll work a whole week for you free to let him know that he needs me here. You'll see how much it will help your place of business. I pointed out to him to look at the grease and stuff all over the floor. Every time they drop a uniform they have to wash it over. When I get through, they won't have to do that. The owner gave no response, but I just went out there and took the job.

"I got me a gallon bucket, a gallon of Naphtha gas and some old rags that were stacked up like a haystack and were going to be thrown away. I got something to put under my knees, went under those pressers while the men and women were running them and I cleaned up all of that stuff. Then the week was up. When payday came on Saturday, the owner touched me on the back and asked if I had turned in my time. I said, no sir, because you told me that you couldn't pay me and I told you that I was going to work for you for free. Then the owner told me to tell the secretary every hour I had worked and she will pay me for that. Also, tell her to give you an extra ten dollars. I received my pay. As I returned from the secretary's office, the owner asked me to go downtown with him. We went to the key place. He had keys made for all of his laundry pick-up and drop-off stations at Fort Hood; for his main place on Rancier (where his big building was); and for his building in Temple. Then he gave all those keys to me. He said to me, "I'm not going to give you only one job; "I'm going to give you two." I had the job of cleaning up at the big place, the job of delivering and picking up clothes to and from the laundry stations and also the main laundry. I worked for this owner for a little better than three years. Almost all of my work was done at night. The workers began complaining and threatened to strike when they learned that my pay was much higher than any of the laundry workers and they had hardly ever seen me at the laundry. You see, I just took that job and I made more money at it than any job I had ever had. The laundry owner said that he had to let me go. I left this job, and later got eight-hour employment at the Fort Hood PX. I worked there for several years before my retirement."

D. S. and Gertrude Freeman
Love of Country and Community
D. S. Freeman

We arrived at Fort Hood in November of 1955. The closest place that we could find a house to live in before the houses in Marlboro Heights were built was in Belton, Texas. Therefore, we purchased a house in Marlboro Heights because we didn't have a place to live. When we first arrived in the Marlboro community my wife, Gertrude, didn't like the area. There were not many people in the community at that time; therefore, we had just a few neighbors. The first dwellings that were built in Marlboro Heights were the apartments on Stetson Avenue. After the apartments on Stetson, then, our house and a few others were built on Terrace Avenue, Highland Avenue and Lewis Drive. These houses were put up in a whisk. They were built very quickly.

There was no church in Marlboro Heights when we first got here until Rev. Abercrombie came to Killeen and the church was started. He had gotten out of the Army and was living in Waco. He drove a taxi at Fort Hood, and he spent a lot of time at the bus station because of this. Later, a barrack was moved onto the present location and the renovation began. My wife was not a charter member of Marlboro Heights Baptist Church. She joined after it was organized and with the other ladies in the community became an active worker in the church. The men in the community and I would bring chairs on Sunday that we borrowed from Fort Hood so that the people would have somewhere to sit. When the church opened in 1955, it only had hard benches for its seating.

The city was different at that time. The city citizens and the Marlboro Heights community relationships were also different than today, some forty years later. There was no means of city transportation to and from the community. We had to use our own cars. We could do some shopping downtown, but even though we could, we often sensed a reluctant welcome when doing so. We definitely couldn't go downtown to eat in those places. They were all off limits to us. We stayed here thirteen months before I was reassigned to another military post. My wife, Gertrude, remained in Marlboro Heights at that time. I never was reassigned back to Fort Hood; therefore, my wife later joined me at one of my duty stations. Mrs. Polly, my neighbor, took care of renting our house. I came back TDY only one time to make needed repairs on my house.

In January, 1973, I retired from the Army at Fort Stewart, Georgia and returned here to live. We decided that since we had done so much work on the house, we would make Killeen our home. The community had grown. The city had also grown, and the atmosphere had changed for the better. In addition to my military duty, my contributions to making the community better in this area came through my employment. The nature of my work was in community and humanity building. After my retirement I went to Brown Barbering School in Austin, Texas. I worked a year at Fort Hood as a barber, worked with the Texas Youth Council (TYC) at Gatesville, Texas and finally worked at the Texas Department of Correction (TDC) as a supervisor. I retired with a disability in January 1985, and continued to reside in the Marlboro Heights community in the home that I purchased in 1955 until 2010 and beyond.

Godfrey G. and Nonie F. Langrum
Committed Community Leaders and Supporters
Research Team and Faye Langrum Woodard

Godfrey and Nonie Langrum were among the early community builders residing in Marlboro Heights. Both are charter members of Marlboro Heights Missionary Baptist Church, which had its opening in 1955. Godfrey was a native Texan and Nonie a native of Mississippi. They were a military family. Godfrey by U. S. orders had been assigned to Fort Hood, Texas. They were active in the community. His ministry service in the church included that of deacon, trustee, finance committee member, Sunday school teacher and Sunday school superintendent. He was active in the community as a member of the Veterans of Foreign Wars (VFW) Post 9191 of which he was a former Commander. He was also a member of New Light Lodge #242, Prince Hall Mason and member of United Supreme Council 33. He received the honor of "Honorary Past Grand Master," the highest honor in the Blue House Masonry on his 90th birthday. He had distinguished himself in Freemasonry over several decades of continuous service since 1938 and had been a member of New Light Lodge #242 since it was established more than thirty years ago. He was the lodge's oldest member. He also received honors for participation in other area community organizations.

A great deal of Nonie Langrum's community work centered on her church and its ministries. Her involvement in the Parent Teacher Association and her service to Girl Scouting in the Marlboro Heights community were also welcomed contributions. At Marlboro Heights Missionary Baptist Church, her service included the positions of deaconess, chairman of the pulpit committee, corresponding secretary and member of the mission ministry and the senior choir. She was an active member of the Marlboro Elementary School Parent Teacher Association and served as a classroom mother for many years and giving support to the school and its various activities in many ways. Working with the Girl Scouts and the scout leaders was an area in which Nonie Langrum demonstrated and shared many of her skills as an organizer, through her arts and craft skills and in coordinating Girl Scout projects such as the annual cookie sale and preparation for camping trips. Their daughter, Faye, was a member of the Brownie Scout Troop when Nonie began working with the scout leaders as a parent aide. She was dependable and helpful. You could count on her to volunteer and assist with the coordination of the cookie sales, chaperone camp outings and parade events, teach and help with arts and crafts projects. She continued to support the scout program as Faye moved to the next levels of Girl Scouting. She also shared her time and resources, along with her talent to ensure that the projects were a success. As a member of the Eastern Stars, Nonie Langrum also participated in many of their community projects. Both Godfrey and Nonie Langrum are now deceased, but we acknowledge their leadership and service as community builders.

Willie Gibson
Soldier, Businessman and Municipal Public Servant
Willie and Katie Gibson

My husband, Willie Gibson, and I came to Killeen, Texas in the fall of 1955 on a military assignment with the U. S. Army. He obtained recognition as a trailblazer in the Fort Hood-Killeen area almost twenty years before he became the first African-American Councilman in Killeen. In 1955 his military assignment at Fort Hood, Texas brought recognition to Willie Gibson as the first African American top grade sergeant major to serve at Ft. Hood. Fort Hood was recently integrated and had never had an African American military personnel over a unit. Willie was assigned as a battalion sergeant major. His contribution to the military and to the community toward promoting a better relationship and understanding among the civilian and military communities was significant far beyond that which we have realized it would be. After he retired from the army in 1962, he entered the business world and later the world of politics. He was successful in all three areas.

Willie Gibson and I were owners of the Marlboro Barber Shop. It was named for its location in the predominately black area of town called the Marlboro Heights addition. It originated as a residential business with the garage being converted for the shop at our home on Hillside Drive in Killeen, Texas. In 1962, two operators, Willie Gibson and the late Clifford Young, provided the barbering service. At that same time Willie Gibson was also employed part-time at the Barber Concession on Ft. Hood, Texas. Therefore, it became necessary to hire another employee, Edna Johnson, the wife of SFC Earl Johnson, was hired as the barber shop's third barber.

As the barber business thrived, it was necessary to find a larger place to accommodate a three-chair shop. Therefore in 1968 Roy Hamilton, manager of Roby's Motel on East Business Hwy 190 leased us the ample floor space needed. The barber shop operators in this new location were Willie Gibson, the late Clifford Young and the late Andrew White. When Marlboro Barber Shop moved to Roby's Motel, the Hillside space was rented to Mildred Dillard of LaMil's Beauty Salon. In a short while the Roby Motel property was sold, and new owner had other plans for the entire area; therefore, the barber shop moved again.

In 1969 a property at 2807 Terrace Drive in Marlboro Heights was purchased and remodeled for a three-chair barber shop; a three chair beauty shop; and a pool table and sauna room. The beauty shop operators were Mary Redrick (formerly Hardeman), Clarice Burnett (formerly Gibson) and LaJune Crews, who later made a permanent change of station (PCS) with her husband to Germany. The beauty shop became a source of opportunities for several other beauty shop operators to receive experience working at Marlboro Beauty Shop. Among these were Marisa DeBose, Bevlon Mustiful, Tommy Poindexter and Jewel Williams. The newly remodeled Barber/Beauty Shop at 2807 Terrace Drive also had three barber operators: Willie Gibson, the late Clifford Young and a new barber, Jean Woolridge.

On October 16, 1976, the Marlboro Barber and Beauty Shop was incorporated, a goal we had accomplished with which we were very pleased. In October 1979, fire caused extensive damage to the building and equipment on Terrace Drive; thus, relocating was again necessary. The Marlboro Barber Shop returned to Hillside Drive. During that time Willie Gibson had earned his broker's license and spent a great deal of time pursuing real estate interests. Mary Redrick decided to open her own shop. Clifford Young and Mr. Gibson temporarily operated in the back of Stylistic Beauty Shop, which was owned by Hortense Gilkey and located on Zephyr Road. After a period of working in temporary conditions, Willie Gibson returned to his shop on Hillside Drive. Clifford Young opened a shop downtown in Killeen on Avenue C and worked there until his demise in March 1985. Having retired from full-time barbering, Willie Gibson still had a few old faithful customers by appointment, and he was thankful to God for the opportunity he had to have known and serviced so many wonderful customers. As business leaders in the community, we facilitated the expansion of entrepreneurship in the areas of barbering and cosmetology for many Blacks by providing a place for beauticians and barbers to exercise their skills and later become entrepreneurs in their own businesses.

Willie and I left our mark on the Marlboro community not only as business leaders, but for the contribution of our personal skills and talents in the ministries of our church, Marlboro Heights Missionary Baptist Church and through the community organizations in which we provided leadership or held membership. Our three daughters, Clarice, Letha and Sheri are among the successful youth of the community and are now responsible and productive adult citizens in the communities in which they reside.

Willie Gibson is also a trailblazer in politics for Blacks in Killeen. By far, one of his most significant achievements for him was becoming the first African-American Municipal Councilman of Killeen, a position previously held only by whites. Willie Gibson realized there was a need to have a representative on the council to express the views and desires of the voters, especially minorities. The local citizens convinced him to seek this slot. He agreed to give it a try. In the spring of 1972, there were three seats vacant for councilman-at-large. Willie Gibson ran but was narrowly defeated by twenty-two votes. Many people who previously supported him in this endeavor encouraged him to run again, which he did. The voter's response received from the citizens in his first election resulted in his running in a second election. Willie Gibson entered his second political race for City Councilman-at-large in 1973. He campaigned in a field of seven candidates vying for one of the three at-large seats. His platform was stated in a newspaper ad which appeared in the Killeen Daily Herald.

Citizens of Killeen:

I am soliciting your vote when you go to the polls to elect your city council. I am seeking the position of councilman-at-large. I have entered the race because I can be of service to you by serving the people of Killeen. Our city has shown record growth each year, and we expect it to continue to do so. The areas

93

of construction, city government, city improvement and the extension of services have been a probable visible sign of this growth. We must work to keep this progress orderly and beneficial.

I believe that we should continue these programs and projects that will benefit all of our citizens. We should continue to support improvements in law enforcement, which will keep our city a safe and a desirable place to live. I also believe that we should continue to extend existing services, programs and facilities.

So that you will know more about me and my qualifications to hold the position of councilman-at-large, I present the following information. I am a native of Texas, and have been a resident of Killeen for nineteen years. I reside at 2709 Hillside Drive with my wife, Katie, and our three daughters: Clarice, 16, Letha, 13 and Sheri, 6. I am the owner and operator of Marlboro Barber and Beauty Shop of this city. My family and I are members of the Marlboro Heights Baptist Church, where I am a deacon and the financial secretary.

My civic activities include membership in the Veterans of Foreign Wars, in which I am a charter member, and for four years served as Quartermaster; secretary of the Central Texas Consistory #306; as a 33rd Degree Mason; treasurer of the New Light Lodge 242; member of the Killeen Chamber of Commerce; secretary for the last six years of the Barber Local #778 AFL-CIO; member of the Board of Directors of the Killeen-Harker Heights United Fund, Killeen Library Committee, Central Texas Council of Governments and the Bell/Coryell County Big Brothers Programs.

I received my education and professional training in San Antonio, Texas. Graduated from

Phyllis Wheatly High School; attended St. Phillips Junior College; and graduated from the Alamo Barber Shop College.

After 21 years of service, I retired from the United State Army in 1952 as a sergeant major. During my Army career, I served in many administrative positions as an administrative specialist. I believe that this experience will be beneficial to you as I serve as your councilman-at-large. I am soliciting your vote, and that of every citizen of Killeen. I will serve in this position to the best of my ability, and as your councilman-at-large, I will represent the citizens of Killeen.

The support of each of you on Tuesday, April 2, will be appreciated and properly recognized.

Sincerely Yours,
Willie Gibson

Political Adv. Paid by Emery Davis, 2715 Marlboro Drive, Killeen, Texas

This ad during the Killeen City Council 1974 election campaign clearly and specifically established this candidate's strong platform in the interest of all citizens of Killeen. It introduced him as capable of fulfilling the position and made a sincere appeal for the votes of all citizens. Now better informed of this candidate the results on April 2, 1974 were historic for the city of Killeen. Willie Gibson was elected. He became the first Black City Councilman in the history of Killeen, Texas. When the votes from the four wards were counted, Willie Gibson was among the top three candidates receiving votes and a winner on his second attempt in the political arena. (See Killeen Daily Herald Chart.): *Dr. Sidney Young, the incumbent, was also re-elected to his seat.

Candidates	North	South	East	West	Total
Dr. Sidney Young	179	274	21	92	760
Dr. Sidney Isdale	163	254	151	115	683
Willie Gibson	63	258	82	117	520
Stanley Cohen	97	183	123	96	499
John C. Odom	93	170	124	84	471
Mack Forsythe	67	180	109	102	458
David Ruiz	91	147	11	94	449
J.M. Keefe	96	166	108	51	421
Rev. Ed Green	18	80	26	53	177

Willie Gibson faithfully served the Killeen citizens for six years (three consecutive two-year terms) which is the maximum allowed based on term limits already established by the city charter. His message to the citizens of Killeen expressed in this ad was a commitment of service, which he fulfilled with dedication and integrity during each of his terms of office. At the end of his tenure, he was honored by local church congregations, fraternal organizations, city officials and friends in appreciation for the unselfish and selfless service rendered and a job well done. It was a remarkable day and unique tribute. His concern was to make a better community life for everyone. Therefore, he represented and served not only the minorities but all citizens as a whole. By his very presence on the council, he was certainly instrumental in maintaining and furthering the harmony and goodwill already in progress. He was also a forerunner for others who would strive to continue responsible and progressive city government. There were many citizens that believed that he could make a difference in the lives of ALL people of the Killeen and Fort Hood Area.

Willie Gibson was not only well respected in the Marlboro Heights community and by African-Americans, but he was also highly respected by citizens throughout the city and neighboring communities. His valuable services as a member of Marlboro Heights Missionary Baptist Church and in his many community activities were well known. During all of those years in military service and public service most of all, his family—Katie, his wife, and daughters Clarice, Letha and Sheri were a reliable and productive support system for him. Willie Gibson did make a positive difference in the city of Killeen, just as he did in the lives of military personnel assigned to his care in1955. Citizens continued to recognize the dedicated and effective service of Willie Gibson during his tenure in city government and long after his tenure as a Killeen City Councilman ended.

Bobby and Cloerine Brewer
Community Leaders and Champions for Justice
Cloerine Brewer

I first came to this city in 1954 to visit my brother, Samuel Mack Williams, who was in the Civilian Conservation Corps (CCC). He was here helping to build Camp Hood, which later became Fort Hood. My husband, Bobby Brewer, and I returned to this city in 1956 to live and experienced the housing shortage. When we arrived in Marlboro Heights, housing was so scarce that sometimes two families would live in one house. At that time segregation was so prevalent we could only live in certain areas of the town. Marlboro Heights and Simmonsville were the designated communities for Blacks to live and both were located just east of the city limits of Killeen. The city's attempt to run a bus every hour in the Marlboro Heights community was unsuccessful. However, we could ride downtown for about twenty-five or thirty cents on the intercity bus that ran down Highway 190 from Killeen to Temple or get a cab which was quite expensive.

In the early years, the need for places of worship became the focus in the community. The first church for Blacks was Simmonsville Baptist Church. The year 1951 commemorates both the anniversary of the official naming of the church under a Baptist minister and the anniversary of the official edifice in which to worship. The founding pastor was Reverend John Wiley Bosier. In later years, Reverend A. R. D. Hubbard became the pastor of that church. Then, Marlboro Baptist Church was organized in 1955 and became the second church in the community. Reverend Roscoe A. Abercrombie became the founding pastor of this church. Some three years later, a Pentecostal Church was organized in Simmonsville, and Reverend E. M. Green became the founding pastor of The Holy Tabernacle Church of God in Christ. As the community grew, other churches were later organized. There was the Serviceman Church on Zephyr Road, which was organized by a serviceman, SGT Smith. After he left Fort Hood, several ministers were pastors of that church, sometimes under the denomination of the IME Church and sometimes as other denominations. In 1964 Anderson Chapel African Methodist Episcopal Church was organized. It was the first AME church in the Killeen, Harker Heights and Copperas Cove area. Reverend Arthur Anderson was the founding pastor of this church. We were called colored people at that time, so these were the only churches that colored people could attend in Killeen.

There were very few organizations of different groups for military and their dependents in the community. During the early years when our husbands went away on military assignments, the church was where many families spent much time involved in the activities of the ministries of the church. Then later on, organizations such as the Progressive Civic League, the VFW and the VFW Ladies Auxiliary were formed. The first attempt to organize a chapter of the NAACP was initiated by Rev. R. A. Abercrombie during the Sixties. After a small response from his congregation and the Marlboro Heights community, he opened up memberships from the Waco Chapter in which he was a member. The membership dues were 50 cents and some adult and youth members of the church took out a membership. However, later the urgency of establishing a chapter in Killeen became more evident as incidents began to occur in the community. One such incident that sparked the assembly of community persons and their formation into a committee was the announcement of the closing of the Marlboro Elementary School at the end of the 1969 school term. The purpose of the committee was to seek a resolution to the announcement in order to keep the neighborhood school open. Their protests were to no avail. The school was closed as announced. However, through the concern and diligent work of a self-appointed committee, the support of the community and the assistance of the nearest NAACP chapter, the Killeen Branch NAACP was organized and received its charter in 1970. Clyde Williams was elected president; Willie Jefferson was elected vice president; and Reuben Hatcher was elected secretary-treasurer.

A Masonic organization was also formed. The masonic family in this community is considered to be one of the oldest Black establishments in the city of Killeen. We have our own building which is located on Thirty-Eighth Street. The organization includes the Eastern Stars; the Heroines of Jericho; the Golden Circle; Arantha Court; the Blue House Masons; and the Consistory which consists of Thirty-Second Degree Masons; Your Temple; and Your Thirty-Third Degree Harges Rites. Under the masonic family you also have the Daughters of Issi which is the ladies auxiliary for the Shriners Temple. There was also one other club formed in the 70s. It was a club for the women called the "Waiting Wives Club." I was a charter member of this club. This was a club where many of the wives got together while their husbands were in Vietnam. It was more of a social club.

Community involvement was very important to our family. My community service also included tenures as PTA president, both at the local school level and at the school district level. While working with PTA, I served as Haynes Elementary School's PTA President, and later served as vice president and president of the Council of PTAs in the Killeen Independent School District. This Council was composed of the executive officers and the presidents of about eight or nine schools that had local PTAs. I was the first Black to serve in this position in the Killeen Independent School District (KISD). As President of the Council of PTAs, I attended the National PTA Conference in Nashville, Tennessee. I believe that I was also the first council president to attend a National PTA Convention representing Killeen Independent School District. Our family had not only been active in the community life of the Marlboro community, but I have also been involved in the activities of the City of Killeen and of

Bell County. I have served as a worker in many political elections as a voting clerk at the voting precincts and assisted with the voting booths. My husband, Bobby Brewer, and I have always been interested in politics to a certain extent, but not nearly as much as maybe we should have been. Bobby was always active in the community and in his organizations. He found himself being a trailblazer in his employment. In the early 70s, he was the first black route salesman for the Martin Linen Company out of Waco, Texas. He was also the first black landfill supervisor for the city of Killeen. He was a willing advocate for the community and supported many efforts along with me in the political arena.

The Killeen Independent School Board had never had a minority or black serving on the School Board prior to 1990; however, there had been candidates that came forth from the black community to run for a seat as trustee. Powell Brook (1978), Hallie Tolbert, Jr. and Patrick Booker (1983), Janice Harris (1985) and I, Cloerine Brewer, were all unsuccessful in our campaigns for school board trustee. After the election was over, my campaign committee agreed that it was time to initiate a strategy to accomplish our campaign goal. It was decided that we would try to change the system under which candidates were elected to office. There were many hours and many days of work and meetings with the Killeen Independent School District Superintendent and the Board of Trustees. We worked very hard trying to get the school board to agree to adopt the election system of single member districts in the city of Killeen for electing board trustees. All efforts failed in that area. The committee's next decision was to take the case to the courts. Litigation began when a group of concerned citizens retained Attorney Walker from Little Rock, Arkansas. I was a Plaintiff in this lawsuit; also T'chia Gilmore, who was Korean; and Humberto Flores, who was Hispanic. The lawsuit made big news in Killeen and the Central Texas area because no one had ever challenged the way that school board members were elected. The case was rejected by both the state and district courts on appeal. While we lost in the legal arena, there was a change on the horizon for Killeen ISD. More jobs became available for Blacks. In 1990 Fannie Flood was appointed to fill the unexpired term of one of the trustees on the KISD School Board and she became KISD's first Black to serve in this position by appointment. At the end of this appointed term, she campaigned for re-election to the same seat on the KISD Board of Trustees, but was unsuccessful in winning the seat. In 1992, Dr. Edward Wagner was the first Black to be elected to the Killeen Independent School District Board of Trustees and served until 1997. He served as vice president of the board during 1996-97. Brenda Coley became the second Black to be elected to the Killeen Independent School District Board of Trustees in 1996 and served until 2007. She also served as president of the board during her last three years and is the first Black to serve as School Board president in the Killeen Independent School District.

The request for recognition of Dr. Martin Luther King Jr. with the renaming of a street in his honor emerged in the political arena of the city of Killeen when Alice Gilliam, a Marlboro Heights resident, initiated a campaign for this cause. Her first request to the council for either 38th Street or Business Highway 190 was denied. However, a portion of FM 2410 was later approved. The official naming of a Dr. Martin Luther King Jr. Boulevard occurred on May 13, 1990. I am so grateful that I had the opportunity to participate in fulfilling the request of Alice Gilliam, which was to see the project to completion.

As I reflect on Killeen in 2008, I remember the Killeen that I visited in 1954 and returned to make it my residence in 1957. I see a transformation within Killeen that is definitely very evident to those of us who arrived here in the very early years as Black residents. Overcoming the inconveniences and the obstacles that were encountered; being forgiving of the rejection we faced as responsible citizens of the community; having the courage to stay in spite of our experiences; and as Blacks, having had the opportunity over the years to have been involved in making significant contributions to the growth and prosperity of this city, make our determination to not give up on doing well but with faith know there will be better days in Killeen for all of its citizens. We are glad to be community builders. Our children are adults now and are responsible citizens and we are sure that they appreciate the importance of becoming involved in community building where they now reside.

Eugene and Merdine Talley
Making a Difference through Community Outreach
Merdine Talley

Eugene Talley moved to the Killeen area in 1956 when he received his military assignment to Fort Hood. After Eugene and I were married in 1960, I moved to Killeen. Eugene is a native of Tennessee and I am a Texan. There was no housing available for my husband's rank on the post at the time of my arrival; therefore, we first lived in Belton, Texas. Housing for Blacks in Killeen was also very limited. Blacks lived in the Marlboro Heights and the Simmonsville communities, and many blacks commuted daily from surrounding towns to Killeen and Fort Hood. I did housework for pay while living in Belton. Later, I began doing housework in Killeen. I would ride to work with my husband and stay late after my regular work hours were over, waiting to ride back to Belton with him. This job paid twenty-five dollars a week. Our first child was born in September 1962, and I became a fulltime mother while Eugene deployed for the Cuban Crisis in October, 1962. Our immediate and extended family now includes my husband, Eugene; son, Cedric Talley; daughter, Michelle Talley Alexander; grandsons, Carlton Talley and Michael Alexander; and Gwen and Catina Lowe. Michael was born in Germany and all remaining family members are Texans.

We accompanied Eugene on his tour to Germany and when we returned in 1966 the housing situation was better but employment opportunities were not. We purchased a house in the Marlboro Heights Community. Jobs were hard to find. I had personal experiences that were discouraging when I applied for jobs and was told that there were no openings and then learn that in fact there were openings; or after having called to verify that a position was still open and being told it was closed upon my arrival. One of my greatest disappointments in job hunting occurred when I arrived for an interview and was told to wait and nobody came to interview me. The business closed but no one ever called me in for the interview. However, not all of my experiences in job hunting produced disappointments. My family also had positive employment experiences. I worked at a day care center and a cleaners and laundry station. My husband served his country in the Army for twenty-six years and worked civil service for an additional fifteen years.

As responsible citizens since the 1960s, our family's contribution to community building for many years continues to be our outreach ministry. I have a passion for helping others, visiting the sick, encouraging neighbors and friends, supporting and engaging in the work of mission. Also included are acts of kindness delivered to lift the human spirit by giving unexpected expressions or tokens of love and care. I am committed to mission outreach and find much joy in giving, sharing and encouraging. This is our mission in the community. I am grateful to God and my husband that it has been possible for me to do this. Without his support my involvement would not have been possible. Our outreach to others has become our ministry. We love God and family. Friends and people in general are also important and valued by us.

Over the years, I have served in the ministries of my church as church recording and financial secretary and as a trustee. I was in the Missionary Society, the choir, Pastor's Aide Workers and Willing Workers ministries. Our children have also been involved in the Sunday school and youth activities of the church. Cedric was "Mr. Sunbeam," and Michelle was "Miss Anderson Chapel" both were activities that were sponsored to benefit the church. Service to my church and to the community has brought much satisfaction in my life.

We have had challenges in life and have been blessed to overcome them. We have celebrated the happy experience of the birth of our two children. We are grateful for their accomplishments as college graduates and the careers they are following. We were thankful that sad incidents do not last always. As an infant, Cedric swallowed the metal end of a pencil and the matter was resolved without resulting in a health problem. We value the importance of education for our children and for other children so that they can enrich their lives. I was one of the students in my high school class who graduated with honors. Eugene was able to become a Sergeant Major in the U. S. Army. Both Eugene and I have even taken some courses at Central Texas College in Killeen and in Germany as adults. Our adult children are both KISD graduates. Michelle was one of Manor Middle School's first Black cheerleaders. She is a Prairie View A and M University graduate with a bachelor degree in business administration and a Master's degree. She is the business manager for the School of Continuing Education at Houston Community College. She has received honors as "Ms. Business," "as Homecoming Queen" and "Woman of the Year."

Cedric's high school involvement included student council treasurer, member of the band and tennis team. He was voted class favorite his senior year in high school. He was also a member of his college national honor society. After graduation, Cedric worked for Bastrop Independent School District (BISD) as a computer technician. He has been the owner of Cedric's Computer Consulting since 2002.

Our military experience allowed us to do a lot of traveling. We visited Paris, Luxemburg, Belgium, Austria, Germany, Garnish, and Jamaica; we've taken a family cruise and more. However, we were happy when we returned home to Killeen. As long time residents we are proud to have been contributors to the community building that produced a better community in which we live.

L. V. And Lizzie Anderson
A Creative Sunday School Setting
Lizzie M. Anderson

My husband, L.V. Anderson, and I arrived at Ft. Hood in December 1958. The family first lived on Terrace Drive in Marlboro Heights. We are both native Texans. L.V. is from Jonah, Texas, and I am from Taylor, Texas. I was born in Thorndale, Texas. In fact, my twin brother Charlie and I were the first African American twins born in Thorndale, Texas. L. V. was reared and educated in Jonah and Georgetown. He had worked as an ammunition inspector. He served in the U. S. Army from September 1942 to 1958. His last military assignment was to Ft. Hood, Texas.

From Terrace Drive we moved to Harker Heights, where we were the first African American family to buy there. Harker Heights did not have a church for African Americans at that time; therefore, I held Sunday school under my carport. Reverend R. A. Abercrombie sent Reverend Norman Shaw to preside over the Sunday school, and Mattie Alford was the Sunday school teacher. The funds raised from the Sunday school were used to purchase the first piano that was placed in the new sanctuary of Marlboro Missionary Baptist Church. Reverend Abercrombie was a good leader. He cared about the church and about the community and his leadership helped build a close knit community in Marlboro Heights. I was baptized at Marlboro Missionary Baptist Church and I served as one of the presidents of the Lydia Circle.

I thank the Lord for Professor Dock Jackson. The parents felt that he was good for the school. The teachers looked after the children and they really helped us rear our children. During those days the teachers were able to chastise our children. Everyone in the community was concerned and cared.

In 1963 our family moved back on Zephyr Road in Marlboro Height. My mother lived with me at that time. We felt safe as residents of the Marlboro Heights Community. Many nights we slept with opened windows and opened doors and only latched screen doors. As residents of our community and the city of Killeen, we contributed in community building by being responsible citizens. I worked outside the home for the wife of General Bruce, the first General of Ft. Hood from 1958-1967. I never had any problems with segregation and I never had a problem with people mistreating me. Several years later, we purchased a home on Muir Drive and moved away from Marlboro Heights. We are parents to two daughters Barbara Anderson Simpson and Christa Anderson Gibson. Our three sons are Michael, Dexter and Patrick. Our children are adults now. They all attended Killeen High School. Dexter and Patrick graduated from Killeen High School. Michael went into the Army. My husband L.V. Anderson is now deceased. He was a member of the Glad Tiding Pentecostal Church in Killeen. My desire is to always grow closer to the Lord.

Willie and Georgia Miller
The First Black Owned Cleaners in Killeen
Willie Miller

My wife, Georgia Miller, and I are long-time members of the Marlboro Heights Community. We owned and operated the first black-owned dry cleaners in the city of Killeen. Our business, "Community Cleaners", was located on East Business Highway 190—just east of the Marlboro Heights community. In the early years of the fifties and sixties the availability and accessibility of a dry cleaner in our new community that had limited means of transportation and other restrictions as a community; the cleaners was a convenient resource. The service of the Miller family's Community Cleaners made a significant contribution to community building and in expanding the entrepreneurial spirit of the community. I am a United States Air Corp Veteran and was one of the early African American business leaders in the community. I am a native of Elgin, Texas. We are homeowners in the Marlboro Heights community and the parents of a son, Ricky Miller.

We are members of Marlboro Missionary Baptist Church. I served as chairman of the deacons and trustees boards. Georgia served in the Deaconess Ministry and the Senior Women Ministry. The Miller family's entrepreneurial spirit was motivating for the creation of other business ventures during those early days in the Marlboro Heights Community. Leon O'Neal, Napoleon May, Willie Gibson, Milton Williams and I opened a car wash during the 1960s. The automatic carwash was located on 8th Street in Killeen. Each member of this five-member team was a resident of the Marlboro Heights community and co-owners in this new business venture. In later years, I gained employment with Texas Utilities (TXU) and retired from TXU's employment after over twenty years of service. Georgia was employed at Fort Hood. She retired as service manager at the Fort Hood laundry after many years of service.

Mildred B. Anderson Debose
Killeen High School's First Black Graduate
Mildred B. Debose

I hold a unique distinction in the history of Killeen, Texas. From an historical point of view, I was the first Black graduate of Killeen High School. In fact, this recognition equates to my also being the first Black high school graduate in the Killeen Independent School District. This information appeared in a Bell County Journal stating that Mildred B. Anderson Debose was the first black graduate of Killeen High School, having received her diploma at the end of the first semester in January 1958. When Nathaniel Anderson Jr. moved his family in 1953 from Cameron to Ft. Hood, where he had been working since late 1942 or early 1943, we lived in the civilian barracks at Fort Hood. At that time my sister Ardella and I were in high school, but were not allowed to attend school in Killeen. We were issued bus tickets from Walker Village to Killeen and from Killeen to Belton, where T. B. Harris High School was located. After eight months the school board stopped issuing the tickets from Walker Village to Killeen, and we had to find our own transportation or walk to Killeen to catch the bus to Belton.

After two years of riding the bus to Belton, Ardella Anderson, the older of the two and a senior in high school, told her father that she didn't want to graduate from T. B. Harris High School in Belton. So, he let the girls return to Cameron where Ardella graduated. By then the Killeen schools had been integrated. I returned to Killeen and entered Killeen High School where John Little, Sr. was principal. I graduated at the end of the first semester, becoming the first African-American to graduate from Killeen High. My family is now in its third generation of KISD graduates, and at this writing has the fourth generation's family members presently enrolled in Killeen Schools.

In 2004, I participated in a lecture session at the "Center for African-American Studies and Research" located at Central Texas College. I shared the oral history of Nathaniel and Murtha Anderson's family in Killeen.

On May 11, 2008, Simmonsville Missionary Church, its youth members and some Killeen citizens honored me in recognition of my unique place in Killeen's history as Killeen High School's first Black Graduate. Tierra Martin, a youth member, spoke of the Brown vs. Board of Education of Topeka, Kansas, and the influence this graduation might have had in Killeen. Cyanna Bedford, Orlando Moore and several other youth members paid tribute to me. Killeen's Mayor Timothy Hancock presented me a plaque for my contribution to the city and also a proclamation honoring me with a "Mildred Anderson Debose Day". Former Mayor Maureen Jouett presented to me a gift on behalf of the Killeen Branch NAACP and told of my accomplishments. Former City Councilwoman Dr. Claudia Brown dedicated a special *Ode to Mrs. Debose* for my accomplishments. She compiled the ode by talking to my close friends and family. My message focused on the youth assuring them that they can obtain any goal that is set before them. I encouraged them to rise above gang banging, drugs, social injustice and ignorance. I also reminded them that they are Americans and that American ends in "I Can."

The name of Mildred Anderson Debose is etched in the education history of Killeen, Texas. Long before Killeen developed into the city that we know now, her parents and a core of early residents dared to settle in the area and become the families that formed the foundation for establishing a community in which Blacks initially resided.

Reverend Hubert E., Sr. and Mildred B. Debose
Service in Ministry, Business and Community
Mildred B. Debose and the Task Force

Reverend Hubert E. Debose Sr., an ordained minister, and I are both natives of Cameron, Texas. He is a graduate of O. J. Thomas High School in Cameron, Texas and I hold the distinction of being) the first Black graduate of the Killeen Independent School District. He began his ministry to preach at Marlboro Missionary Baptist Church under the administration of the Reverend Dr. R. A. Abercrombie. He served on the ministerial staff at Marlboro Baptist Church where he was an associate to Pastor Abercrombie. Prior to accepting the "call" to the ministry, Hubert E. Debose, Sr. was employed in a medical career for thirty years as an X-ray technician at Darnall Community Hospital at Fort Hood, Texas. He was later called to pastor Independent Missionary Baptist Church in Rosebud, Texas, and Sweet Home Missionary Baptist Church in Gatesville, Texas. He currently serves as pastor of the first and oldest church founded by Blacks and for Blacks at its origin in Killeen. This church is Simmonsville Missionary Baptist Church. It was organized in the early fifties. Now under the current leadership of Reverend Hubert E. Debose, Simmonsville Missionary Baptist Church continues to progress with growth in membership, in spiritual experiences and opportunities and in its physical expansion.

Reverend Hubert Debose, Sr., as one of the spiritual leaders in the local community and within Central Texas, and I touched lives in many different ways. As a team in ministry, he and I reach out in the community providing leadership in spiritual services, giving service to causes that benefit the community, and addressing needs that will make the area a better place to live. For instance, Reverend Debose, with his congregation, demonstrated leadership in projects for the betterment of the immediate community. He was instrumental in joining the city and the Simmonsville Community in a co-op pilot project to make the neighborhood a safer place for families and to provide recreational opportunities for the youth, as well as, the adults. The place of interest was A. A. Lane Park, founded in 1964 in Simmonsville and named for a popular little league coach. At one time, the park enjoyed the status of being one of the city's premiere softball facilities for many years. When Reverend Debose saw that this neighborhood park in Simmonsville had become run down and the perfect site for late-night illicit activity, he stepped into action. He approached the city officials, and as a result of this contact, the city formed a pact to rehabilitate Lane Park. The city provided the funding for equipment and labor, and the church congregation's job was to initiate community involvement for the purpose of rejuvenating and monitoring the activities and the care of the park. In another instance of community outreach, Reverend Debose provided community leadership in the recognition of two former community leaders who had served the citizens of Killeen well. He was one of the sponsors for a recognition event for Killeen's former Mayor Raul Villaronga and the former City Councilwoman, Rosa Hereford, who served well in their positions. These were services needed at that time and Rev. Debose responded. There are still other instances of service to the community.

His service extends beyond his local service in this community. He holds several ministerial roles including: Chairman of the Foreign Mission Board in the Missionary Baptist General Convention of Texas with Dr. B. V. Clark, its President. He has served as Moderator of the Good Hope General Association in Waco, Texas. His responsibilities in this office require us to travel to locations outside of the United States, such as Belize and Germany. He was instrumental in taking forty-three persons who were in the Missionary Baptist Convention of Texas to Belize and Central America. Twelve of these persons were from Simmonsville Missionary Baptist Church. I was blessed to sponsor three of these persons. The trip was rewarding. Seven young men accepted Christ as their personal Savior.

On February 20, 2002, the Center of African-American Studies and Research was officially opened in the Oveta Culp Hobby Memorial Library on the Central Texas College Campus in Killeen,

Texas. One of its objectives is to bring in speakers to participate in its forums about Black issues. One of the lecture topics was about the early life of black families in Killeen. On November 12, 2004, I shared the oral history of my family during a lecture session of the "Center for African-Americans Studies and Research." I spoke about the experiences of my father and the family during their early days in the Killeen area. You can read about my father and mother, Nathaniel and Mertha Anderson in this book. My family was among the Black trailblazers who began establishing a community for Blacks in Killeen.

We were blessed to be parents to five children: Marisa, Lisa Ann, Angela, Hubert, Jr. and Keenan. They are adults now. All are graduates of the Killeen Independent School District, and became responsible and contributing citizens in the communities in which they reside. Hubert E., Jr. is now deceased. However, after Hubert Jr. accepted the "call" to the ministry he obediently and willingly exercised his gift of ministry with the youth of Simmonsville Baptist Church and with the youth of Memorial Baptist Church, in partic-ular. The Debose family, as longtime residents, has watched Killeen come of age and establish itself as a diverse and progressive city. The roots of Killeen run deep in the lives of these two community leaders who willingly pitched in over the years to give back to the community through their service and their skills as a mentor to beginners in their careers of cosmetology and a mentor to beginners in God's ministry. The Debose and Anderson families' contributions have made the city a better place in which to live and we have been blessed to be community builders in the community and city in which we reside.

Robert and Wadella Heath
The Spirit of Compassion
Wadella Heath

Sgt. Robert L. Heath came to Fort Hood in March of 1959 and his family was scheduled to join him later. While waiting for his family's move to the area, he accompanied Sgt. Pierce, a fellow soldier, to see Godfrey G. Langrum in Marlboro Heights in search for a house to rent. When Mr. Langrum told Sgt. Pierce the amount of the deposit and the amount of the rent, the total was too high for the fellow soldier to pay. Sgt. Heath had already been told that there were two thousand military families waiting for housing on the post; therefore he paid the twenty-five dollar deposit and the eighty-five dollars and rented the house at 2714 Terrace Drive for his family. Sgt. Pierce's wife and son had come to Killeen for Memorial Day and now they had no place to live. Therefore, Sgt. Heath let the Pierce family stay in the house until his family arrived in the area. He then took a four day pass to go home and bring his family to Killeen. The family included me, his wife, and four children: Christine, Gwendolyn, Robert Lee and Gary Heath. When we arrived here, the only housing that had been built for Blacks were on Stetson, Highland, Hillside, Lewis, Marlboro Drive and Terrace Drive. It was in June and the weather was about one hundred degrees. We had no fan in the house. Sgt. Pierce's family still had not found housing. Therefore, we let them stay with us. We had two bedrooms, a living room and a kitchen. They shared one bedroom; we shared one bedroom; and the children shared the living room. The people at that time were very close to each other and cared a lot for one another.

We moved to Longview Drive in September, 1960. I remember well that we closed the loan on the house one week and my husband came home with orders the next week. It was my choice that I would remain in Killeen because it was a place where my children could run and play freely, and it also provided the safety and security that they needed while they were growing up. I wanted to work, but jobs were very hard to find. One of the neighbors told me about Colonel and Mrs. Goodman who lived on the post. They needed somebody to do day work and I got the job doing day work for Colonel Goodman, Colonel Batch and Colonel Boyer. Rebecca White and I served receptions and open house events on the post together, and we enjoyed doing it.

My involvement in the community allowed me to do many things to help the growth in Marlboro Heights. From 1960-1964, I worked with Boy Scouts and Girl Scouts and from 1965-1970 worked only with the Girl Scouts. When I worked with Girl Scouts, a city bus came to the Marlboro Heights community and would take the Girl Scouts to Judge Duncan's Ranch. The bus would return in the evening to bring the scouts back to Killeen. The next day the bus would repeat this service, if needed. During the early sixties, I helped to get the Ladies Auxiliary of the Veterans of Foreign Wars started and later became the president of that auxiliary in 1963. I also was the first district president for the Ladies Auxiliary of the Veterans Foreign Wars. Katie Gibson was my sponsor for this position. From 1959-2002 I also served as the coordinator or principal of Vacation Bible School at my church and was a member and great supporter of the Marlboro Elementary School PTA. One evening I said to Dock Jackson, the principal of Marlboro School, at one of the PTA meetings, "You can't even find a job around here in Killeen," and he said, "We are going to renovate this school and we will be adding a kitchen and lunchroom." Well, sometime later when I was on Business 190, which is now renamed Veteran Memorial Blvd, Dock Jackson said, "Mrs. Heath, the job in the lunchroom is yours if you want it. Just go and talk to Mr. Peebles who is the business manager of the Killeen Independent School District." I was hired for the job, and Willie Mae Knight and I were the first Blacks that worked in the lunchroom for the Killeen Independent School District. When it was time for workshops to be held Willie Mae Knight and I were told by the superintendent that we will be paid to stay home while the rest of the lunchroom workers went on to the workshops. This procedure later changed, and I attended many workshops just as the other lunchroom workers did.

I worked at Marlboro School until the school closed at the end of the 1968 school year. The Federal Department of Health, Education and Welfare (HEW) identified Marlboro Elementary School as a segregated school. When the school closed, the employees and students at Marlboro were integrated into the faculties, staffs and classrooms of the other KISD Schools. I was sent to Nolan Middle School. Prior to my assignment, there had not been a Black person on that kitchen staff there. However, being an Army wife and being accustomed to working with people of diverse backgrounds—also because I love people—I was able to get along with everybody. My food service director came to me and said that they had another workshop and schooling at Southwest Texas University in San Marcus, Texas and that she wanted me to go. I went, and that same year in November I became manager. This assignment was just one year after I was at Nolan. Having made this accomplishment, I made up my mind that I was going to the highest peak. The next year I attended classes at Texas A and M University in College Station, Texas and everything they offered, I took it.

The following year the food service program needed an assistant director. My director came to me again and informed me that she would submit my name for assistant director. I got all of my credentials together and took them and submitted them to the KISD business manager. The school board accepted me for the position with no problem. I became KISD's Assistant Director of Food Service in 1973. That next year when I got to the administration building, I wanted to go to North Texas University in Denton, Texas. My director supported my desire to participate in the program by recommending to the KISD business manager that I be given the opportunity to attend. The school district sent me to North Texas State University that summer. This brought me even closer to attaining the goal that I had set while I was cafeteria manager at Nolan Middle School. During this time I also earned an associate degree in Applied Science at Central Texas College. I also completed all requirements of a food service program and became certified with the State of Texas and nationally in food preparation and management.

In 1976, the food service director died and I was appointed the first black director of the Killeen ISD food service department. It was my responsibility to set up all programs and workshops. All of the training programs were set up under my direction. In addition, I started the first Black Senior Citizen Program in the Killeen School System. There were many experiences, many opportunities, and many friends over the years. I have served on the governor's committee for the aging in Austin, Texas, and I was the first black to serve in this position. I became the first District 12 Food Service Director for the KISD School District in this area and was the first black to serve in that capacity. In an event sponsored by the Killeen Chamber of Commerce, I became the first recipient elected as the Athena Woman in 1986. The Bluebonnet Council of Girl Scouts honored me as a 2007 Woman of Distinction. I was blessed to retire from KISD, having given thirty-three years of service. This was service that I enjoyed sharing. My retirement years are bringing me much satisfaction. I continue to be involved in the life of the community. My organizational memberships and affiliations include: Marlboro Missionary Baptist Church, and later, Greater Peace Missionary Baptist Church; Texas and Killeen Retired Teachers Associations; KISD Retired Food Service Workers Organization; the Masonic Order of the Eastern Star, Starlette Chapter 455, and American Business Women's Association. I am thankful that I have had an opportunity to successfully serve in positions of trust and accountability.

My support system in all of my endeavors is my family. My husband, Robert L Heath, Sr., retired from the U. S. Army with more than twenty years of service to this country. He has always been committed to taking care of his family. Our four adult children and their families have lived or are continuing to live productive and responsible lives. Robert Heath, Sr. died on March 24, 2008.

Gary Lawrence Heath, our youngest child, died on February 8, 2007. Gary proclaimed a true belief in Jesus Christ early in his life, and in keeping with God's plan for his life, found peace and trust in knowing that Jesus could weather any storm. He was a veteran of the U. S. Air Force Reserve and received an honorable discharge for his military service. After completing his military assignment, Gary worked twenty-one years and nine months as a mail handler in civil service for the U. S. Postal Service.

Robert Lee served in the United States Marines, bravely and loyally defending our country. He completed his high school requirements while in the Marine Corps and has attended junior college. Robert Lee is a civil service worker. He is an immigration detention officer with the Flint Group.

Gwen resides in the Killeen area with her family. She has chosen as her occupation of interest serving as a para-professional in the field of education. She is employed by the Killeen Independent School District and is a member of the classroom support staff in the Special Education Program. She works with special needs students.

Dr. Christine Diggs is now a resident of the state of Virginia. She pursued and obtained her doctorate degree in psychology, has her own practice in counseling and related services and is Director of the Counseling Center at Virginia State University. She was the first Killeen High School graduate who previously resided in the Marlboro Heights Community to achieve a doctorate degree. She is representative of many of the youth from this community. She is a goal setter and an achiever. Dr. Christine Diggs has also held numerous leadership offices in her church, community and school affiliations. Her career has spanned a variety of employment opportunities. However, according to Dr. Christine Diggs, the most important position that she has held is that of being mother to her children Bobby, Nikki and Scott. They have given her experience as taxi driver, chief cook and chairperson of the housecleaning team. Her motto is simple and straight forward: "I can do all things through Christ who gives me strength" (Philippians 4:13).

Willie and Rev. Bertie Sworn
Family, Ministry and Service
Reverend Bertie Sworn

In 1959, the Sworn Family made a permanent change of station (PCS) from Germany to Fort Hood. Killeen was segregated at this time, which meant there was very little housing for Blacks. Therefore, we moved to Temple, Texas and Willie drove from Temple to Ft. Hood for work each day. In March of 1960 the family was able to move from Temple to Killeen. Our first address was a small frame house on Lewis Street in the Marlboro Heights community. We heard about new houses being built on Longview Drive in Marlboro Heights by a company from Austin, Texas, and we purchased a house on Longview Drive. The family then became an integral part of the community. I became involved in community service related to school, scouting, church, ministry outreach and volunteer service with the Red Cross. Educators and parents worked well together during these years of the 1960s. In 1963 I was elected PTA secretary, and in 1964 I was elected PTA president. The PTA encouraged parents to get involved so that our children would have the things they needed for a quality education. As more families moved into the area the school became overcrowded and another first grade class was added. The PTA became an active tool in helping the school obtain materials and other items needed by putting on talent shows, carnivals and banquets as fundraisers. We purchased fans for each classroom, the curtains for the stage and the shrubbery that adorned the front school grounds. The Marlboro School PTA was chartered into the National PTA in 1965 under my leadership as PTA president. Lea Ledger was the National PTA president and Marlboro School was accepted by the National PTA Convention which was held in Houston, Texas. As PTA president I also served as Marlboro's representative to the Killeen Council of PTAs. In spite of obvious racial discrimination we would not let our children be denied opportunities to be involved in activities in the city. Therefore, during 1966 the PTA and the school entered its first float in the downtown Killeen Christmas Parade. Our PTA involvement brought blacks and whites together. Then in 1968 Marlboro School was declared racially unbalanced by the Health, Education and Welfare Department (HEW) and was closed by the Killeen Independent School District. My children were assigned to East Ward Elementary School due to the closing. I went to East Ward and continued to work with PTA and was elected vice president of East Ward Elementary School's PTA.

Girl Scout troops continued to exist in Marlboro Heights for African-Americans during the 1960s. The scout leaders in the Marlboro Heights Community at that time were Wadella Heath, Alice Douse, Bertie Sworn, Mrs. Brown and others. The black and white scout leaders held their meetings together, but the troops and leaders of the troops were not integrated until later. With the help of my husband, Willie Sworn and other parents, we transported our scouts to Camp Kachina for weekend and summer camp. His community service was vital to the success of the community's Girl Scout Troops during those early years.

In 1964 Anderson Chapel A.M.E. Church was established and the church was named in honor of the founding pastor, the Reverend Arthur Anderson of Lampasas, Texas. Reverend Anderson's wife, Mary; the Sworns: Willie and Bertie; the Douses: Marion J. and Alice; the Haydens: Velma and Freddie; Mary Manjang; and Eddie Johnson became the charter members of Anderson Chapel African Methodist Episcopal Church. As founding members of Anderson Chapel AME Church, Willie and I both served faithfully for many years. Willie served as a member of the Board of Trustees and Board of Stewards. I worked in many leadership positions as choir director, church secretary and Missionary Society president.

During 1971, I started volunteering with the American Red Cross as secretary and later became the first black to be hired as a caseworker. I worked for eighteen years at the American Red Cross, serving in positions as caseworker, office manager, Director of Services to Military Families and as Disaster Director. I received an Associate Degree in Social Work from Central Texas College. I also received numerous continuing education awards and certificates. Our ministry and community service made a difference in the lives of others in the community. Building a better community through community service and ministry has been very rewarding.

In the 1980s I returned to my "call" into the ministry to which I was first called at age twelve. I answered the call again in 1982 and became a member of Anderson Chapel AME Church ministerial staff. I continued my Outreach Ministry and community service of teaching Bible study at Christian Farms, a drug and alcohol rehabilitation Center. In 1984, I was appointed pastor of Thomas Chapel AME Church in Copperas Cove, Texas. Members and friends who know of my labor as pastor of Thomas Chapel recognize that, although I was not the founder of that church, God blessed me to exercise the leadership necessary regarding the acquisition of land for the church; that was purchased, the renovation and the refurbishing of the church structure into a fine facility. Therefore, it is noteworthy to credit me with the title "builder" of Thomas Chapel AME Church. My tenure as pastor, supported by the membership and my husband, Willie, was very fruitful and richly blessed.

We are parents to four adult children. They all attended Marlboro Elementary School, and all four graduated from Killeen High School and attended college. Deborah is the administrator for several family business ventures and her husband, George is a certified public accountant (CPA). Willie is a department supervisor in an industrial firms in Houston and his wife Linda a bank employee. Constance (Connie) is an LVN in the healthcare field and has worked in San Antonio, Killeen and the Temple areas. Vanessa has completed training as a medical specialist. She works as a teacher's aide with students with special needs. She and her husband Robert Stewart reside in Killeen.

Willie Sr. served during the Korean and Vietnam Wars. In May of 1982 he retired from the Army with the rank of Master Sergeant after thirty-one and a half years of military service. He gave fifteen years of additional service as a civil service employee. After retirement he was employed as a school bus driver by the Killeen Independent School District. Willie received an associate degree in auto mechanics from Central Texas College. He was also a former member of the VFW and the American Legion of Killeen.

James W. and Frenetter W. Conway
Committed to the Spirit of Volunteerism
James and Frenetter Conway

God has been very kind to Frenetter and me, as well as to our seven children and thirteen wonderful grandchildren. Thank you for the opportunity to share a bit of our life experiences with you and all of our other friends who may remember us from our stay in Killeen/ Fort Hood. I certainly have fond memories of the period from April 1959 to October 1963 when we called Killeen/Fort Hood home. The VFW was first to afford me the opportunity to get acquainted and form friendships with Mr. Langrum, Captain Talmadge Foster, Sergeants Gibson, Bell, O'Neal, Priestly, Doggett, Scotty and many others whose names escape me now, but friends nevertheless. Many of the early families who were residing in the Marlboro Heights community prior to 1964 probably remember me as one of the scout leaders in the community. Others may remember my leadership as one of the commanders of the General Benjamin O. Davis VFW Post 9191. Still others may remember my involvement in various community services, activities and projects. However, that same spirit of community service that I demonstrated within this very young developing community of Marlboro Heights has remained an important part of my way of life in Montgomery, Alabama. In fact, there have been many and various opportunities for community service available to me and my commitment to render service whenever and wherever these opportunities exist.

I was the 1991 recipient of the "Alexis de Tocqueville Society Award" in recognition of my dedication, compassion and my lifetime of service to the community where I now reside. The award was presented to me by The Montgomery Area Alexis De Tocqueville Society. This organization was created in 1972 by United Way of America to recognize persons who have rendered outstanding service as volunteers in their own community or on a national level. Rarely a day would go by that I was not involved as a volunteer in services and activities such as:

- Being concerned for the handicapped in many different ways, individually or through organizations, to improve their way of life.
- Showing great consideration for the needs of the elderly by being involved in the area's Council on Aging and giving service to this organization in a number of different capacities.
- Showing great interest in the community food bank with service to the organization.
- Establishing a mentoring program for juniors and seniors to take part as interns with businesses during the summer months or for other opportunities.

My list of services as a community volunteer over the years has been extensive. The review of the complete record of my community service by the Society resulted in my selection for this honor. Thinking back to April 1959 through October 1963, you may remember that I willingly rendered service as a volunteer and community builder to Marlboro Heights while there. Enjoying a spirit of volunteerism in your community or city can result in opportunities to make a significant difference for others.

I am Frenetter Conway and I remember our tour of duty at Fort Hood and Killeen. I recall that friendships made the difference for me in Marlboro Heights. When the Army installation closed at Fort Polk, Louisiana in early April 1958 we moved to Fort Hood, Texas with four children. My husband had secured a house in the 2700 block of Terrace Drive and our children attended Marlboro Heights School. We met really nice people there and we joined Marlboro Heights Baptist Church where Rev. R. A. Abercrombie was the pastor. The friendships that I made as a resident in the Marlboro community overshadowed and soothed the disappointments I experienced upon arriving in the Killeen area. Employment for Blacks, especially black women, was limited to laundry on Post at sixty-nine cents per hour or cleaning in the BOQ at one dollar per hour. I had worked for the government for five years as a clerk or clerk typist. However I could not get beyond the personnel office. I was accepted for work at the laundry after going on interviews two or three times each week for positions for which I was qualified. After two months of humiliation, I went to God in prayer and in fasting. He opened the door for me to get employment at the commissary. One cannot adequately describe the humiliation that black women had to endure trying to secure a job in the Killeen/Fort Hood area during those years. Nevertheless, the friendship and warmth that we received from our neighbors and acquaintances in the Marlboro Heights Community compensated for some of the hurt that you felt from the discrimination you had to endure. These friendships and our love have lasted over these many years. It is my hope and prayer that those hurtful things that happened back then will never return to haunt other dependents that have to accompany their husband, father or mother to a military installation in our country. We now reside in Montgomery, Alabama and are making a positive difference in our local community as community builders and Volunteerism.

Dr. Rudolph and Missionary Pearl Jackson
A Servant Pastor for the Master
Reverend Dr. Rudolph Jackson

In 1959, I moved to Killeen with my father, the late Superintendent E. M. Green; my mother, Mrs. Catherine Green; and my sisters and brothers. My father is the founding pastor of *Church of God's Holy Tabernacle God in Christ*. There was no Civil Rights Bill at this time in history. Segregation was alive and well. Blacks were not allowed to eat with white people in the front of a café, or ride in the front of the bus. Even though the schools were integrated, the town was not. The population in Killeen at that time was about twenty thousand people, not counting the military. I attended Killeen High School which later became Fairway Middle School. I was sixteen when I came to Killeen. I didn't know many black people at the school when I started because I went to work the next day after I arrived in Killeen. My older brother who was here when I came had a job for me at the

Bluebonnet Café washing dishes. My pay was five dollars a day, seven days a week. If I took a day off, I did not get paid for seven days. I left Killeen in the 1961 and moved to Denver, Colorado for about four months. When my father Elder Green was sent overseas to Germany, I came back home to Killeen to be with my mother, my sister and my brothers. My father, mother, one sister and three brothers are no longer with us. I am the oldest of the children yet living.

I have seen this city change in a very positive way. The growth that has taken place is for the best. But like everything there will be some negative that comes with growth. There were only two churches for black families to attend in Killeen when my father started God's Holy Tabernacle Church of God. They were Simmonsville Baptist Church and Marlboro Baptist Church The church on Zephyr Road next to the VFW was started after God's Holy Tabernacle Church of God by a soldier whose surname was Smith. There was a community center that was operated by the Progressive Civic League. It was where teenagers would come on Friday night and dance and have a good time. All in all, it was a fun place to be. At that time this was basically all we had for the black youth. The young people would also hang out at a house on the corner of Lewis and Stetson. We called it the Sweet Shop. However I don't remember the name of the family that lived there. There were movies on Fort Hood, but my brothers and sisters didn't go to movies.

My ministry has been blessed. At the death of my father, Superintendent E. M. Green, on July 13, 1983, I was appointed pastor of God's Holy Tabernacle Church of God in Christ. I was installed as pastor on October 25, 1983. My wife Pearl Jackson is a missionary for the Killeen District. She works along beside me. The church continues to make a contribution to the community's progress by providing the spiritual support to our members and the citizens of our community. We are also community builders and we continue to assume our role and perform our responsibilities in this process.

Tommy and Shirley Adanandus
Civic and Community Volunteers
Shirley Adanandus

We came to Killeen in July 1959 when the Army gave Tommy military orders for Fort Hood, Texas. Tommy is a native of Texas, and I am a native of Arkansas. Our immediate and extended family includes Toni Edmondson Mills of Smyrna, Georgia; Ronald Edmondson of Tulsa, Oklahoma; Steven Edmondson of Ft. Worth, Texas; Della Adanandus Bush of Kennesaw, Georgia; Jennifer Adanandus Miller of Marietta, Georgia; Mark Adanandus of Killeen, Texas; and Linda Adanandus Scott of Lithuia, Georgia. We first resided on Marlboro Drive in the Marlboro Heights community from July 1959 to March 1961. We later moved to our present home on Jefferies Avenue which is still in the Marlboro Heights community. We resided at the Jefferies location from March 1961 to October 1962 before leaving the area twice; but always returning to the same address. There were only two neighborhoods opened to colored people when we arrived in Killeen. These neighborhoods were the Simmonsville and the Marlboro Heights communities.

There was also a shortage of rentals in the area at that time. Therefore, prior to our moving to the Fort Hood area we were told to stay where we were until the sponsor could secure housing. Tommy attempted to rent a house in Copperas Cove, but was told by the agent that she could not rent to colored folk. Finally, the family was able to move into a duplex on Marlboro Drive, which was much nicer than we expected since reading about the living areas available to Blacks in *Jet Magazine*.

Killeen now had a new population of residents who needed services other than housing. We quickly experienced that shopping in the local ladies clothing stores or the department stores was difficult for Black customers. Often it was simply the non-availability of assorted shades of cosmetic products and shades of items like ladies hosiery for Blacks. These items were limited in Killeen during the early years. I remember experiencing a shopping situation when by just inquiring about the availability of such items as hosiery or cosmetics resulted in my receiving poor customer service from the salesperson. In addition, there was a practice during the fifties when Blacks also experienced being denied the opportunity to try on clothes in some stores when attempting to select a potential purchase.

Blacks also experienced that civilian jobs were hard to find and that for those who found a job the pay was very low. Tommy was in the Army and I was a stay-at-home mom; therefore, I did not seek any local employment. However, after retiring from the Army, Tommy worked at Burger Chef on Business 190 (now Veterans Memorial Boulevard) and Highland Avenue six days a week, ten hours a day. He only cut back his work schedule at Burger Chef to part-time so that he could attend Central Texas College (CTC). After receiving his associate, degree employment opportunities opened for him. He was hired by the Hillandale Hospital (now Metroplex) as a purchasing agent and he remained in that position until his retirement in 1995. My work experience in the Killeen/Fort Hood area included employment at the Post Exchange; cook at Hillandale Hospital; receiving clerk at the Sears Catalog Store; operator and service assistant for Centel Telephone Company. I retired in 1998 as a teacher's aide.

We are members of St. Joseph's Catholic Church. Tommy is a member of the Knights of Columbus, where he has served as Deputy Grand Knight and Faithful Navigator. His community involvement included serving on the Killeen Planning and Zoning Commission in 1973-1974; and membership in the Veterans of Foreign Wars Post 9191. My involvement includes service as president of St. Joseph's Altar Society, President-elect of the Knights of Columbus Auxiliary in 1997, and prior to holding that position; I served as the society's secretary. In addition, I am a volunteer at Metroplex Hospital in Killeen and a member of Metroplex's Clown Troupe. My work with the youth of the community included serving as a mentor in the Killeen Independent School District's (KISD) Host Program and as a Brownie Scout leader in the early seventies.

Our family values family, religion, our faith, education and friends. All seven of our children graduated from Killeen High School. Tommy and I, as well as six of our children, attended Central Texas College in the Killeen area. Tommy and Mark received their bachelor degree from the University of Central Texas. Linda, Mark and Toni received associate degrees there. Linda then continued her college education and received a Bachelor of Arts degree from the University of Texas in Arlington, Texas.

Tommy is an avid golfer. He excelled in the sport of golf, and I also play the sport a little. We are proud of our adult children who are responsible contributing citizens within their communities. We still reside in the home that we purchased in 1961 in the Marlboro Heights community and where we made our contribution to the city and its citizens as community builders.

Roy and Della Hamilton
A Passion for Food Preparation and the Social Scene
Roy Hamilton

I am a Texan. My father, Maurice Hamilton and I shared the stage in the preparation of Bar-B-Q, and providing restaurant service at Fort Hood and Killeen for many years. When my Dad left Lampasas, and began his first food business in Killeen. I was a fifteen year old high school student who took over the whole Bar-B-Q business that he left in Lampasas. In fact, I added to it. I was in total control of the whole thing and I would rush home from school and get things going for the evening. Working with food has always been a great interest to me. I also worked at Ft. Hood when we all moved to Killeen. I started working with the food service department as a bus boy and got moved all the way up to assistant food manager while on Ft. Hood. It was quite an experience. However, I left the food service business for a while and pursued other interests.

I had another dream. It was a passion for business and to establish myself as a trailblazer by following my dream as a pioneer in creating the social scene in Killeen. My wife, Della, is a native of Florida and a longtime resident of this community. We have been known for bringing entertainment to the social scene of the city. Music and entertainment can add to the quality of life in a community and be a source of relaxation, fellowship and fun among friends. We began creating the social scene and brought entertainment to Killeen for African Americans and others.

In 1967, I began my first social spot in Killeen and for more than 30 years, I was either owner, or manager, or in partnership or was associated with several social clubs. My career came full circle in 1990 when Dad passed away. I returned to my first successful and enjoyable occupation in food service as owner and manager of Maurice Bar-B-Q, the oldest black business in the Killeen/Harker Heights area. Just as I did with the Maurice Bar-B-Q business when I took it over in Lampasas, I have in fact added to the Maurice Bar-B-Q business in Harker Heights. We renovated in 2004 and added a spacious dining area for family and friends to dine and fellowship. This expansion also provides a relaxing atmosphere for customers. We have expanded the entrees on the menu and provide quality service in food preparation that adds a touch of Texas class to any and every event. We have still maintained a viable business of the 21st Century, and we still give service at Maurice Bar-B-Q with a smile. It is always "service" that makes a difference.

CHAPTER 3

1960-1969:
Decisions that Opened
Neighborhood Opportunities

—〰—

A greater influx of African Americans who were mostly military families continued to arrive in Killeen and Fort Hood in this decade. These arrivals represented a population increase of foundation builders that added to the existing contributions and accomplishments of community builders. This decade marked the beginning of African Americans' involvement within the city beyond that in their neighborhoods. By the mid-sixties African Americans began to receive some access to community opportunities within the city of Killeen and responded by seriously investing their efforts in the opportunities that were presented. It was in this decade that African American youth were given access to use the city's public park and swimming pool. In 1964, a request was made to the Killeen city leaders by fifteen active duty African American military personnel asking that our African American children be able to use Condor Park, Killeen's first public park, created in 1954. Then, in the mid-sixties, LTC General Ralph E. Haines, commander of III Corp and Fort Hood, gave his support to the concept of open housing in Killeen for all military personnel and their families. With this decision and the support of Killeen's city leaders, housing within Killeen was opened up to African Americans to rent or buy houses in other areas of the city than Marlboro Heights and Simmonsville.

This was the beginning of a transition within the city. The initiation of this practice released some of the restrictions that limited African Americans' freedom to rent or purchase a house in other parts of Killeen. It also allowed families to become a part of the larger community of Killeen. In the mid-sixties of this decade, the school district integrated junior high schools. In addition, the police force was integrated when Cordus Jackson became the first African American to join the Killeen police force. Cordus Jackson later became a Captain in the Killeen's Detective Department.

As we approached the late sixties, the expansion of open housing within the city benefited minorities in their search for housing and resulted in diversity in the neighborhoods. This allowed for the establishment of some long lasting neighborly relationships in the city among families, co-workers, school age children and younger children. Better human relations began to develop and Killeen became a more diverse city in Killeen Texas where retirees and civilians had chosen to live and raise their families. African Americans who arrived in Killeen in this decade witnessed the beginning involvement of African American families in the larger community. In this chapter you will read about their stories of service, contributions, accomplishments and the challenges they encountered. However, they persevered and can now be designated as community builders in the city of Killeen.

Milton and Jewel Carroll
Faith, Family, Friendship and Education
Jewel Carroll

In 1960 the Army gave Milton Carroll orders for Fort Hood, Texas. We arrived and discovered that the economic, social and housing conditions were not so good. With only sixty-one houses for rent in the area, we made a decision to purchase our home in the Marlboro Heights community right away. I did not like the area when we first arrived, but over time fell in love with Killeen. We felt that during those early years the Marlboro Heights community was a safe place for the children to play and to visit friends. I have fond memories of the children in the neighborhood playing ball in the shopping strip where Gibson's Variety Store and later King Savers Grocery Store were once located. Our family first worshiped at Simmonsville Baptist Church. We later joined Marlboro Baptist Church, where I helped each year with Vacation Bible School. This was then the highlight in my life. My community involvement expanded and in 1969, I worked with children at the Marlboro Heights Community Center. This building is now a multi-service center and is still located in the circle intersection of Rev. R. A. Abercrombie Drive, Highland Avenue and Terrace Drive. Years later our family joined Anderson Chapel AME Church. Our children served in the youth ministries there; Milton served for many years on the Board of Trustees and media ministries while I served on the Stewardess Board and sang in the Chancel Choir. My involvement in the church ministries and community work helped me to overcome my shyness.

From 1986-1993, I worked with students as an instructional aide in the Killeen Independent School District (KISD) at Haynes and Hay Branch Elementary Schools. Now I am a KISD Retiree and retirement gives me more time to engage in my passion for gardening. After Milton's military career, he became the owner of Carroll's TV Rental and Repair Shop from 1974-1985. It was located on 8th Street in downtown Killeen. In 1986 the family started a new business, M and J Home Repairs. Milton enjoys building, construction, electronics, farming and ranching.

Family time together, friendships and education are important to us. All four of our children—Gwen, Jackie, Janice and Roy—graduated from Killeen High School, earned their college degrees and have touched the lives of the youth in their communities as educators. These young adults now have families and are giving back to society as they influence the lives of the students and youths at schools; as they work in the ministries of their churches; and as they live in their communities. As parents we feel really blessed that our children have grown into responsible and contributing adult citizens. In their interview survey for the Tapestry project all four siblings expressed their gratitude as a tribute to Milton and me, for making education so very important to and for the family. They believed that their parents' encouragement and support, along with their desire to achieve, contributed to their success. Our son Roy held the distinction of integrating Friendswood High School faculty in the Friendswood School District as its first African American faculty member. During his tenure there, he remained the only African American faculty member. In 2005 our family experienced the demise of our son, Roy Milton Carroll. We later moved from Killeen and became residents of Waco, Texas.

Tilmer and Mary Manjang
Love and Prayer Make the Difference
Marilyn Manjang

My parents, Tilmer and Mary Manjang, are native Texans who were both raised in the San Marcos area. They arrived in Killeen in 1960. Tilmer Manjang had been assigned to report to Camp Hood. He retired in 1962 with twenty years of loyal service to his country in the U. S. Army. Upon arriving in Killeen, they moved to the Simmonsville community. There were a few white families living in this community at this time. However, they began moving away after several black families moved in. Most blacks lived in Belton during this time. My parents experienced instances of discrimination. Eggs were occasionally thrown at their house. Someone also once threw a blasting cap at their trailer house and unknowing to my parents, my brother, who was a young child, began playing with it. The cap exploded and this young child almost lost his eyesight. It was a difficult and trying time, but they persevered.

After retiring from the Army, my father worked for several years on Fort Hood and later became self-employed. He held several jobs throughout his lifetime. He operated a fruit stand in Killeen for over thirty years. He was known for providing fresh fruit and vegetables for the citizens of Killeen. In addition, he was a handyman and an unbelievable fisherman. People from all walks of life encountered Mr. Manjang, either through his fish tales or his long talks about having the "sweetest" watermelons in town. He helped many youngsters purchase their school clothing or other necessities by allowing them to work with him during the summer months.

He was affectionately called the "singing fisherman" by family and many friends. He enjoyed helping people when they were down and out. He even assisted in the building and the renovation of the original structures of Anderson Chapel AME Church when it was located in Simmonsville's old city jail. He also assisted in making the second structure, which was located on Jefferies Avenue, usable both outside and inside by building the boardwalk sidewalk to make it possible for entrance into the building on muddy days. He repaired inside the building to include the sanctuary and the restrooms; and made modifications and adaptations where needed. The men of the church were all overseas serving our country. My father was the only man we had to depend on, and he willingly gave his service, accepting no pay for his work even though he was not a member of Anderson Chapel AME Church. Ted Tilmer Manjang sang in the choir, served in the brotherhood and occasionally played the drums at St. John Missionary Baptist Church in Killeen where he was a member. He truly loved his pastor and the members of the body.

My mother, Mary Manjang, a dedicated Christian, joined Simmonsville Baptist Church under the pastorate of Reverend Hubbard after relocating to Killeen. She was an active member for four and a half years. Upon leaving Simmonsville Baptist Church she became a founding member of Anderson Chapel African Methodist Episcopal (AME) Church in February 1964. She is an ordained deaconess and a lifetime member of the Women's Missionary Society of the African Methodist Episcopal (AME) Church. She has been an active and contributing member of the church for more than fifty years. During this entire time she has served as a class leader and has taught the young children's beginners' Sunday school class. She served as an usher for nine years and in later years was a member of the choir. She loves her church and like helping people. She regularly visited the local hospitals, nursing homes and the homes of the sick and shut in. She also worked at the church's mission house twice a week to give out clothing and food to those in need. The church honored her and another missionary of the church, Lester Hamilton, by naming the local missionary society the "Hamilton-Manjang Missionary Society." And the church's two mission houses are also named the Hamilton-Manjang Mission House I and II. This is an outreach ministry of the Women's Mission Society of Anderson Chapel AME Church.

She began her employment career with the Killeen Independent School district in 1970. Upon her employment, she was assigned to work in the cafeteria at Fairway Middle School. She worked there for two years and then transferred to Killeen High School. Mary helped feed many students hot meals for twenty-five years. Students loved to go through her serving line because they knew that she would give them an infectious smile and an extra-large serving of food.

My father and mother are the parents of five adult children: Kenneth, Pameler, Stanley, Marilyn and Dennis. They are all responsible adults and are doing well. Kenneth resides in Utah and the others remained in Texas. Each has chosen an area of interest that was pursued as a career, and each is using his or her career in making a contribution to the communities in which they now live. Kenneth is the owner of an electronic service. Pameler and Marilyn are educators in the Spring Independent School District in Texas. Stanley is owner of an auto mechanic shop. Dennis works in the area of security. Tilmer Manjang passed away on February 8, 2003, after a brief illness. Mary Manjang maintained her home in Killeen, Texas.

Charles and Bobbye Wade
Advocates and Friends to Scouting
Bobbye Wade

My husband, retired SFC Charles "Skipper" Wesley Wade, III, was a native of Chicago, Illinois where he received his education from public and private schools. He entered the U. S. Army on June 20, 1950. I am a native of Arkansas and was reared and educated in McGhee, Arkansas. After graduating from McGhee High School in 1957, I went to Chicago to work. My first job was working in the order department at Montgomery Ward. It was there that I met my future husband, married and moved to Texas in 1960. We lived in Temple and Belton before moving to Killeen. When we arrived, we found Marlboro Heights to be a friendly community. Families helped other families; the school had positive expectations for the students and the children, even as teenagers were respectful. We are the parents of seven children. Three of our children were born at Fort Hood. My husband loved this area, but I did not like the terrain. I had become accustomed to beautiful green grass, tall trees, rivers and natural lakes in Arkansas. I had never heard of man-made lakes before coming here.

During the Sixties, I was not employed outside of the home. My life was concentrated on being the very best housewife that I could be. I also had the opportunity to become engaged in community life and found it enjoyable as I worked with the Boy Scout Troops under the direction of Scoutmaster James Redwine. My family left Killeen and went to Germany. We had the opportunity to do a lot of touring in Germany. We returned to Fort Hood and the Killeen area in 1972. This time, both Skipper and I worked with the Girl Scouts under the direction of Girl Scout leader Martha Scott. We had a yellow Volkswagen bus, and that bus went to Camp Kachina and to West Fort Hood many times, transporting Girl Scouts to camp and to other scouting activities. Skipper was always involved in this transportation. It was rare for men to be given special awards for girl scouting, but Charles Wade was honored in 1974 for his dedicated service and contributions to the Girl Scout program.

Charles retired from the U. S. Army on September 30, 1972. His tours of duty during his twenty-two years of service included the Republic of Korea and the Republic of Vietnam. We were both active members of Anderson Chapel AME Church in the Marlboro Heights community, working in various ministries of the church. I began working for Army and Air Force Exchange (AAFES) and remained there for ten years before resigning to attend Central Texas College where, in May 1986, I graduated with an associate degree in General Studies. My last employment before my retirement included five years with the Killeen Independent School District's Food Service Department. Our children have all become responsible adults now and have families of their own. "I am excited about this project to preserve the history of our community; and while my health is not the best, I will work tirelessly on seeing this project to fruition." We are community builders.

Willie C., Sr. and Geneva Vanarsdale
Family, Military and Community Service
Willie C. Vanarsdale, Sr.

I am a native of Pickens, Mississippi, and was inducted in the military on January 28, 1943, at Camp Shelby, Mississippi. Many times my food consisted of horse, goat and potatoes during the first part of my military career. While at Fort Bliss I was the bodyguard for the heavy weight boxing champion Joe Louis. I was assigned to Company I, 366th Infantry Regiment, an all-Black Infantry Regiment commanded by Colonel Quain. My military orders brought me to Ft. Hood, Texas. I worked part time as Master of Arms from July 1960 through August 1961 in the Ft. Hood NCO Club. I spent a tour of duty overseas and was reassigned to Fort Hood for three years. I retired from the Army on May 1, 1966, and became self-employed. My employment after retirement included:

- Working in the trucking business with Andrew Temple, one of my neighbors, from May 4, 1966 through January 1967
- Working at a gas/service station from February 1967 through April 12, 1967
- Working with the Post Exchange from April 14, 1969 through April 12, 1971
- Employment with Civil Service at Ft. Hood from April 13, 1971 to December 1997
- Employment with the Killeen Independent School District as a school bus driver from April 1988 to May 1994

- Working for several years in the position of Custodial Contract Coordinator in the Service Branch of the Logistics Division at Darnall Army Community Hospital, Ft. Hood, Texas

My wife Geneva and I are the parents of six children: Virginia, Yvonne, Veronica, Vinson, Willie Jr. and Debra. We also adopted a grandbaby into our family. We moved into a newly constructed home on Longview Drive in the Marlboro Heights community on December 16, 1960. There were very few activities, places or events in the Killeen area in which Black people could work or participate when they arrived at Fort Hood. My wife worked part time in homes as a housemaid cleaning, washing and ironing. In the sixties I joined Marlboro Missionary Baptist Church but later became a charter member and deacon of the Greater Peace Missionary Baptist Church. I was actively involved in organizations and activities in the community. In 1963, I became a member of the Veterans of Foreign Wars (VFW) Post 9191. Later in 1968, I was elected Youth Director of the Progressive Civic League in Marlboro Heights. I was also elected and installed as the 1972-1973 Post Commander for the General Benjamin O. Davis VFW 9191. I am a member of the NAACP, the New Light Lodge #242 of the Masonic family and the American Association of Retired Persons (AARP).

Education is valued in our family. All six children graduated from Killeen High School, and four of the six siblings have attended college. Virginia Vanarsdale, the oldest daughter, was the first African American female from Killeen High School to receive a Parrie Haynes Scholarship Award from the Killeen Independent School District. She attended North Texas State University, Denton, Texas known now as The University of North Texas. Virginia R. Vanarsdale Whitfield resides in Arizona; Debra Vanarsdale White, Yvonne D. Vanarsdale Barlow and Veronica R. Vanarsdale Peters still reside in Texas. As adults, they are responsible residents of their communities. Our two sons, Vinson and Willie Jr. Vanarsdale are now deceased. Willie, Sr. left a legacy of service to his country, his church and his community. He and Geneva Vanarsdale have left a legacy of care and compassion to their family. Willie and Geneva were community builders.

Narvella Freeman
Giving Back to the Community
Narvella Freeman

My husband Benjamin and I moved to Fort Hood as a military family in 1960 with our children: Sammie, Oliver Louis, Leonard and Debbie Freeman. We lived on Post until 1962, when we relocated to Marlboro Heights because Ben was deploying to Germany and we had to clear quarters. During our stay on Post, the two older boys, Sammie and Oliver Louis, had to ride the bus from Fort Hood to attend school in Marlboro Heights. We were already living in Marlboro Heights when Leonard and Debbie began school in this community. We purchased a house on Jefferies Avenue in Marlboro Heights, and our children walked to school. Jefferies Avenue had only a few houses occupied when we moved here. There were houses being built on each side of us, but our house was the first one occupied on my side of the street. Later, Jefferies was opened to Zephyr Road, and even later it was opened south of Zephyr Road. Anderson Chapel AME Church was organized and they moved a building on Jefferies for worship. Our son, Oliver Louis, put the first coat of paint on this old barracks building after it was there for a year or two. Our children all attended school in the Killeen Independent School District from elementary to high school. Our family members are all natives of Taylor, Texas.

I graduated from high school in Taylor, Texas. I always wanted to be a nurse and had everything I needed to go to college. I was ready to go to Prairie View A and M College after high school graduation, but my principal failed to send my transcript in time for my admission. Later, I attended Houston Tillotson in Austin. Being a student there, I worked at the Deaf, Blind and Orphans (DBO) School in Austin, Texas. I also worked at one of the hospitals in Austin.

In the Killeen area I worked for the Army and Air Force Exchange System (AAFES) for many years, but my interest in nursing never left me. When I lived in Taylor—this was before I had children—I had expressed to a doctor for whom I worked that I wanted to attend the Johns School of Nursing. The doctor responded that he would work that out. Several years after I had moved to Killeen, I received an offer that I could now enroll in the Johns School of Nursing. However, this was after I had moved to Killeen and had my four children. Therefore, I could not accept that offer. My interest as a healthcare provider stayed with me over the years, and after my retirement from AAFES, I went back to school and obtained my certified nurse's assistant (CNA) license. I saw an opportunity to provide healthcare service and fulfill a desire that was always a part of me. I was successful in obtaining my license, and I began doing private home care. I have also taken care of some prominent citizens in the Killeen area during their illnesses. Most of the private care requests that I receive are the results of referrals by the families of previous patients that I had cared for. I am so grateful that I have had the opportunity to achieve my dream, which was to provide healthcare service to others. I am a member of Anderson Chapel AME Church and give support to the mission of the church. For years I served in the music ministry, and now I am active in the health ministry of the church. I still reside in the Marlboro community. I am among the few original homeowners that still reside on my street.

My adult children attended or are graduates of Killeen High School. They are responsible and productive citizens in their communities. Sammie, who was a very industrious teenager and young adult when growing up, is a prominent entrepreneur and businessman as CEO of Diverse Food Group in Missouri City, Texas. He is now fulfilling a lifelong goal that he set early in life. Many people remember him for his outstanding work ethic, even as a teenager. Oliver Louis joined the Job Corp before finishing high school. From there, he joined the Army. He and his family reside in Houston, Texas. He is the veteran of the family, and he served his country with honor and courage. He is caring, helpful and dependable, and you'll find him busy with various jobs.

Leonard and his family also live in Houston, Texas. He began demonstrating his talent, the gift of art, at the early age of three.

He has more than twenty years' of experience as a self-employed artist. In that time he has amassed a body of work that encompasses every area of art production, from freelance illustration to commissioned portraits in oil. His achievements have been featured in many notable publications. His lists of clients include major corporations, advertising agencies, Christian ministries and individuals. He is the recipient of many awards from businesses and organizations that have commissioned him to do various types of work. As a Christian, he emphasizes the need for spiritual growth through the use of art. He is a "self-taught artist" with no formal continuing art education to his credit. However, his self-education is always ongoing. He now has his own art gallery in the Houston area and has participated in art shows in many cities and states. He also has talked with students in elementary and high schools about art. In high school, Leonard created a portrait of Dr. Charles Patterson, which was an outstanding likeness of his principal.

Debbie has been associated with law enforcement agencies and related services ever since her graduation from high school. She served fourteen and a half years with the Killeen Police Department; eleven and a half years as a dispatcher; and three years as a PBX Operator. She also served two years with the Copperas Cove Police Department as a dispatcher and three years in Copperas Cove as a secretary for a criminal investigator; and one year with the city of Houston Police Department. Debbie has also served as an administrative tech with the Department of Public Safety for fifteen years. She and her family reside in Killeen, Texas.

Curtis and Flora Durry Jones
Memories and Lasting Friendships
Flora Jones

My family came to Killeen in 1961 because my husband was stationed at Ft. Hood. We resided at that time in the Marlboro Heights community. Our immediate and extended family included: my husband, Curtis; daughter, Lalita Durry Williams; two grandkids, Alicia Williams and Malcolm Bonner; and one great-grandchild, Curtis Williams. We are natives of Alabama and Florida. When my family arrived in this area, we found the families in Marlboro Heights friendly and helpful, which made our adjustment to the area much easier. The neighborly spirit that existed among the families provided my family with many memories and some lasting friendships. However, there were conditions that required some concern in many of the households. Housing was limited for Blacks during this time. Even though some houses were being built in the Marlboro Heights community by a local building company. Job opportunities were also limited for Blacks, except those in or employed by the military. My husband and I had jobs and careers in the military and civil service, as well as employment experiences with the Quartermaster laundry. There was no bus transportation from Marlboro Heights to downtown Killeen, and many families had either one vehicle or no vehicle. I vividly remember the signs of discrimination.

Family relationships are very important to us because we value family, love and unity, and the love we have for one another as a family was very important to us. We have always aspired as a family to help others. We wanted to be community builders, and my greatest contribution to this goal has been in putting forth my efforts in maintaining the neighborly atmosphere that I found in the Marlboro Heights community and being the best citizens that my family could be in this new developing community. As a family and residents we knew that working together even during times of adversity was necessary if our community was to grow into a desirable place for our children to live. It was also my hope that the city would become more accepting of Blacks in Killeen, and as the years passed, we began to see changes for a better life for Blacks.

Our family also values education and encourage others to pursue it. I achieved two years of college, and Curtis achieved his associate degree. Our daughter, Lalita, completed her college program and now works for the State of Texas Department of Human Services as a caseworker. Our family left the area in 1972 when my husband, Curtis Jones, was relocated to Free Port, Texas, with his job. All of these memories and the lasting friendships we made in Marlboro Heights, Killeen and Fort Hood will always be important to my family.

Ernestine Hill Warren
Teacher, City Councilwoman, and City Mayor
Ernestine Hill Warren

I am a native Texan, and I have shared residencies in Killeen and Rosebud, Texas my home city, for more than thirty years. After giving more than fifty-three years of public school service to the students in that community, I retired as a teacher from the Rosebud-Lott Independent School District. My love for learning was evident early in my life and resulted in my graduating from Wilson White High School as valedictorian of the class. In addition to earning the Bachelor of Science Degree from Texas College in Tyler, Texas; Masters of Education Degree from Prairie View University at Prairie View, Texas, and pursuing advance studies from Baylor University in Waco and the University of Texas in Austin, I also obtained my certification as a reading specialist.

Throughout my years in education, I have been an active participant in many educational activities and associations that have the interest of delivering the best education possible to students. I have served as president of the Local Falls County Texas State Teachers Association (TSTA). In 1988, I was nominated for Who's Who among American Educators. In 1992, I was included in Who's Who among American Teachers. In 1994, I received the Teacher of the Year Award.

Membership in Phi Delta Kappa, Waco, Texas has kept me focused on education. Even after retirement I find time to serve as first vice president of Falls County Retired Teachers Rosebud, Marlin and Lott Texas Association. I hold membership in the Killeen Area Alliance of Black School Educators. I try to stay in touch with education's best practices and give back to the community as a tutor of students in the Killeen schools. I have also become a mentor to a former student.

My community involvement includes active participation as a member of Greater Peace Missionary Baptist Church in Killeen, where I continue to share my gift for teaching as a Sunday school teacher. My community service involvement includes: Life Membership in Delta Sigma Theta Sorority Inc., a public service organization. I am one of the Charter members of the Killeen Alumnae Chapter of Delta Sigma Theta Sorority, Inc. and served as the chapter's second president. My service as block captain for heart fund drives and four years of service as chairperson for the March of Dimes Walk America, has kept me in touch with the community over the years.

My service in the political arena has given me the opportunity to serve the larger community of Rosebud, my hometown, where I was reared and educated. In 1999, I served as a board member of the West Rosebud Neighborhood Association. This experience was followed by two years of service on the Rosebud City Council. Later, my most noteworthy contribution in the political arena was my opportunity to give my service as a four-term mayor of Rosebud, Texas. Giving back to the community in service in positive ways is important to me. My adult daughters also share this interest and this practice. They are also responsible and productive citizens in their communities. My work and service gives me much fulfillment. Good citizenship practices and service make our city a better place in which to live and work. Giving back to the community is a purposeful goal for community builders.

Cordus, Jr. and Tommie Jackson
Public Servants Making a Positive Difference
Tommie Jackson

My husband, Cordus Jackson, Jr. and I came to Killeen in August 1961 from the Bryan and Caldwell, Texas areas. When Cordus Jackson, Jr. was growing up on his father's farm near Caldwell, Texas he had one dream for his future–which was to become a policeman. His dream was realized in December of 1961. It was at that time that Cordus Jackson, Jr. joined the Killeen police force as a part-time patrolman under Chief of Police Cooper. His employment established a historical fact in the history of local law enforcement in Killeen. Cordus Jackson had become the first African American policeman in Killeen, Texas. On October 1, 1962 Cordus Jackson became a full time patrolman on the Killeen police force and held this position of patrolman for six years. He earned another promotion on November 1, 1968 when Chief of Police Don Cannon announced the promotion of Patrolman Jackson to the position of police detective. This promotion established a second historical fact in the history of local law enforcement in Killeen. Cordus Jackson also became the first African American detective in Killeen, Texas. Killeen had a new chief of police in 1970. His name was Charlie W. Mitchell. The quality of Cordus Jackson's performance as a detective had again earned him a promotion to supervisor of detectives with a rank of lieutenant. Chief of Police Mitchell made this announcement. In this new position, Detective Jackson replaced Detective H. E. Shelton, who became the assistant to the Chief of Police. Detective Jackson was later made Captain of the Detective Department, and was then the State of Texas' highest ranking police officer. He accepted invitations to speak at churches, schools and many organizations about law enforcement. The residents of Marlboro Heights and Simmonsville were very proud of Captain Jackson's achievement in law enforcement and often spoke about his accomplishment to others who were new arrivals to the community. These achievements were also well received throughout the city-at-large by the citizens with a sense of pride, humility and thanksgiving. Detective Jackson became a respected role model in the community for many of the youth. He received numerous awards during his employment with the Killeen Police Department to include: The Officer of the Month and Commendation Awards, which were signed by City Manager Lloyd E. Moss and Mayor R. Q. Bay and other City Officials. In 1973 Detective Jackson left the Killeen Police Department and was employed with Lindy, Wells and Michalk Law Firm as an investigator and continued giving service back to the community.

I began teaching at Marlboro Elementary School in the Killeen Independent School District (KISD) the year *I* arrived in the city. I graduated from Prairie View A and M University in Prairie View, Texas and earned both my Bachelor Degree and my Master of Education Degree there. *I* taught fourth-grade at Marlboro Elementary School until its closing in 1969. The closing was to correct what the Department of Health, Education and Welfare (HEW) determined was a "dual school system." Marlboro's faculty, staff and students were assigned to other campuses in the school district. My new campus appointment was to Peebles Elementary School where I taught fifth grade until my retirement. I spent thirty-six years teaching the youth in Killeen and those in Caldwell where I had previously taught. After my retirement in 1990, I joined the Texas and the Killeen Retired Teachers Associations. I was elected treasurer for the local organization and faithfully served in this position for more than ten years.

We are members of Greater Peace Missionary Church in Killeen, Texas and faithfully serve in mission and other ministries of the church. We are the parents to four adult children. Belintha, Artie, Rhonda Kay and Patricia, They are all graduates of Killeen High School and are responsible and productive citizens in their community working in their chosen areas of interest and are giving service back to their community through their chosen careers. Belintha resides with her family in Bryan/College Station, Texas and has a career in computer information with an analyst organization. Artie is a graduate of Texas State Technical Institute (TSTI) in Waco, Texas and with his wife Michelle are owners and operators of Artie's Heating and Air Conditioning, Inc. It was established in 1982 in Killeen, Texas. Our daughter, Patricia, is a part of the administrative staff of the A/C and heating business. Their business not only provides service to communities in and around Killeen, but also provides employment to persons in the area. Our daughter, Rhonda Kay, pursued a career in cosmetology. They are goal setters, achievers and community builders in their own rights.

We are also community builders. Our contribution to the progress of Killeen as it exists in the 21st century is greatly valued. Cordus has given dedicated and selfless service for the safety and protection of all citizens and my devoted and committed service to the education of several generations of youth resulted in their development into responsible and productive adults.

Reuben W. and Catherine Hatcher
Community, Country and NAACP Service
Reuben Hatcher

My military experiences share historical insight about a soldier's life in the early days of the military. I was drafted into the Army on August 4, 1942. In the early years of a segregated Army, there were few combat units available to which black soldiers could be assigned; therefore, Blacks were mostly assigned to support units. I am a native of Wilmington, Connecticut. It was in the military that I met Catherine Frances Chase, who later became my wife. In 1961 we moved to Mineral Wells, Texas. Then my military assignment brought me to Ft. Hood, Texas in 1965. In April of 1965 we became members of Marlboro Missionary Baptist Church under the pastorate of Reverend R. A. Abercrombie and remained members for many years. In May 1994 we became charter members of the Greater Peace Missionary Baptist Church in Killeen under the pastorate of the Reverend J. A. Moland. We continued our faithful involvement in the church's ministries and activities. I also received my commission as a public notary and made my services available and convenient for the community.

Upon our arrival, Catherine and I first resided in the Simmonsville community, but later moved to the Marlboro Heights community. Both Catherine and I made notable contributions to the progress of the Marlboro Heights community and to the larger community—to include Killeen, Ft. Hood, Harker Heights, Nolansville and Copperas Cove—through our work as civil rights advocates. Our work in the NAACP reached both the state and national levels because as lifetime members, we were actively involved in local, state and national activities. Voter registration, Killeen Independent School District concerns, community concerns and personal concerns of citizens also received our interest and assistance. My contribution to the work of the Killeen Branch NAACP and of the community has had a positive effect in the life of the community. My long-time loyal and faithful service as secretary/treasurer and later secretary of the Killeen Branch NAACP and my committee work in the interest of the students of the community are most memorable. As early as the mid-fifties, Pastor Abercrombie and others began advocating for a Killeen Chapter of the NAACP. After there had been other unsuccessful attempts to organize a local branch of the NAACP in Killeen, eight other citizens and I met with Mr. R. Dockery, Regional NAACP Chairman, for the purpose of forming an adult chapter of the NAACP. Again, these nine persons were an insufficient number for a quorum; therefore, we were called a committee and charged to get more members. This committee, along with the support of other citizens in the community, recruited a sufficient number of members, and an NAACP Charter was granted to Killeen on July 2, 1970.

Prior to the formation of this NAACP committee, I had been actively involved in another community action group using as its name, "Committee to keep our School Open for Marlboro Heights." This committee was in response to an action on the part of the United States Health, Education and Welfare Department (HEW) to close the Marlboro school at the end of the school year in 1969. The Killeen School Board announced the closing. I was named the corresponding secretary for this committee, and I forwarded many protest letters, as directed by the committee, to the Killeen Independent School District Superintendent and Board of Trustees; to the U.S. Commission on Civil Rights; to the Texas Civil Liberties Union; and other agencies and individuals. These letters shared community concerns about elementary school-age students' welfare and their protection to and from other schools, which they would have to attend that were outside their neighborhood.

My dedication to my community work paralleled my commitment to my military experiences. When I retired May 22, 1972 at Ft. Hood, my military experiences involved a history of thirty years of honorable service that would bring me unexpected honors and recognition. In 1996, during President William Jefferson Clinton's administration, I received an invitation to the White House to be the special guest of the family of the late Staff Sgt. Edward A. Carter, Jr. (Sgt Carter was a former member of the 12th Armored Division who had distinguished himself in combat action in Germany on March 23, 1945.) The invitation was requesting my attendance to a historic occasion on January 13, 1997, during which time President Clinton would bestow the military's highest decoration, the Medal of Honor, upon the first seven black World War II heroes. I had been a member of Company D, and Carter was assigned to Company No. 1 (provisional), both units of the 56th Armored Infantry, 12th Armored Division. I appreciated the invitation, but did not attend due to health reasons.

My next honor came more than twenty-seven years after my retirement when I was honored with special recognition as a Bronze Star Medal Recipient. I was told of this honor in 1999 that I had been authorized the bronze Star Medal, which is the fourth highest medal awarded in combat. The Bronze Star recognized me for my combat service against armed enemies during World War II in the European-African-Middle Eastern Theater of Operations with Company D, 56th Battalion, and 12th Armored Infantry Division, from April 26 through September 1945. While researching the files of Black World War II veterans for consideration for the Medal of Honor, my authorized Bronze Star Award was discovered. As a result of that research, President William Clinton, in Washington D.C., presented the nation's highest award to seven black World War II veterans, of whom only one was still alive to accept the medal. Then, many miles away from Washington, D. C., on May 31, 1999 Lt. General Leon LaPorte, III Corps and Fort Hood Commander, presented the Bronze Star Medal to me, Reuben W. Hatcher, at the age of eighty years old. The ceremony took place during the Memorial Day Celebration at the Killeen Community Center in Killeen, Texas with family members and friends in attendance. I had also been the recipient of many other awards and recognition during my thirty years military career. Reuben W. and Catherine F. Hatcher will long be remembered for their contribution to community building through their advocacy for civil rights, community progress and honorable military service.

Richard, Sr. and Hazel Daniels
A Steadfast Communicator

Hazel Daniels arrived in Killeen from Morgana, Louisiana in September of 1961 to live with my aunt and uncle, Mr. and Mrs. Aristide Brown. I first worked on Post in the homes of colonels and lieutenant colonels, but later proceeded to pursue training in some applied skills. I attended Cosmetology School in Waco, Texas. I also attended business school and completed IBM training on computers. After this training I was employed in 1969 as an operator with Mid Texas Telephone. At that time, two other employees and I were the only three African American operators on the company's staff. I have continued to work in the field of communication for thirty-seven years. The name of the original company changed from Mid Texas Telephone to Centel. It later changed to Sprint Centel, then to Embarq. Since my retirement, the name changed to Century Link. Throughout these changes and prior to my retirement I remained in each new company's employment.

Richard, Sr. had come to Fort Hood and Killeen before I moved here. We are parents to three adult children who all live in Texas. Our youngest adult child, Richard, Jr., lives in Killeen. He is a graduate of Killeen High School. He attended Stephen F. Austin University and earned both his bachelor and master degree in the field of kinesiology. Richard Jr. returned to Killeen and is now employed by the Killeen Independent School District as a physical education teacher in one of its elementary schools and as a coach at Killeen High School. He, like many other former Marlboro Heights youths, accomplished the goals that he set for himself. Now he is giving back to the community and to the city of Killeen as a responsible and productive citizen.

Our family has been active in the community life of the Marlboro Heights community. We are members of Marlboro Missionary Baptist Church. I have been actively involved in the activities of the city of Killeen and of Bell County. For years I have served during political elections as a voting clerk, manning the precinct's voting stations and assisting with the voting booths. It has given me the opportunity to be of assistance to the citizens in exercising their right to vote. I have also been involved in an important issue that had a significant impact on the students, teachers and families in the Marlboro Heights community. I worked with the NAACP and was involved in the Marlboro Heights community's attempt to keep Marlboro Elementary School opened for the students of the community. I was among the delegation of concerned citizens representing the desires of the community by meeting with the Killeen Independent School District Superintendent. Our family is proud of our service as community builders. It was for the development of a better community.

Reverend Elmer and Adalee Snell
Faithful Soldiers in the Lord's Army
Rev. Elmer Snell

I came to Killeen, Texas, in 1961 and was stationed at Ft. Hood, Texas. A year or so later I received orders for Germany. This was during the Berlin Crisis. Having completed this tour of duty, I returned to For Hood, Texas. My second tour of duty was spent in Vietnam, and after serving that tour I was again stationed at Fort Hood. I married Adalee Hamilton Snell, the daughter of Maurice and Lester Hamilton and returned to Germany for my third tour of duty and again returned to Ft. Hood. I joined Anderson Chapel African Methodist Episcopal (AME) Church. I taught Sunday school for more than a year and accepted my call into the ministry. After receiving my ministerial training I was given a charge as pastor of Griffin Chapel AME Church in Llano, Texas at the Central Texas Annual Conference of the African Methodist Episcopal Church. My appointment was made by the Bishop. I commuted weekly to Llano as pastor and rendered service to that community.

My wife Adalee was a blessing to my ministry. She served at Griffin Chapel as a stewardess, the church musician and wherever she was needed. The Lord blessed my ministry throughout my appointment there. We have nine children and along with other family members, they all blessed our ministry. Adalee and I are grateful for the support that they gave. When I retired as a pastor, we returned to Anderson Chapel in Killeen. I re-joined the ministerial staff there and became actively involved in the visitation, prayer and Sunday school ministries. My wife rejoined the choir ministry. After my retirement from the military, I worked for Zip Cleaners, a local cleaning company and had my second retirement.

Over the years I watched the city of Killeen grow from a small town to what you see now. There have been many homes, businesses, schools, churches, as well as many civic and social organizations established in this city. I also witnessed a city government and its people working together to bring about this growth. Killeen became a city where my family and many others families chose to live. Through my outreach ministry my contribution as community builders expanded beyond Killeen, Fort Hood and Harker Heights and was blessed.

Evans and Rose Washington
Honorable Military and Community Service
Zawanda Washington

Our parents, Evans and Rose Mary Washington came to Killeen, Texas, in 1961. They are both from Mobile, Alabama. As a career military man in the U. S. Army, my father was assigned to Fort Hood, Texas, as a part of 2nd AD. After living in temporary accommodations, they purchased their first home. It was a small blue house located on Highland Avenue in Marlboro Heights. They are the parents of three adult children: Tchelinda, Cassandra and Zawanda. Two of the daughters live in the Killeen area, and the eldest daughter resides in the greater Houston area. Their grandchildren are Marcus, Paris and Maryrose. The family traveled extensively prior to returning to the Greater Killeen Area in 1979.

My dad served in active duty in Jackson, Tennessee, from 1976-1979 at the National Guard. He was a part of 1st Calvary during his duty station at Fort Bliss in El Paso, Texas, from 1973-1974. Hildesheim, Germany was one of three overseas tours the family experienced. Mannheim, Germany and Baumholder, Germany were the other two stations where my dad was assigned. After deciding to retire in this area our parents purchased a home in Harker Heights, Texas where they have lived for the past twenty-seven years. Our dad retired in 1982 and immediately joined civil service, working at Range Control. After fifteen years of service with civil service he took a temporary hiatus. When Fort Hood decided to become a closed Post after the terrorist attacks, Dad went back to work at Fort Hood, Texas as a security guard and in 2006, he reluctantly retired again.

Our Family has continually been active in area churches. We were initially members of 19th Street Chapel. When we moved to Harker Heights, we became members of Marlboro Missionary Baptist Church. Currently we are active members and charter members of

Greater Peace Missionary Baptist Church where our parents serve as deacon and deaconess. They are also actively involved in several ministries which include mission, the brotherhood choir, ushers and Sunday school. Over the years, my mother has also been involved in community service. She has been recognized as a 2008 Woman of Distinction by the Girl Scout Council of Central Texas. Our parents celebrated their golden wedding anniversary on June 10, 2006, with a gala affair at the Officer's Club at Fort Hood. They entertained family and friends from near and far. They continue to be a viable and encouraging influence in our community. They are community builders. Their service as community builders has been valuable.

Walter, Sr. and Louise Clark
Family, Love and Prayer Make the Difference
Lucky Clark and Task Force

In 1961 my father, Walter Clark, Sr., arrived at Fort Hood, Texas, with our mother, Louise, and four children: Walter Jr., Rosemary, Delores and me. He was a native of Scotland, Georgia, and our mother, a native of McRae, Georgia. Our family members became longtime residents of the Marlboro Heights community, where we became homeowners and involved in the life of the community. My father became an independent trucker after his retirement from the military and in this occupation, as would be expected, he traveled many miles across the USA adding even more mileage to the travel experiences that he had while in the Army.

My Mother's involvement in the community was varied. Her employment was in the area of food service management, and she was blessed with a gift for preparing delicious and appetizing meals, as well as, mouthwatering dessert dishes. The family became members of Anderson Chapel AME Church. My mother's leadership as Sunday school superintendent for over twenty-seven years made an impact on the youth of the church, as well as the on the adults of that congregation. She also served in the church's stewardess ministry where she had the opportunity to be involved for many years in providing service for two very important sacraments of the church: Holy Communion and Baptisms. Her faithfulness to her responsibilities contributed to the accomplishment of the church's mission. She also accepted the opportunity to be involved in community service and was as a member of the Killeen-Cove, Hood Special Olympics Board. She continued to maintain membership in the organization, supporting her son, Walter, Jr., and the many other persons with special needs for many years. Her service, together with other board members and parents, ensured that opportunities for wholesome activities were available to these Special Olympians. Walter Jr. was a Special Olympics participant and experienced success and recognition in track, shot put, golf, and bowling. These successes build character, confidence and self-esteem within a Special Olympian.

Their adult children: Lucky Clark, Rosemary Clark Tisdale, and the late Delores Clark Johnson—are graduates of Killeen High School and they became productive contributors to the Killeen community through their chosen careers. For many years Lucky's employment has been management in the jewelry industry; Rosemary's as a registered nurse; and. Delores chose to give back to her community in her early years in retail clothing employment. In later years her community involvement contributions were to the community in which she resided. The Clark family members are community builders who contributed to making this community a better place to live. Walter, Sr., Louise and their daughter Deloris Clark-Johnson are now deceased.

Marie Henderson
The Joy of Teaching
Marie Henderson

I am a native of Oklahoma and was born and reared on my Papa's farm in Vian, Oklahoma. My father was a farmer/rancher who raised white face Herefords cattle . . . the same kind that President Lyndon Johnson used to raise. I received my elementary and high school education in Vian. After high school I attended Langston University and graduated with a B.S. degree in elementary education. Growing up on a farm was rewarding and challenging in many ways. You learned how to walk and run fast (our means of transportation) at an early age. If you said the word "snake," suddenly, Wilma Rudolph didn't have a thing on me. I am number eight of nine children. There are only three of us living. It was fun growing up in a big family. We had our good times and bad times. Papa was a man of honesty and integrity and he set high standards for us which we had to abide by.

My mother died at the age of forty-two. From then on Papa had to take over. He raised all of his nine children and two grandchildren by himself. We could not have asked for a better father. My oldest sister played a major part in helping out. She was very kind to all of us. So you see, I hailed from a strong foundation that was developed by strong parents, a loving sister and a determined spirit led by a man whose mission in life was to make a better world for his children.

Welcome to Texas! The year was 1962. I arrived in the great state of Texas with two children, Lloyd and Meeker, ages seven and two. Dock Jackson, Jr., principal at Marlboro Elementary School, gave me my first opportunity to teach in Killeen. Wow! I was overjoyed! Mr. Jackson was very kind, understanding, courteous and supportive to all of his teachers and staff. The teachers that I worked with were an awesome group. Tommie Jackson and I taught fourth grade together. She made sure that I knew the rules in Texas. We quickly became best friends.

In my opinion teaching is one of the most rewarding and challenging professions on earth. Teaching has given me the opportunity to expand and enrich the minds and lives of hundreds of young people. Knowing that I have made a difference in the life of a child is the experience that I value most in life. This experience is validated when a former student returns after high school or college and thanks me for their experiences in my third grade classroom and attribute part of their success to learning gained while a student in my class. Words fail to adequately express the feeling of pride, joy and accomplishment when I am reminded that my purpose in life was to simply. . .teach. To me teaching was a calling which I responded to wholeheartedly.

During my forty-three year tenure in education I had the privilege of teaching at various places in America and Europe, to include: Washington Elementary in Moffett, Oklahoma; Wurzburg Elementary in Wurzburg, Germany; Douglas Elementary in Lawton, Oklahoma; Kumpf Elementary in Kansas City, Missouri; Marlboro, Meadows, Nolanville and Willow Spring Elementary in Killeen, Texas. While my teaching experiences were vast, I am most blessed to have thirty-two years in Killeen Independent School District (KISD), from which I received my fondest experiences and memories. In KISD, I was not only afforded the opportunity to teach but to learn as well. I became a great teacher as a result of being led by many incredibly talented colleagues and principals.

Currently, I am a retired teacher; however, my lifestyle is not retired. I am actively involved in my church and community where I continue to teach, mentor, support and give whatever service I can. I even find time to regularly attend a local gym, where I work diligently to stay fit. My pride and joy of life are my two children, currently residing in Kansas City, Missouri, and Burlington Township, New Jersey, and my two granddaughters who are now in high school. Well, to sum things up, I am honored to have enjoyed a life of service and serving others. A phrase from an old song says it best: "If I can help somebody as I pass along, then my living will not be in vain." Community Builders touch lives of many and make a positive difference. These lives touch others. Maria Henderson has been a builder of humanity in this community.

Marion J. and Alice W. Douse
A Committed Team in Service
Alice Douse

 My husband, SFC Marion J. Douse, and I arrived in the Killeen/Fort Hood community in June 1962 during a very hot, dry summer with change of station orders from Fort Polk, Louisiana, to Ft. Hood, Texas. We were accompanied by our four daughters Cathy, Michelle (now known as Mtisha), Glenda and Carla. My husband whom I call M.J. and I are formerly from Florida, and as a family we had resided in Pennsylvania, Georgia, and Florida and now in Texas. In addition to making adjustments to the very hot weather we also experienced the uncertainty of finding housing for the family. We found ourselves exceeding the allowable stay for guests in the Ft. Hood guest house, but we were not forced to leave. We went out daily searching for a place to rent, first in Killeen, then later in Copperas Cove and Temple. After having driven through the Marlboro Heights community many times we really wanted to live in this community. We learned of a local contractor who was building in Marlboro Heights and contacted the company to purchase a house. We were very happy when our application was approved. We finally located a rental in Temple. It was in substandard condition but provided temporary housing until the construction of our house was completed. M. J., commuted weekly from Temple to Fort Hood during that time.

A few weeks before the Killeen schools opened a new school year in 1962, the house was almost completed except for some minor finishing jobs and the contractor agreed to let us move in early. We traveled to Killeen on the day prior to our move and worked inside the house. On the next day while awaiting the arrival of our household goods we discovered that the bathtub had a crack in it and had to be replaced before passing the final inspection. However, we moved in anyway and workers came in for a few days to finish up the work and replace the tub.

The new school year began with Cathy, the oldest daughter, enrolled at Nolan Junior High; Mtisha (Michelle) the next oldest daughter enrolled at Marlboro Elementary; and Glenda our third daughter enrolled at the Ft. Hood Under School. Carla, the youngest daughter, remained at home with me. I was an experienced teacher when I moved to Killeen; however, I did not work for about a year and a half. During this time I began volunteering as a PTA worker and officer. Then later I served as a Girl Scout troop leader.

Two years after our arrival to Killeen/Fort Hood, another opportunity for community involvement and service was presented to us, and in 1964 M. J. and I joined with eight other persons to establish a new church that we named Anderson Chapel African Methodist Episcopal Church. This was the first African Methodist Episcopal Church in the Killeen area. The ten founding members were Frederick and Velma Hayden, Willie and Bertie Sworn, Mary Manjang, Eddie Mae Johnson, Marion J. and Alice Douse, Rev. Arthur Anderson, the founding pastor and his wife, Mary Anderson. All the founding members were residents of Killeen except Rev. Anderson and his wife, Mary. They were residents of Lampasas, Texas and commuted for ten years to serve this church. As a founding member, M. J. served as the church's first treasurer and one of the first stewards and trustees. I served as the church's first Sunday school superintendent and one of its first Sunday school teachers. Our daughter Cathy served as the church's first pianist. Since its humble beginnings over fifty years ago, we have remained active members of Anderson Chapel AME Church. Over the years we have faithfully served in various ministries of the church, as leaders to the youth and adults, and as supporters of other church leaders and events. The church is now a supporter of local, regional and global missions. We have been committed workers who value making a difference and giving back to the community.

After more than 20 years of loyal military service to his country, including service at Ft. Dix, Ft. Bragg, Ft. Benning, Ft. Sam Houston, Ft. Valley Forge and Walter Reed Army Medical Center in Washington, DC; also two tours to Tripler General Hospital in

Hawaii, and a tour each to Korea and Vietnam, SFC Marion J. Douse retired in 1973 at Fort Hood, Texas. He held a unique classification in rank of being the only specialist seven (SP7) at Fort Hood for a period of time during the decade of the sixties. After retirement he gave additional years of civil service in the area of health services as a licensed vocational nurse (LVN). In 1974, M. J. served on the Killeen Planning and Zoning Board for two years. He then accomplished two of his educational goals by earning his certification in hotel and motel restaurant management, and also earning his Bachelor of Science Degree in Business Administration. He has provided independent auditing services for some public service organizations over the years, and has been supportive of numerous local organizations such as Special Olympics, Central Texas Cruisers Track Club, and other causes. His charitable and philanthropic contributions have been responsible for the establishment and sustainability, for a period, of various projects, including a learning center.

Since our arrival in Killeen, I have had many opportunities to give service to my community. In 1964, I was employed by the Killeen Independent School District and began to expand my service in the field of education. I began as a sixth-grade teacher at Marlboro Elementary School. At that time, because of segregation it was the only school where Black professional educators could be employed in the school district. Dock Jackson Jr. was Killeen ISD's first Black principal and was my principal at Marlboro Elementary School. In 1966, I was reassigned to Pershing Park Elementary School as a sixth-grade teacher and integrated the professional staff as Pershing Park's first Black teacher. I remained a teacher at Pershing Park until 1975 when I became Killeen Independent School District's (Killeen ISD) first Elementary School Science Consultant. A year later in 1976, I was appointed chairperson of Killeen ISD's Talented and Gifted Committee with the responsibility of planning Killeen ISD's first Talented and Gifted (TAG) Program. However, during that same year (1976) I was appointed assistant principal to Pershing Park Elementary School, and due to the assistant principal appointment I relinquished my position as chairperson to the Talented and Gifted Committee. My appointment as principal of Haynes Elementary

School was made the following year in 1977, and I became the first Black woman to serve as a principal in a Killeen ISD school; and the second Black principal employed by the school district since 1954. My tenure at Haynes Elementary School on Zephyr Road lasted nine years, and in June 1986, I was appointed by the Killeen ISD Board of Trustees as the inaugural principal of the newly constructed Hay Branch Elementary School. I remained principal at Hay Branch for ten years until my retirement in 1996. During my tenure in KISD my greatest joy was the opportunity it offered to touch the lives of the youth of this community as a teacher and administrator and to work with educators, parents and citizens in the community.

My community affiliations in organizations also gave me opportunities for service. They gave me many opportunities to work for a better quality of life for myself and for others through organizations and events such as the NAACP, Killeen Alumnae Chapter of Delta Sigma Theta Sorority, Inc., Prairie View Alumnae Club, Central Texas Chapter of Phi Delta Kappa Fraternity and the Killeen Area Alliance of Black School Educators. Over the years, I became the recipient of several awards from different groups in the community which included the Jefferson Award, Fort Hood Good Neighbor Award, Classroom Teachers Texas Administrator of the Year Award, Cornerstone Baptist Church Top Ladies of Distinction Award, Bluebonnet Girl Scout Woman of Distinction Award, U. S. Army Community Service Award, AME Church Outstanding Service Award, the Exchange Club Golden Deeds Award and others.

Our daughters Cathy, Mtisha (Michelle), Glenda and Carla are Killeen High School graduates. They are also educators and have earned post graduate degrees at the master level. Cathy's employment has always been at the college and university level. Mtisha and Glenda are employed as special education teachers at the elementary and secondary school levels. Carla, a former speech pathologist and kindergarten teacher is now a grants administrator for Title I programs in her school district. Our daughters are also community builders in their own communities. They have been honored and recognized in their own rights by professional, religious, public service organizations and have embodied a servant's spirit by actively participating in church, civic, political and public service organizations.

In reflecting back over the more than fifty years since our arrival at Killeen/Fort Hood, our family's involvement in the community stayed focused on service and involvement in projects and activities that provided personal growth to us and to others. We are thankful for the many opportunities we experienced. Our family's experiences as community builders have taken us on a rewarding journey and have produced fulfillment in our lives. Our community has changed for the better. We now have a very diverse community with people working, worshiping, and living in communities together as well as governing the city together. However, the community must continue striving to become more inclusive in order to enhance the quality of life for its entire population. This is important because community building is for everyone. Community building is a team effort of contributions shared by citizens in different careers and professions, races and ethnicities through businesses, schools, churches, organizations, community and our homes.

Alexander and Nora Vernon
Championing Veterans and Military Families Rights
Alexander Vernon

My family and I arrived in the Killeen/Ft Hood area at the end of August 1962, just four days before Labor Day. My wife Nora and my children Linda, Robbie, Alexander Jr., Yvette, Annette and I had traveled by train to Temple, Texas. I was an E-6 upon my arrival to Ft. Hood. My assignment to Ft. Hood came about when I had been picked up by a unit that went over to Europe as a single unit for the German build-up. We lived in the Post's guest house while looking for housing in Killeen. At that time Simmonsville and Marlboro Heights were the only two communities in the Killeen/Ft. Hood Area where Blacks could live. In most cases the housing for Blacks in these two communities were segregated and the housing in Simmonsville was often substandard. My family was able to locate a house on Terrace Drive in Marlboro Heights just next door to the home of Sgt. Milton Williams and his wife Julia.

My wife registered a complaint with the G-1 about the inadequate housing situation for minority military families and garnered his promise to move us into military quarters as soon as possible. In the meantime, my wife and the kids decided to take a trip to the Panama Canal Zone to see our parents and family. Upon their return to Ft. Hood, we were called and subsequently moved into the Pershing Park housing area.

After two years I was promoted to the rank of warden officer and my Army career was going very well. In 1964 a new Post Commander, General Ralph E. Haines, arrived at Fort Hood and made quite an impact on the quality of life for Black soldiers and their families. Killeen was still very segregated at the time and Blacks could not freely enter businesses in town, receive services, or enjoy activities. General Haines met with community leaders and asked that minority servicemen and their families be treated fairly and welcomed in the Killeen community. In Killeen at that time, the only businesses that we could visit to eat out were Maurice's Bar-B-Q Restaurant and one night club in the city. During this same time approximately fifteen active duty military personnel wrote a letter to the mayor of Killeen asking that our Black children be able to play and enjoy activities at Conder Park, a city recreational facility. After a few weeks the mayor approved the request.

In 1965, I received orders for Vietnam, and my family had to move off-post. By this time an Austin-based construction company had begun building a sub-division of single-family houses for minorities in Marlboro Heights. I left for Vietnam three days before the house was completely finished. My family moved into our new home on Haynes Drive and our kids enrolled in Marlboro Elementary School under the guidance of Principal Dock Jackson.

When I returned from Vietnam in 1970, my wife decided to apply for a job. However, it was no easy task for Blacks to find a job in Killeen. She had always worked before coming to Ft. Hood, and after approximately nine months, she was employed at Ft. Hood as a secretary for the Officers' Club System. It was about this time that our family began to adjust to our life in Killeen. My wife was working; the kids were doing quite well in their school work; and the Marlboro Heights community was attracting new families. It was also during this time that Killeen started to grow because there were now two major combat divisions stationed at Ft. Hood. It was really a great change from what we saw when we first arrived here in 1962. Killeen had begun to accept the diversity of the military lifestyle. I remember back then when a few mixed-race couples arrived here; they would be transferred to another post overnight. But soon the townsfolk became more tolerant. When I first got here, I wrote every congressman in the state of New York asking to get out of Ft. Hood. But, after doing two tours to Vietnam (November 10, 1965 to September 23, 1966 and January 3, 1969 to January 1, 1970) I began to feel more comfortable about the area. During my two tours to Vietnam, I earned the Vietnam Service Medal with a Silver service star and two Bronze Service Stars, the Republic of Vietnam Campaign Medal and the Bronze Star Medal with one Oak Leaf Cluster. I also served two tours of duty in Panama. After each tour I received orders to go right back to Ft. Hood, and I felt that the Lord had given me a message; so I decided to call Killeen my home. I have been blessed beyond my dreams as I served in the United States Army for twenty-two years, ten months and twenty- two days. I retired from active duty at the rank of Chief Warrant Officer.

After my retirement I was employed as an investigation detective for eleven years with the Killeen Police Department. My next civilian employment was with Lockheed Corporation at Ft. Hood, Texas. Since retiring from my third career, my wife and I traveled and enjoyed life in Killeen. I remain a life member of the Veterans of Foreign Wars (VFW) 9191, District Fourteen in Killeen and have served in numerous service and leadership positions at the state and national level, and continue to strive to make the lives of veterans and their families better. In 1995-1996, I was named "State Commander for the Veterans of Foreign Wars (VFW), Department of Texas," the first Black to hold this state-wide office representing the interests of over 113,000 veterans. A highlight of my service was being selected by the Jewish War Veterans to be part of a delegation to tour Israel and meet with political leaders in 1998. In addition, I was selected vice-chair of the Texas Veterans Commission, December 1999. "I am proud to be here in Killeen" Both Nora and Alexander Vernon were dedicated community builders. Alexander Vernon's work in the interest of veterans everywhere is his legacy to the United States of America and to his fellow brothers and sisters in arms.

Edward and Sammie L. Hornsby
Productive Service that Makes a Difference
Sammie L Hornsby

Edward, a native of Oak Grove, Louisiana, was drafted into the United States Army in 1949 in St. Louis, Missouri. We were united in marriage in 1957. Edward's military assignment brought him to Fort Hood, Texas in 1962 and we resided in Temple, Texas until moving to Rev. R. A. Abercrombie Drive (formerly Parkhill Drive) in Killeen, Texas. After living in Killeen for four months Edward received orders for deployment to Fort Wainwright, Alaska. In September of 1962 Edward was off to Alaska; however, the family did not join him in Alaska until November, 1962. We were stationed in Alaska until September of 1965 when Edward was reassigned to Fort Polk, Louisiana, and not to Fort Hood as we all desired. The family returned to Killeen for approximately four months, alone. Then, Edward was fortunate enough to trade assignment with an individual stationed at Fort Hood who desired to be stationed at Fort Polk, Louisiana. In less than four months we were all back in Killeen. Edward's next military orders were his assignment to Fort Riley, Kansas, during the early months of 1967. The family remained in Killeen until the end of the 1968 school year before we joined him in Fort Riley and remained there until Edward's retirement. On September 1, 1969, at Fort Riley, Kansas Edward Hornsby retired from the U. S. Army after twenty years of honorable military service and the family elected to return to their home in Killeen after his retirement.

Upon our return home we both continued our employment careers at Fort Hood, Texas. Edward worked at the Fort Hood Commissary as a master butcher for twenty years, retiring in 1991; I worked civil service for thirty years. My last 15 years of service were performed at Carl Darnell Army Hospital (formerly Darnall Army Hospital) as a Supervisor; Supply Technician /Accounting Technician/System Administrator in the Data Conversions and Files Section, Logistics Division, under Headquarters Health Service Command, Fort Sam Houston, and San Antonio, Texas. I retired from civil service on January 4, 1994.

We were blessed with five children. Our oldest daughter graduated from high school in Junction City, Kansas and our other four children are Killeen High School graduates. They are productive achievers who are giving service back to their community in positive ways. Daughter Jacquelyn M. McKinney is an Occupational Therapist for the Dallas Independent School District; Robert Lee Daniel III's now retired, provided years of service at the State of Texas Comptroller Office in Austin, Texas as a Manager and in Account Maintenance; Charlton P. Hornsby Sr., P.C., Attorney-at-Law is Board Certified and the owner of the Charlton P. Hornsby Law Firm in Beaumont, Texas; daughter Germaine M. Hornsby, a LaMar University graduate is an assistant in the law firm. Byron K. Hornsby is an Implementation Specialist for Sprint in Fort Worth, Texas.

There has been tremendous growth in Killeen since we first moved into the Marlboro Heights community. We have witnessed the growth from one high school to four high schools from three elementary schools to thirty-two; from two middle schools to eleven; and Special School/Programs from one to eight. *NOW THAT'S GROWTH!* We have seen Killeen move from one major highway entrance, Business Highway 190, to another entrance, Central Texas Expressway. In the early 1950s there was one store on Business 190. I believe the name was "One Stop Grocery." There were no restaurants for Blacks, only one barbecue stand, "Maurice Barbeque," owned by a Black man named Maurice Hamilton. There were no hotels/motels. Most of the Blacks lived in Marlboro Heights or Simmonsville. The city of Killeen now has a myriad of restaurants, hotels/motels, businesses and shopping centers. Killeen has had its first Black Mayor and first Black City Manager. After over fifty years, we still reside in the Marlboro Community. Edward and Sammie Hornsby, two loyal citizens, community builders have not only personally contributed to the progress of a better community, but have also nurtured productive achieving children who now are giving back to the communities in which they reside and have also become community builders in their own rights.

Ollie Louise Redwine
Dedicated & Committed to Mission
Ollie Louise Redwine

My husband, James, and I moved to the Killeen-Fort Hood area in 1962 as a military family. We have two sons. During James' active duty assignments, the family traveled in many parts of the world. My two favorite assignments were Germany and Hawaii. I am a native of Wadesboro, North Carolina. We later moved to the Marlboro Heights Community in 1968. As a member of Anderson Chapel African Methodist Episcopal Church I serve with the Missionary Society ministry. My mission service extended into all levels of missionary work for the African Methodist Episcopal Church. I was recognized for my faithfulness and dedication to the work of the local mission activities sponsored by the Hamilton-Manjang Missionary Society. I also serve in the Music ministry of the church.

Education and my personal development are important to me. Therefore I became a member of the International Training and Communications Club (ITC), and the Central Texas Branch of Toastmasters International. I also attended Central Texas College pursuing a degree in Chemical Dependency. My community activities included the Federal Women's Club and the Ladies Auxiliary of Veterans of Foreign Wars, Post 9191.

I adopted the three sons of my late brother and raised them with my two sons. They attended the Killeen Schools just as our two sons did. I value family and helping others. One of my hobbies is cooking and I do that well. Two other hobbies that brought me much pleasure are: sharing encouraging words and brighten a person's day through random acts of kindness to others. My service as a community builder became a part of my work in missions and my ministry in the Missionary ministry of my church. I retired from Civil Service with 29 years of service as an Accountant Technician Supervisor at the Fort Hood Commissary. I have had a fruitful life. I strived to be a benefit to the community.

Colonel (Retired) Junious W. Smith, Jr. and Eula Mae Smith
A Family Sharing "Firsts" Experiences
Linda Smith Pelton

In June, 1963, my late father Colonel (Retired) Junious W. Smith, Jr. requested and received a transfer to 1st Logistical Command at Ft. Lee, Virginia. The reason was that 1st Log was being moved to Ft. Hood, Texas, and he wanted to move the family to Texas because he was contemplating retirement. He and Mom were from Burleson County, Texas. The family consisted at the time of Major Smith; Eula Mae Smith, our mom; and the children: Linda (sixteen), a student at Killeen High School; Buster (fourteen) and Ronald (twelve), both students at Nolan Junior High School; Erma (nine) and Zelma (eight), who attended Marlboro Elementary; and Susan (five) who attended kindergarten on Post (Fort Hood). At this time, the then Major Junious W. Smith was the "first" African American field grade officer assigned to Ft. Hood. We moved on Jefferies Avenue in the Marlboro Heights community. Our mom, Eula Smith, became secretary to Mr. Dock Jackson, the principal at Marlboro Elementary School. In fact, she was the "first" secretary of Marlboro Elementary School and "first" African American secretary hired by the Killeen Independent School District.

In December 1963, the family moved to Patton Park, the field grade housing area, where we were the only black family there. We were also in a new school attendance zone. I became a student in the first senior class at the new Killeen High School on Thirty-Eighth Street. Buster and Ronald attended Fairway Junior High; Erma and Zelma attended Meadows Elementary and Susan joined mom at Marlboro Elementary School.

In April, 1965, our father went to Vietnam. We moved back to Marlboro Heights on Longview Drive. The Robert and Wadella Heath family was one of our neighbors. We all transferred to our school's attendance zones at Rancier Junior High and Marlboro Elementary. I graduated from Killeen High School in May 1965 and went to Prairie View A and M University. Mrs. Alice Douse, a Marlboro Heights resident, was attending graduate school there and would often bring packages to me from Mom. Susan's first grade teacher was Mrs. Vera Nelson. Buster and Ronny were the athletes of the family and in 1964-65 my brother, Busters, attended Killeen High School. Our family worshiped at the chapel on Post, but two of my school friends, Mabel May and Ruth Elise O'Neal, brought me to Marlboro Baptist Church for worship with them. When dad went to Vietnam, Mom and the family joined Marlboro Missionary Baptist Church.

I am a graduate of Killeen High School, Prairie View A and M University and Mary Hardin-Baylor of Belton, Texas. I have been an educator since 1971 and began my career as a special education teacher at Marlboro Elementary School. I later held the position of Parent/Community Coordinator in the Killeen School District. I am also a former KISD principal of Haynes Elementary School located on Zephyr Road. After my retirement as principal I continued to serve as a mentor and evaluator of future teachers and school administrators. My husband, Johnny, and I have four children: Dr. Stephanie Pelton Miller, a social worker with the Killeen Independent School District; also Michael and Stacey, graduates of Killeen High; and Matthew, a graduate of Harker Heights High School.

My siblings are now productive citizens giving back to the communities where they reside. Buster retired as an E-8 at Ft. Bragg, North Carolina having given loyal service to his country; Ronny has a degree from Prairie View A and M University and Southwest Baptist Theological Seminary. He resides in Houston, where he is a Harris County Probation Officer and the Director of Christian Education at Mt. Ararat Church. Erma is a journalism professor at San Francisco State University in California. Her degree is from UTY, Columbus. She credits her love of language and writing to Mrs. Thelma Jackson, her fifth grade teacher at Marlboro Elementary School. Zelma works for the Texas Registration Budget Office. She has a degree from the University of Texas and Trinity University. Susan is a writer for the Austin American Statesman. Her degree is from the University of Texas.

Erma, Zelma and I were Girl Scouts. I attended the *first* formerly segregated camp session at Camp Kachina on Belton Lake in 1964.

"Today, Black Girl Scouts and their parents in Central Texas may not be aware of the fact that their opportunities to attend integrated sessions of Girl Scout activities and events resulted from a petition presented to the Board for Bluebonnet Girl Scout Council in 1964 by a service leader from Fort Hood and a African American mother, my mom Eula M. Smith. They petitioned the Board for the Bluebonnet Girl Scout Council to have all sessions of activities and events integrated." The response to this petition was that the next session of Girl Scout activities and events were open to all girls and I, Linda Smith (Pelton), Junious and Eula's daughter, was the "first" African American girl to attend a Girl Scout session that was not "designated integrated." *Prior to the Board for Bluebonnet Girl Scout Council's acceptance and approval of the petition for integration of all sessions of scout activities and events, African American scouts could only attend sessions that were designated integrated while others sessions were closed to African American scouts.*

African American Girl Scouts, former Girl Scouts, and their parents also may not be aware that more than fifty years after I, Linda Smith (Pelton), participated in my "first" scout session of events open to *all* scouts, in 1997 I was elected to the Board of the Bluebonnet Girl Scout Council, which owns Camp Kachina and served on the board until 2000. A few years later I was elected president of the Bluebonnet Girl Scout Council and became its "first" African American president of the board for the Bluebonnet Girl

Scout Council. The Board for the Bluebonnet Girl Scout Council served twelve and one half counties in Central Texas, including Bell County and all sessions of scout activities and events are open to all Bluebonnet Girl Scouts.

Our father and our mother are both deceased now. They both were role models, and they were constant encouragers and supporters of the accomplishment of the goals of their children and grandchildren.

Community builders on many occasions find themselves actively involved in working to make a difference not just for their personal good, but also for the good of many others. Eula Smith and daughter Linda, with the assistance and encouragement of a supportive family, "opened a window" in Girl Scouting that has made this organization a more just and fair builder of confidence in girls. In addition, this "opened window" has resulted in an organization that is truly representative of the precepts taught in scouting. Do community builders make a difference? Absolutely! I believe and I know that community builders do make a positive difference in lives.

Jacqueline Bailey Stabler
A Door was opened for Others
Jackie Stabler

James Bailey, a soldier with orders assigning him to Fort Hood, Texas, and me, a native of Washington, D.C., came to the Fort Hood area in 1963. Our four children—Sheila, James Jr., Katrina, Wendy and also my husband's nephew—were with us. We moved into the Marlboro Heights community and only black families, most of whom were military, lived there. I was pregnant when we arrived in the area. In October of 1963 I went to the hospital at Fort Hood to deliver my baby; sadly our baby was stillborn. In an attempt to make contact with a funeral home for our baby's burial in the city, I was told that no funeral home in Killeen or surrounding areas handled black bodies. We were also told that we needed to contact a black funeral home in Temple, and I did that. Our child was buried in Temple, Texas. In addition to being saddened, I was very angry about the denial of burial service in Killeen. Therefore, I called my uncle in D. C. and explained to him what happened. He advised me to contact my Congressman in Maryland, the last place that I was living. He also advised me to take the information that we had to the Post Commander. We also did that, and it was then that we learned that all funeral homes in Killeen and surrounding areas had a contract with the government. Therefore, they could not discriminate against persons who requested their service. As a result of this incident, shortly thereafter, the Killeen area funeral homes began serving all races that requested their service. This experience for us was unexpected. However, it opened a door for others.

The reality of a second incident that our family experienced left us with an impression that prejudices may exist in the town. It occurred in downtown Killeen at a drug store. We went there to purchase hamburgers for our family. In fact, we ordered eighteen sandwiches. In the meantime I sat on the bar stool, while waiting for the hamburgers to finish cooking and was told that I could not sit down on the stool while waiting for my order. My inquiry to be sure I heard the employee's statement correctly brought a response that I cannot sit while waiting. We left the business as newcomers without purchasing the hamburger and began making our adjustment to the town. However, as we would experience other unpleasant events during the year, it affirmed for me, a newcomer, that African-Americans were not welcomed in this town.

My family was fortunate to find housing in Marlboro Heights because there was a housing shortage. Mostly substandard housing existed in the Simmonsville Community at that time, but new and up-to-standard housing existed in the newly developing community of Marlboro Heights. Housing there was very limited until builders could complete the construction of additional ones. Jobs were also hard to find, or they were not available to African-American applicants even when they had the skills to perform them. I applied for a job as a stenographer only to find out when I returned to check on the status of my application, it was discovered that someone had assigned a code to it that meant that I was seeking a maid position. However, my family remained in the area and I became a community builder.

On a brighter side, our family did find places of worship, and our church involvement in the community included attendance at Saint Joseph Catholic Church and membership at Anderson Chapel AME Church. As a family we value maintaining family relationships. Our family gatherings are full of fun and bring much laughter when we get together. However, life brings happiness and brings sadness. The loss of our baby was a time of sadness for the family; and a divorce in 1973 from my children's father brought sadness. Then, over twenty years ago, I started my own business as a wedding planner. My company is called "Weddings by Jackie," and my business continued to do well. This venture has brought happiness.

My children have also brought me much happiness. Our family values education. All four of our children are Killeen High School graduates. My oldest daughter, Shelia Bailey Timmons, a senior underwriter for a major insurance company in Dallas, has a Karate School in Mesquite. My son, James Bailey, Jr., for over eighteen years has been an electrician in Houston. My third daughter, Katrina Bailey Washington, a Killeen resident, worked in insurance for about ten years and is now a real estate agent. My youngest daughter, Wendy Bailey White, has worked for Delta Airlines for years in Florida. She has just completed school as a medical transcriber. My mother, Margie Williams, is living with me now and this has also brought much happiness. The joys of my life are my six grandchildren: My oldest grandson, Clay (Myster) Bailey has worked for NASA for over nine years and has made outstanding accomplishments. He has acquired two master degrees.

A community event that brought me much happiness and a feeling of accomplishment as a community builder giving back to my community occurred in September 2000. I was coordinator for the Marlboro Heights Community Reunion. Mrs. Alice Douse and Mrs. Wadella Heath were chair and co-chair. On Saturday morning, September 2nd, we gathered for "get acquainted time" in Marlboro Park. That evening, a banquet was held at the Central Texas Homebuilders and we had great attendance. On Sunday morning,

September 3rd, a praise and worship service was held at Melba Joe Park. Rev. Charles Maze, Pastor of Mount Zion Missionary Baptist Church of Temple, Texas, preached. Rev. Maze grew up in the Marlboro community as a youth. A picnic was held after the worship service. On Monday morning, September 4th, the reunion participants returned to Marlboro Park to enjoy a send-off breakfast. The memorable weekend ended with former and current Marlboro Heights' participants bidding each other goodbye as they left to return to their homes in the Killeen-Fort Hood Area and in various cities in Texas and abroad.

Willie and Dorothy Holmes
Encouraging Service and Achievement
Dorothy Holmes

My husband, Willie Holmes, and I are natives of Mississippi. We were raised in the Delta. Willie entered the Armed Forces, went all over the world and made a career out of the Army. His military service spanned over twenty years. We arrived in Killeen, Texas in June, 1963, from Las Cruces, New Mexico. We first had to find a place to live but could not find one in Killeen. Therefore, we decided to drive to Belton to look for a house to rent. Our trip was a success because we did find a house in Belton right beside the T. B. Harris School. We were so happy. We lived in Belton for a year and a half while Willie drove daily to work at Fort Hood, his duty station. Soon Willie got orders to deploy to Germany. I didn't want to live in Belton while he was overseas, so we decided to move to Killeen in 1965 and build a house in the Marlboro Heights community. The community was so beautiful and clean. We lived close to the Marlboro Missionary Baptist Church and Marlboro Elementary School. We were also closer to Fort Hood.

We were very happy living in the Marlboro Heights community. The family got involved in community life. The children and I attended Marlboro Heights Baptist Church. The people in this community were so friendly and were from all walks of life. That was a blessing. The children attended school and I started working at Fort Hood. Willie was a member of St. Joseph Catholic Church where he was actively involved in the activities of the church. He attended Sacred Heart Catholic School when he was growing up in Greenville, Mississippi and he was a strong believer in volunteerism. He received many honors and awards for his faithful service. St. Joseph Catholic Church also honored him as "Man of the Year."

Now retired from the Army, and after making the transition from military to civilian life, Willie received an associate degree in automotive technology from Temple Junior College. He continued to serve God and his country through his church and community. My husband is deceased now, but I still live in our home and I'm glad that I moved here. I really like my community.

We are the parents to five adult children and seven grandchildren. They all are doing well. All of our children went to college and are living productive lives. Valerie and Andre graduated from high school in Prince George County and attended college at Virginia State University. They both graduated from Prairie View A & M University in Prairie View, Texas. *Valerie* taught for several years at Prairie View A & M University and at Southern University in Baton Rouge, Louisiana. At this writing, she is now a counselor in the Channelview Independent School District, near Houston, Texas. *Andre* is a special education teacher in the Houston Independent School District (HISD). Maurice and Tonya are graduates of Texas State Technical Institute (TSTI) in Waco, Texas. *Maurice* is owner of "Holmes Services." He does contracting in building construction and building repair services. *Mark* is a state official with the Texas Department of Criminal Justice. His employment with the Texas Department of Criminal Justice (TDCJ) spans more than twenty years. He has received several honors and awards in recognition of his work as a college student and as an employee in the Texas Department of Criminal Justice. He was named "Outstanding Student" by the UH's Chapter of Alpha Phi Sigma, the National Criminal Justice Honor Society while a student at the University of Houston-Downtown.

He was recognized as "Outstanding Professional Development Officer of the Year" by the Texas Department of Criminal Justice Institutional Division. He also received the Dr. Martin Luther King, Jr. Award at the University of Houston at Clear Lake. *Tanya* is the coordinator for the student organizations and foreign programs at the South Texas College of Law in Houston, Texas. She is also a music producer. Her music has been aired on the radio in Houston, Texas, and has been selling internationally in the UK. "Do Something." *Asida Soul* was selected as Album of the month for Soul Brother Records in London. Tanya is strongly involved with the fight against HIV/AIDS Awareness. I am so proud of our children. Willie and I are valued community builders who have made our community a desirable place to live.

The Wesley and Moland Family
Spiritual leader, Educators and Achievers
Brenda Wesley

The Wesley family came from Arkansas to Killeen when SFC Steve L. Wesley, my dad, was assigned to Fort Hood. Our family members included our dad, Steve; our mother, Bernice; and their children, Brenda and Stevie. Ronnie was later born at Fort Hood, Texas, in 1963. My dad was engaged in his military assignments, and my mother was an educator in the Killeen Independent School District. Our dad died in 1973. Later our mother married J. A. Moland. The Wesley children at that time were truly blessed to have J. A. Moland as a father. This extended family blossomed in all areas emotionally, spiritually and academically.

Rev. J. A. Moland was "called" to preach the gospel. The late Dr. Bernice E. Moland worked her way upward through the educational structure from teacher to administrator. She advanced through appointments in the Killeen Independent School District from teacher to facilitator to assistant principal to principal, and finally to Special Assistant to the Superintendent of Killeen Independent School District (KISD). She was one of the two Black educators who had earned a doctorate degree in education in the Killeen Independent School District. Dr. Bernice E. Moland gave more than thirty years of service as an educator. Our parents motivated us to succeed, spiritually and academically. All of the Wesley children attended Marlboro Elementary School. We all went to college and later into the work force: Ronnie, as a lawyer; Stevie, as a businessman; and Brenda, as a soldier and teacher.

The Reverend J. A. Moland, as pastor, and the late Dr. Bernice E. Moland assisted in the founding of Greater Peace Missionary Baptist Church in Killeen, Texas. This church not only ministers to the spiritual development of the community, but also ministers to the physical needs of families and individuals in the community with items such as clothes and food. Dr. Bernice Moland served as Director of Church Training Union; Director of Curriculum; and Advisor for the Women's Willing Workers Auxiliary. She passed away in 2004. The Reverend J. A. Moland, also an educator, taught in the Killeen Independent School District (KISD) for over twenty years. His teaching assignments included Nolan Middle School, the Alternative Center in Nolanville and Haynes Alternative School. He is an active speaker at civic and community events such as Black History observances. Rev J. A. Moland and Dr. Bernice E. Moland were also co-owners of J's Christian Books and Church Supplies in Killeen.

I, Brenda Wesley, attended school at Marlboro Elementary School in 1962 before there was integration. After sixth grade I attended Nolan Junior High School which was integrated. I have only pleasant memories about Nolan. I attended Killeen High School with enthusiasm. Attending Roo Country included getting good grades and being a member of the first girls' sports track team in Killeen. I was also the first Black selected for the Killeen High School Tennis Team. However, in 1972, I went to Arkansas to take care of my grandma and did not play. I earned my Associate of Arts Degree from Central Texas College in 1975, and my Bachelor of Science in Education from Mary Hardin-Baylor in 1976. In 1978, I attended the U. S. Army Institute and received Army commendations, achievement medals and also the Korean Defense Ribbon and Army Service Ribbons. After my tour of duty in the Army, I taught school in Monterrey, Mexico. I also worked as a substitute teacher in the Killeen Independent School District.

Stevie L. Wesley, my brother was the first Black president of the student council at Manor Junior High School. He excelled in sports and did very well academically. He is a graduate of Killeen High School and was awarded a basketball scholarship by Temple Junior College, where he attended. He earned his bachelor's degree from North Texas State University. He resides with his family in Grapevine, Texas. Dr. Ronnie D. Wesley, LL.D., also my brother, began kindergarten at Marlboro Elementary School; attended Clifton Park Elementary, Nolan Junior High School and graduated from Ellison High School. He was vice president and president of student council at Nolan. He also served as president of the student council at Ellison High School and was the first Black to hold that position. He received many honors in junior high and high school. Ronnie graduated from Baylor University with a Bachelor of Science degree in 1985. He received a doctorate of law degree from the University of Texas at Austin, Texas. Ronnie passed away in 1991. His last job was as an attorney for the treasurer of the State of Texas. Our mother passed away in 2004 but not before leaving a heritage for us to cherish. The family of J. A. Moland and the late Dr. Bernice Moland is another family of community builders that has contributed to their community and to the city of Killeen in ways that made this a better place in which to live.

Alice Gilliam
Dr. Martin Luther King, Jr. Boulevard Advocate
Kimberly Gilliam Davis

Alice and Floyd Gilliam moved to the Killeen-Fort Hood area in 1964. We were a military family that included a daughter, Kimberly, and two sons, André and Lamont. Alice was a native of Louisiana. In addition to her role as a mother, she was a respected member of the Marlboro Heights community, a staunch member and supporter of Marlboro Heights Missionary Baptist Church of Killeen. She served in several of the ministries there and was devoted to the church nursery and Junior Mission. My mother was one of the first African American businesswomen, as a successful Avon Independent Sales Consultant, for over twenty-five years. Through her mentoring efforts, she helped other women to gain financial independence and her salesmanship helped to provide for our own family. For many years she was also employed by the Killeen Independent School District as an instructional aide for students with special needs. My mother "possessed a faith that she practiced every day of her life." She won countless "souls to Christ" through her evangelistic work and continuous dialogue with people from all walks of life. As a mother she filled our home with love. As adults, my brothers and I can only hope to follow her example. My brothers and I are graduates of Killeen High School. We are now responsible and contributing citizens of the communities in which we live and are giving back to the community through the careers we have chosen. I was among the first group of computer technologists hired by the Killeen Independent School District when it initiated its computer program for all of the elementary schools. My family is delighted to be included in the long list of community builders in Killeen.

My Mother initiated the first campaign to name a street in Killeen in honor of Dr. Martin Luther King, Jr. She solicited the support of her pastor, Reverend R. A. Abercrombie, church members and other families in the Marlboro Heights community to accompany her to Killeen City Hall to present her request to the city council. As she waited for the council members to deliberate upon the request, her health continued to fail. Because of her strong passion for the success of this endeavor, she designated three close and dedicated supporters Reverend R. A. Abercrombie, Calhoun Smith and Cloerine Brewer to ensure that the project was taken to completion. In July of 1987, Alice Gilliam died not knowing the outcome of her efforts. Former Councilwoman, Rosa Hereford, joined these three friends and with community residents fought for three years after her death to get a street renamed. In 1990 the council unanimously approved a stretch of Highway FM 2410 from Veterans Memorial Boulevard to the city limit's line adjoining Harker Heights for renaming. Alice Gilliam's dream was realized on May 13, 1990, at the official ceremony of the naming of Dr. Martin Luther King, Jr. Boulevard in Killeen, Texas.

Charles and Verda Jarmon
An Outreach Ministry and Education Mission
Verda Jarmon

I moved to Killeen in August 1964 as a single young woman to teach in the Killeen Independent School District. Charles came to this area as a soldier with assignment orders to Fort Hood in July of 1964. I resided in Marlboro Heights from 1964 to 1966, and Charles resided on Post at Fort Hood from July 1964 to 1966. We met in September 1965 and were united in Holy matrimony on June 18, 1966, at Fort Hood. When Charles and I first arrived in the Killeen/Fort Hood area (1964), our impression of Killeen upon our arrival was that it was a small country town with a population of around 25,000, dominated mainly by Fort Hood. The housing conditions were limited and some of the soldiers and their families had to live in other places, such as Belton, Temple and other surrounding communities.

Entertainment and recreation at that time for young adults were very limited. Clubs on and off Post and the movie theater on Post, were the primary sources of entertainment and recreation for Black young adults. A few restaurants for dining out in the mid-sixties included Holiday Terrace and the Cowhouse Motor Hotel Restaurant. There were no large hotels in the area, just mainly motels. Dairy Queen, Burger Chef and What-A-Burger were some of the fast food businesses that existed. There were just a few churches for Blacks in the mid-Sixties. We joined Anderson Chapel AME Church and became actively involved.

As a new teacher my first impression of Marlboro Elementary School was that it very well kept. My classroom, with my name above the door, was very spacious. I immediately fell in love with it on first sight. Then on the first day of in-service when all the teachers reported to their campuses and I met all of my fellow co-workers, I got the feeling that the faculty was going to be like a family to me. They made me feel more at home. It was a great beginning for me, a first year teacher who was fresh out of college. My principal, Dock Jackson (now deceased), whom I held in high esteem and to whom I am grateful, placed me under the guidance of an exceptional teacher, Vera Nelson, who literally taught me the "ins" and outs" of teaching, especially first grade. The skills, wisdom and experience I gained from her made me, in my opinion, a number one superior teacher. I enjoyed every moment of my five years teaching at Marlboro Elementary School. I went on to receive numerous awards, accolades and completed forty years of commendable service in the teaching profession. The service I rendered in educating students in the state of Texas and the military dependents in schools overseas has been most rewarding and gratifying for me. I am now happily retired since June, 2004. Building an educational, emotional and spiritual foundation in the youth in these communities was my focus as an educator so they could cope with daily living socially. Helping youth to recognize the source of all they possess and to be informed about the things of the world around them are what teachers who are community builders do.

My husband, Charles, had only two thirteen month tours of duty in Korea and in Vietnam, plus a three-year tour of duty as a family in Bremerhaven, Germany; then the remainder of his military service was spent at Fort Hood until his retirement. While serving a tour of duty in Germany, the Lord blessed us with a beautiful daughter, Cynthia Denise. Cynthia grew up in the Killeen community and attended Meadows Elementary School, Nolan Middle School and Ellison High School. After graduation she attended Texas A and M University in College Station, Texas and graduated in 1993. Her post graduate studies in the Master of Public Administration (MPA) Program were taken at Texas Southern University and the University of Houston, both in Houston, Texas. While growing up, Cynthia was active in her church organizations and activities with the youth. Likewise, she was also involved in community and school activities: the National Honor Society, Keywanettes and Girls' Choir. She now works for Deloitte and Touché, a Fortune 500 company. Her husband, Earl, completed a residency in obstetrics and gynecology. Zachary our grandson is a bright energetic youngster who enjoys playing hockey. Cynthia, along with her husband, Earl, and son, Zachary, reside in Nashville, Tennessee.

With our tour of duty in Germany over and our return to the Killeen-Fort Hood area, Charles and I became increasingly more active in the community and especially in the church where we worked in various ministries—Charles has been a trustee, steward, youth usher sponsor and Sunday School teacher, and I have served as a Sunday School teacher, steward, choir member and as a mission worker in the Women's Missionary Society. My community involvement and membership in several organizations such as: TSTA/NEA; the Killeen Alumnae Chapter of Delta Sigma Theta Sorority, Inc., Phi Delta Kappa; Texas PTA, Texas Classroom Teachers Association, American Business Women Association (ABWA); and Top Ladies of Distinction (TLOD) provided me many opportunities to render my personal service in the community.

Our family is very thankful to Our Almighty God for allowing us to have remained a family from the early 1970s to the present time and grateful to have reared a beautiful daughter; owned some real estate; and are able to retire. Charles retired from the U. S. Army and I retired from teaching. As a family, we have had the opportunity to travel to most of the states in the United States, as well as, abroad. Charles is still raising and selling livestock, which he has done for more than twenty-five years. We are also still helping citizens in this community and some organizations as an Outreach Ministry. We give all the credit to our most Heavenly Father. Our family has a strong faith in God. We uphold high spiritual and moral values. We feel strong about helping others in need and are strong supporters of education. While growing up as a child it was always a dream of mine to become a teacher. What started out as a dream ultimately became reality. Charles and I willingly continue our outreach work together as committed community builders.

Culbertson and Lillian Johnson
Ministry Outreach and Family
Lillian Johnson

I arrived in Killeen, Texas on December 30, 1963 as the wife of Ben Elam, a serviceman assigned to Ft. Hood, Texas. I am a native Louisianan. I graduated from high school in Plaquemine, Louisiana. I am a retired licensed cosmetologist. Life in Killeen has been good for me. When we arrived in this area, we first lived on Parkhill Drive which was later renamed Rev. R. A. Abercrombie Drive in honor of the first pastor of Marlboro Missionary Baptist Church. We made our home on Parkhill Drive from January to April in this little white house across from Marlboro Missionary Baptist Church. On April 30, 1964 we purchased a house and moved to Taft Street. There were only three houses on the street at that time. We were the third family to move there. I soon became involved in the community. I first joined the Servicemen I.M.E. Church and also became a member of the Ladies Auxiliary of the Veterans of Foreign Wars (VFW), Post 9191. My husband Ben Elam died in 1968. I joined Anderson Chapel AME Church in 1969 and worked in many ministries of the church as: President of the Usher Ministry, President of the Chancel Choir and President of the local Women Missionary Society. In addition, I was a member of the Stewardess Ministry and the Mission and Welfare Ministry. I was recognized with an honor naming me a "Life Member" of the Women Missionary Society of the African Methodist Episcopal Church. My work with the Nursing Home Ministry and my volunteer work at the VA Hospital were blessings to me. The Bell County Detention Center recognized me with several awards for my volunteerism.

In 1973, I was married to Culbertson Johnson. Culbertson entered the army in 1943 and his military service spanned over twenty-six years. He holds the distinction of having fought in three wars: World War II, the Korean War and the Vietnam War. He retired from the Army in 1969. Culberson is also a member of Anderson Chapel AME Church and has worked with the Trustee Ministry and the Usher Ministry. Life treated my family kindly in Killeen. Many of our friends, neighbors and family pets over the years have brought us much joy. There was Fidel, a male Pekinese that lived to be sixteen years old. After his death we got Nellie, a female Cocker Spaniel and she lived to be twelve years old. We also had a cat, Minnie, at the same time that we had Nellie. Our cat lived to be eleven years old. Our last family pet was named Boomer, a male Pekinese that lived to be fourteen years old. In December 2000 I will have lived in the Killeen area thirty-seven years. My service in the community through the organizations of which I was a member provided me opportunities to serve others. My focus each day is to work together with others in building a united community.

Clarence, Jr. and Kay Brown
Educators Touching the Lives of the Youth

Clarence and I are longtime residents of Killeen. Clarence, formerly from Waco, Texas graduated from Prairie View A and M University in Prairie View, Texas with a major in physical education. He came to Killeen in 1964 seeking employment opportunities. His first teaching assignment with the Killeen Independent School District (KISD) was at Marlboro Elementary School as the physical education teacher. I am formerly from Bay City, Texas and a graduate of Texas Southern University, Houston, Texas. My first teaching assignment in 1969 with KISD was at Haynes Elementary School. Clarence and I have given many years of service in a career of teaching youth in this School District. He was the first African American male physical education teacher employed in the Killeen School District and assigned to Marlboro Elementary School. He has had the opportunity to work in both a segregated school environment, as well as in an integrated school environment during his tenure in the district. Clarence has also worked in the recreation program for the City of Killeen. His fairness and genuine concern for his students and the community youth established wholesome relationships in the school and community environments. In 1969 he transferred from Marlboro Elementary School to Pershing Park Elementary School and became one of the first three African American males in the district to teach with an integrated faculty. He later transferred to Duncan Elementary School and remained there until his retirement.

My assignment as a teacher at Manor Middle School in 1971 provided opportunities for me to be involved in the transitional years of former elementary school students as they prepared to move into their high school studies. I later transferred to Ellison High School and continued to teach there until my retirement. After more than forty years as residents of the city, and with our employment opportunities throughout those years, we have experienced memorable teaching careers. Clarence's thirty-nine years and my thirty-four years of service to the youth of the community have been a rewarding experience for both of us. We both have made a significant contribution in the lives of the youth we taught and to the city of Killeen.

Our family includes a son, Clarence III; daughter-in-law, Shonn; and three grandchildren: Evan, Ryan and Lily. Clarence III is a graduate of Ellison High School. He received his bachelor degree from the University of Texas in Austin, Texas, and a law degree from Emory University in Atlanta, Georgia. He and his family reside in Dallas, Texas. Clarence, III and his wife Shonn are both corporate attorneys.

Our family's church involvement was formerly with Marlboro Missionary Baptist Church, but is currently with Greater Peace Missionary Baptist Church. My community involvement as a member of Mu Theta Omega Chapter of Alpha Kappa Alpha Sorority, Inc., has provided for me many opportunities to render service to others in the community. Alpha Kappa Sorority, Inc. is an organization that is very actively involved in providing student scholarships; mentoring young girls, giving warm clothing for those in need and many other services in the community. Community building is a team effort; we are on that team.

Rev. Arthur Anderson and Mary Anderson
Founding Pastor Anderson Chapel A.M.E. Church
Rev. Velma Hayden and Alice Douse

The Reverend Arthur Anderson was born in Brazoria County, Texas, on October 22, 1893, to the parents of George and Phoebe Anderson. He was the last of eight children. He became a preacher and was pastor of many churches throughout Texas in the African Methodist Episcopal Church. His faithfulness to his charges of even the smallest congregations to whom he was assigned was evident by his willingness to serve and his determination not to be deterred by distance, weather, or even illness from fulfilling his obligations to God and to his congregation.

He and his wife, Mary Willis McPhaul Anderson, whose residence was in Lampasas, Texas, made a significant contribution to the citizens in the Killeen and Fort Hood area. There had been an earlier unsuccessful attempt to organize an African Methodist Episcopal Church in Killeen during the early days of the development of the Marlboro Heights community. Families moved into the Marlboro Heights community from many parts of the United States. Some who were of the Methodist denomination were traveling outside the city to worship even though there were two Baptist churches, one Pentecostal Church of God in Christ and one non-denominational church in the community. Rev. Arthur Anderson, who was then the pastor of Bethel AME Church in Lampasas, together with his wife, and eight charter members, established the first African Methodist Episcopal Church in the Killeen area. It was organized February 10, 1964, as a circuit church that met twice monthly and Rev. Anderson was given the pastoral appointment as its pastor.

Anderson Chapel soon became a "station church" that met weekly and Reverend Anderson became its full-time pastor. Believers and worshipers now had the opportunity and the convenience to worship locally in their choice of denomination. Now that

Reverend Arthur Anderson's was successful in establishing the First African Methodist Episcopal denomination in the Killeen area, we can acknowledges him not only as the founding pastor of Anderson AME Church (which bears his name), but also the trailblazer who instituted the African Methodist Episcopal denomination in the Killeen area. He served this community for ten years as a spiritual leader until his retirement in 1974. Reverend and Mrs. Anderson were the parents of four adult children: three daughters, Reverend Velma Hayden, Mary Frances Jones Dillon, Arthur Lee Anderson and a son, Amos Anderson. Traveling weekly to Killeen for ten years and through their sacrifices, selfless service and shared resources, they have left a legacy to this community that is significant and greatly valued and appreciated. Reverend Arthur and Mary Anderson are now deceased. They were community builders.

Nathaniel Crawford
Service and Integrity as Military and Civilian
Nathaniel Crawford

I was reared and educated in Charlotte, North Carolina and attended several schools in that city before going into military service. I arrived at Fort Hood in September 1965 for my last tour of duty and now I have been a Killeen resident ever since. Prior to coming to Ft. Hood, my military career took me to many places in the States and abroad. It left me with many memories. I entered the U. S. Army on May 6, 1946. After taking my basic training at Ft. Belvoir, Virginia, I was then sent to Alaska for several months. Upon returning to the United States, I was discharged at Camp Stowman, California. I returned home to Charlotte, North Carolina and married my childhood sweetheart, Eriene Crawford. We are the parents of two daughters: Yvonne C. McNeil and Mary E. Medley, and three sons, Calvin, Ronald and Virgil Crawford. I reenlisted in the U. S. Army in 1947 and was sent to Fort Dix, New Jersey for retraining. I served a short tour at West Point before going to Ft. Bragg, North Carolina, for airborne training. There were several other tours of duty before I returned to Fort Hood in 1965. I served at Ft. Hood four and a half years before retiring from active duty service on January 31, 1969.

I completed my active military career with twenty-two and a half years of service.

On May 21, 1972, about two and a half years after retirement, I began working as a civil service employee at Ft. Hood, Texas. I worked in the Supply and Ordinance Division, Directorate of Logistics and Post Engineers for several years. I retired from civil service on November 24, 1993 with a total of twenty-two years and approximately eight months of service. My combined federal service then totaled forty-four and a half years. My community involvement began when I joined one of the local churches under the administration of the founding pastor, Rev. Arthur Anderson. I became active in the work of the church ministries, serving as a class leader for approximately four years, the steward ministry, and then on the Board of Trustees. I am currently a Trustee Emeritus in my church. My community involvement also includes membership in the Masonic family. I was raised to the degree of Master Mason in the summer of 1972, and elevated to a 32 Degree Mason in 1973. I became a Noble Shriner on February 11, 1975, and was elevated to the last degree of Masonry, 33rd Degree, on October 8, 1999. I am an active member of the following Masonic bodies in Killeen and involved in community activities:

New Light Lodge 242	Master Mason
Central Consistory 306	32nd Degree
Nubia Temple 191	Shriners Nobles
Hodges Commander of the Rites	33rd Degree only

My experiences mirror, in many ways, the experiences of many of the citizens who now make up the Black community of this city of Killeen. It was by way of the Army that many Blacks came and remained to build a community.

Johnny and Mary Owens
Serving others as a Mentor, in Ministry and with a Hobby
Johnny Owens

My family moved to the Killeen area in 1965. My military orders were for Fort Hood, Texas. With my wife, Mary and sons Stanley and Steve, we first resided in Marlboro Heights on Terrace Drive and later moved to Taft Avenue. We are longtime residents of Killeen. We are continuing to enjoy the home that we purchased when we moved from Marlboro Heights. My wife was employed by the Killeen Independent School District as a Food Service Specialist for many years. Prior to my military retirement, I started repairing TVs at my home. I am an advocate of education in whatever field a person chooses to work. I attended various electronic schools during my twenty years in the Army, and then earned a degree in Electronic Technology from Central Texas College in 1972. Every time I had a chance to go to school, I went, and it paid off. My first business venture began in 1972 with The TV Shop. My wife and I worked together in this business venture. Three years later I formed a new business, which was located on Florence Road in Killeen, Texas. When we first got into business, the Texas Electronic Association (TEA) was in existence and this organization taught me the fundamentals of managing a business. I was a member and attended all TEA Management Institutes. I also served as vice president, and then as president, of the Texas Electronic Association. I retired from my business and sold my shares to my partners in the corporation.

Before I retired from my business, customers visiting my shop would see hanging on the wall at Homemaker's Television Service about forty certificates that I, Johnny Owens, the owner, received from training seminars I attended for various electronic companies. During my years as owner of a business, I have had the opportunity to mentor and share my knowledge with others in the business world, as well as, in the church. I have always been willing to share what I have learned and this has been a blessing to me and to others. My training and experience provided me with information that is helpful to know for success in business.

Going into business for me was a natural move after having been in a supervisory role as a non-commissioned officer for nineteen of twenty years in the Army. I retired as an Electronic Maintenance Chief, E-7. My advice to potential business owners is to not get too big too soon. That is one of the biggest mistakes people make. This discussion that I am sharing about the business that I own relates primarily to electronics. However, the following tips that I am offering now can be applied to all business ventures. The electronic service business is very, very high-risk because equipment is constantly being updated. The length of time it takes to get parts, which in some cases could be up to several weeks, could possibly result in a customer deciding to buy a new television instead of having an inexpensive set repaired. Statistics show that the majority of businesses fail within the first year. To properly run an electronics shop, requires a lot of investment in equipment and employee training. All three of the technicians in my shop were college-trained. My advice to young people is to go to college if you can afford it. If not, they should consider entering the military to get as much education as possible. The satisfaction from your job comes when a customer returns and tells you how well you performed on a previous job. On one of the signs that was posted in my shop was a true message. It read "Quality is remembered long after price is forgotten." My final tips for a successful business are:

- Make sure you have the required capital before going into business.
- Be willing to sacrifice for a while until the business is profitable.
- Don't be afraid to work long hours.
- Don't ever say *can't*.
- Hire a certified public accountant.
- Don't try to operate a business without a monthly financial statement, so that you can monitor yourself in case the business isn't working out.

Mary and I are members of Anderson Chapel AME Church where we have been involved in many of the ministries of the church and in sharing the Word with others in homes, hospitals and outside the walls of the church. Mary Owens has been a supporter of the Bible Study Ministry. Full sets of Biblical Commentary, consisting of several volumes, have been donated to individuals who showed an interest in growing and serving as Bible Study teachers. She has also supported the Sunday school and the Missionary ministries. I have served as a Bible Study teacher; Sunday Church School teacher; member of the Steward Board and the Stewardship and Finance Ministry. I am also one of the original members of the Board of Directors for the Richard Allen Community Development Corporation (RACDC) and I served as the first treasurer of the organization.

My hobby of photography has brightened the lives of many families and put smiles on many faces because of the photos that I have taken of their loved ones who may be in their golden years; photos taken of babies just beginning life; photos of families enjoying special occasions; celebrating memorable life moments; experiencing or recovering from hospitalization; also photos because the family just does not have any photographic memories.

Our lives have been enriched, even during Mary's season of illness, and we are grateful that she was well blessed during that time. We take pride in the fact that our adult children are giving back to the community through the electronic and technological industry in the U. S. Armed Forces and in the ministry of our Lord and Savior, Jesus Christ. Building a community requires the work of many people. We are thankful that we have also been involved in the process.

Samuel A. and Mary L. Hankins
Advocating for Children
Mary L. Hankins

 Sam and I are the parents of three daughters: Donna, Adrian and Renate, and three sons: Gerard, Gerold and Jason Hankins. They were all Killeen High School graduates. My husband is a native of Little Rock, Arkansas, and I am a native of Greenville, South Carolina. Sam's work was the military. In 1965 his military orders assigned him to Fort Hood, Texas. We arrived at Fort Hood in September, 1965. We traveled to Fort Hood with another family, Eddie and Clara Coppage, whose military orders were also for Fort Hood. Housing was very limited for Black families. Upon our arrival, our family got the last room that was available in the Fort Hood Guest House. Our traveling friends, Eddie and Clara Coppage, were not as fortunate; they had to sleep in their car. Our family moved from the guest house to Zephyr Road in Marlboro Heights. Then, later we moved to our home on Rose Avenue. My husband retired from the Army as Sergeant First Class in 1971. After retirement, he spent twelve years in civil service with the Directorate Facilities Engineers on Fort Hood.

Rose Avenue is located in a newer housing addition called the Rose Addition. It was another section adjacent to Marlboro Heights where Blacks could live at that time. It was located just south of Zephyr Road and before it was developed, Zephyr Road was the southern boundary of Marlboro Heights. Because of the close proximity of these two neighborhoods, the Rose Addition and the original part of Marlboro Heights was often referred to as Marlboro

Heights and made up a close-knit community in which families looked out for each other. The two areas made up a community where together, we were all rearing our children; supporting our schools; being good neighbors, worshiping and praising our God. Our family joined Marlboro Missionary Baptist Church, but later, my husband and I became charter members of Greater Peace Missionary Baptist Church. Sam was ordained a Deacon of Greater Peace Missionary Baptist Church and he faithfully served in this office until his death on May 31, 1994.

All elementary school-aged children in the area first attended Marlboro Elementary School, but later the younger ones attended Haynes Elementary School. When the Killeen Independent School District (KISD) rezoned attendance areas, our children were moved from Haynes Elementary to Fowler Elementary School. Reuben Hatcher, Mr. Pugh and I visited with Dr. C. E. Ellison, the KISD Superintendent of schools, with our concerns regarding this change. This visit was not only in the interest of each of our families, but it was also in the interest of all families in the community. Families who arrived in the Simmonsville and Marlboro Heights areas in the 1940s, 1950s, 1960s became the foundation groups from which a Black community would build. Therefore, the Hankins family has been active as community builders to ensure that Killeen became a better and safe place in which to live.

Rev. Eddie and Clara Coppage
A Team in Christian Service
Mary L Hankins

Reverend Eddie Coppage and his wife Clara were a memorable spiritual team. Their contribution as community builders made a mark in the Marlboro and Simmonsville communities through their ministry. They arrived in the Killeen-Fort Hood in September 1965 because of Eddie's military assignment to Fort Hood. They joined the Marlboro Missionary Baptist Church in Marlboro Heights and became active and faithful members in the ministries of the church. Clara Coppage was a musician and used her musical gifts as pianist, organist and director of Marlboro Missionary Baptist Church's

Choir. She had served as musician in many locations, including overseas. Eddie Coppage accepted the "call" to the ministry, was ordained and later became the pastor of Simmonsville Missionary Church in 1973. Clara joined him to this appointment. She then became Simmonsville Missionary Baptist Church's musician, and served as the director of the Senior Choir. She later renamed this choir "The Redeemed Choir." Many of the accomplishments of this spiritual team can also be found in the history of Simmonsville Missionary Baptist Church.

In 1980, Reverend Coppage's health began to fail, and after a long illness he departed this life in October, 1982. After Reverend Coppage's death, Clara Coppage returned to Marlboro Missionary Baptist Church and continued to serve as a musician, even though sometimes with limitations and difficulty due to her illness.

Revered Eddie and Clara Coppage were the parents of two daughters, Annette and Sigrid, and three sons, Michael, Gregory and Eddie Ben Coppage. The children were all active in the ministries of the church. They were also students in the Killeen Independent School District. They are all adults now and have established careers and families of their own. Reverend Eddie and Clara Coppage, now deceased, left their mark on the community. Through their service over the years, they became community builders.

James and Hazel Williams
A Former 761st Tank Battalion Soldier and A Wheel of Fortune Winner
Hazel Williams

My husband, the late James E. Williams, and I are parents of four sons: Rene (Sonny), Larry, Reginald, Kevin; and four daughters: Lamora Williams Page, Lorna W. Cole, Lynette W. Willis and Kenitra W. Leonard. We also have a son-in-Law, Jameal Page, who we value as a family member. We moved to Killeen in 1967 to be close to our home which is Temple, Texas and to Ft. Hood. My husband and our oldest son Rene (Sonny) were going to Vietnam. We resided on Gardenia Avenue. At this writing, Rene (Sonny) resides in California, Lamina in Illinois, Lynette in New York, Reggie in

Temple, Kevin in Austin. Kevin is an ordained minister. Larry and Kenitra are in Killeen. Six of our children are Killeen High School graduates and attended Central Texas College in Killeen. Our oldest son and daughter graduated from high school in Germany and North Carolina, respectively. We became members of the 37th Street Protestant Chapel at Ft Hood in 1967. Later we worshiped at the 33rd and 25th Street Chapels. For most of the thirty-eight years, I served as program coordinator and Women's leader at the chapels. My husband sang in the choir and Kenitra helped with the children's church.

James and I have had our fifteen minutes of fame. His occurred when the media learned that he was a former member of the 761st Tank Battalion. It was also then that I learned that he was a public speaker. He spoke at several churches and schools and was interviewed by newspapers from across the state. My first 15 minutes of fame came when I lived in Temple in the mid-40s and was crowned Miss USO. My second experience of fame came in the early 80s, when I was a contestant for two days on Wheel of Fortune. I won $11,350.00 in merchandise.

Our adult children are now responsible citizens in their communities. They are using their abilities, gifts, skills and special talents to make a difference in the careers they have chosen to pursue. Rene (Sonny) has been a DJ for many, many years. He once owned his own music store. Lamona is the manager of a credit union. Lorna is an associate at Sears. Lynette is a receptionist at Belvue. Larry is owner of the J. E. Williams Drafting Company, and also was an Associate at Lowes. Reggie is an operator. Kevin is a minister and employee at IRS. Kenitra is employed at Head Start as a teacher. I have written several one act plays. The James Williams family is so grateful to be able to contribute to their communities in so many different ways and do our part in community building.

Reverend Dr. Fred F., Jr. and Clara Cook
Leaders in Ministry
Dr. Fred F. Cook, Jr.

The Cook Family came to Killeen in July 1967. We are natives of the state of Georgia. The family includes my wife Clara Cook and our children: Charles, Belinda, Cynthia, Fred, III and Michael. We moved to this area because of my orders from the military which assigned me to Ft. Hood, Texas. Our first residence in the Killeen area was on Longview Drive in the Marlboro Heights community. We quickly became involved in the church and made friends in the community. When our family moved to Ft. Hood, the community ties that the family had made in Marlboro Heights remained intact. We kept our affiliation and association with the Marlboro Heights community. We became members of Marlboro Heights Baptist Church. Our community and church involvement included my being ordained as Deacon in the church and my service as president of the Brotherhood. Later, in October 1970, I was licensed to preach. Clara served as a missionary and was faithfully and willingly involved with the children and youth department of the church. Clara Cook was the founder of the first day care center opened at Marlboro Missionary Baptist Church. Our family left the area in April, 1971, and we still cherish the memories of friendships that we made while living in the Killeen/Ft. Hood area. It was a time and a place where we had an opportunity to make a difference in the life of the community in small ways during our three years in the area. We will long remember friends like the Hatchers, Heaths, Gaines, Whites and many others with whom we worshiped; worked together in the ministries; and enjoyed fellowship in their homes.

Education is highly valued by our family. I earned my Master of Theology, Doctorate of Theology, and Doctor of Divinity Degrees. Clara Cook earned her Bachelor of Arts and Master of Arts degrees. The children have also established goals regarding their education. One of our sons has earned his Bachelor of Arts degree, and the other children have either completed or working toward completing educational or training goals. We feel blessed and grateful for the accomplishments.

When the Cook family arrived at Ft. Benning, Georgia, my next duty station, I served as a Supply Chaplain. I became a member of Mt. Tabor Baptist Church and later was ordained in the Gospel Ministry in May, 1972. In 1974, I returned to civilian life and began serving as a pastor in 1975, continuing the mission of community building in Augusta, Georgia, where our family now resides.

Reverend James and Rosa Hereford
Committed Community Leaders
Rosa Hereford

We arrived in the Fort Hood/ Killeen area in 1966 when Buzz was assigned to Fort Hood, Texas. He was born in Martinsville, Virginia and reared in Pittsburg, PA. James "Buzz" Hereford served his country with courage and honor. He retired in 1975 with twenty-one years of military service, and returned to school to complete his college degree. He is a graduate of Mary Hardin Baylor University and has done further study at Texas A & M University. He began a new career as teacher and coach with the Killeen Independent School District in 1979. He was on Fairway Middle School faculty for nine years and also taught at West Ward Elementary School and Brookhaven Intermediate School. He retired from KISD in 1998. James Hereford was civic-minded and presented himself in the past as a candidate willing to assume a civic responsibility in the interest of the citizens of Killeen. He is a member of Alpha Phi Alpha Fraternity, an organization of college educated men with a focus on service and education. His community involvement included serving as Cub Scout Master; a Big Brother; Youth Director for the American Legion's Boys State; local Director of TARS, a program for teenagers with special needs. He was a life member of the Veterans of Foreign Wars (VFW) 9191, American Legion, and Disabled Veterans (DAV).

James Hereford's third career is in the field of theology. He served as an instructor in the Minnesota School of Theology. He accepted the "call" to ministry and served as a minister for True Hands of Hope Ministry. Later, he served a pastor of the Independent Missionary Baptist Church in Rosebud, Texas. The Independent Missionary Baptist Church is the oldest Black church in Rosebud; celebrating its 127th anniversary in 2008. Buzz was also a very loyal supporter of my many activities and endeavors. We are the parents of an adult daughter, Lisa, and are grandparents to a granddaughter, Ashley, and grandson, Taylor.

I, Rosa Shaw Hereford, was born in rural South Carolina in a hamlet named after my family, the Shaws. My early education through high school was received in a two-room school house. After graduating from high school at the age of sixteen, I attended Bennett College in Greensboro, North Carolina, where I became an active part of an era in America's history in a way that is both memorable and significant. I, with my fellow college mates, courageously set on a course for gaining civil rights for all citizens. Because of my participation in the Bennett College student sit-ins, today our nation is a better place in which to live. Because of the courage and the actions we took, many people now enjoy a better quality of life as minorities. I was a twenty year-old college student at Bennett College when I first saw Reverend Martin Luther King, Jr. We, as college students, were involved in the protest to integrate the lunch counters in the department stores. Reverend Martin Luther King, Jr. told us to continue non-violently what we were doing, and change would come. His message made such an impact on my life. As a result of this meeting, I believed that you can make a change non-violently no matter what people would say or do, including them shoving you or cursing at you.

This historic sit-in at the Woolworth's lunch counter near the college in Greensboro, North Carolina, sparked the beginning of a series of discriminatory barriers falling, and eventually, not only the counters were desegregated, but also hotels, movie theaters and other public places integrated. My active participation in the Civil Rights Movement in Greensboro, North Carolina, in 1960-1961 has impacted our nation's leaders, our laws and the citizen's liberties. I graduated from Bennett College in 1961 with a Bachelor of Science degree in Biology. I began teaching science at Albert Harris High School in Martinsville, Virginia. It was in Martinsville that I met and married James Hereford. His military assignment took us to Germany. I became the science teacher at Darmstadt American Junior High School, Darmstadt, Germany, and Kissinger American Elementary School, Kitzingen, Germany. When James' military assignment brought us to Fort Hood, I sought employment and received a contract with the Killeen Independent School District (KISD). I taught science at Fairway Junior High School from 1967-1976. After earning my Master of Science Degree from Prairie View A & M University in 1972, I pursued studies in the field of counseling; earned my counselor's certification from Southwest Texas State University in San Marcos, Texas, in 1976; and served as a KISD counselor at both the elementary and middle school levels. I gave thirty years of service to the education of students and retired from the Killeen Independent School District in 1997.

In addition to my successes as an educator, my public service and community service quickly made an impact within the city of Killeen, in Bell County and in the state of Texas. Multi-tasking is a term sometimes used to describe the process of efficiently managing multiple assignments within a shared time period. My interests and service required the ability to multi-task. As an involved citizen of the West Bell County communities in general, and specifically the Killeen and Ft. Hood communities, I have made very positive and significant contributions in the lives of the citizens. My service was significant in the areas of education as I worked with the youth, my colleagues and parents in the school district. My service to organizations and agencies has been focused on the welfare of our citizens and on making our community a better place to live. I have also affected lives and the development of a very diverse community because of my service in the political arena.

Many who have worked with me quickly recognized the leadership qualities that I possess because I use this skill in everything that I do. Central Texas, and more specifically, the Killeen area, has been the recipients of my service and leadership. I am very grateful for the opportunities to render service and for the accomplishments that, with support of many citizens, have been achieved. For example:

I was the first female and the second Black council member in the city of Killeen's history. I served the maximum three terms of two years each (1984-1990). My six years as councilwoman was very productive and rewarding. After seeing several Latino and Blacks, including my husband, fall victim by narrow margins at the local polls—and after much leadership experience in local, state and national organizations—I decided to launch my own bid for city council. I ran a successful campaign and received the second highest vote total in a seven candidate field for the position of councilman-at-large. I served three two-year terms on the Council and diligently worked to be informed and prepared for my City Council duties. I expressed an interest in the welfare of the city employees and pushed for the council to honor Dr. Martin Luther King Jr. by renaming a street for him in the city. Today, Killeen has a segment of the former FM 2410 named Martin Luther King, Jr. Blvd. This initiative was first brought to the city council as a request by Alice Gilliam, a resident of Marlboro Heights. My commitment to address minority issues and concerns, as well as, majority issues and concerns as they were presented to me as a council member gained for me the trust of the citizens.

My involvement in the political arena dates back to the early 70s. Some of my longtime political involvement includes service as: Precinct 404 Chair (1990 - 2000); Bell County Democratic Women Fund Raising Committee Chair, 1989 - 2000) and Democratic Party State Convention delegate (1970, 1972 and 1974). My leadership abilities are well-known and are not limited only to Killeen. I have given outstanding service locally, regional and at the national level in the areas of education, community service, public service and politics. An additional listing of my service and leadership include:

- Killeen Education Association TSTA first Black President (1974-1975); (1978-1979).
- Killeen Housing Authority three-terms Commissioner (1978-1984).

- Civilian Advisory Council member to the Commanding General at Fort Hood, Texas.
- State Job Coordinating Council member. An appointment by Governor Ann Richard.
- Chairman of the 1st Census 2000 Killeen Complete Count Committee (1999-2011).
- Killeen Alumnae Chapter of Delta Sigma Theta Sorority Chapter President (1984-1986), Chapter Vice President (1982-1984) and have chaired many committees.

My service to my community, state and nation has earned me many honors, among them are:

- Ebony Society Humanitarian Award, October 2001
- Rosa Hereford Day, City of Killeen, August 23, 1997
- Key to the City, City of Killeen, May 13, 1997
- Community Service Award, Juneteenth Street Festival 1995
- BOSS IV Award- Austin Metropolitan Business Resource Center, 1991
- Killeen Alumnae Chapter of Delta Sigma Theta Sorority, Inc.'s Delta of the Year, 1987
- Black Achievement Award-Lyn Industries, Inc., (1st Recipient), 1985
- Joint Civilian Orientation Conference (JCOC 48) touring West Coast Military Installations Member, June 1983
- Recognized as one of the Most Prominent Educators in Texas, 1983.
- Educator of the Year, Killeen Rotary Club, 1980
- Notable American Award, 1976-1977
- Outstanding Young Woman of America, 1975
- Human Relations Award, Texas State Teachers Association (1st Recipient), 1973

After retirement as a teacher and counselor, I have been given another opportunity to serve the youth of this community. I now volunteer as a tutor for all academic subjects except math at the Transformative Charter Academy in Killeen. The school offers an alternative program for high school students who dropped out of the public school system and are now studying to complete their high school courses. I also remained active in my organizations and in politics in the interest of the citizens in the area.

I recognize that my contribution to community building has been important, productive and significant. Thanks to the many citizens who supported me in my endeavors. The accomplishments made could not have been achieved without their support. I am grateful that my life and skills are being used in service to others.

Bernard and Mary Jenkins
Reflections: Leadership + Service = Positive Change
Mary Jenkins

My husband, Bernard Jenkins, our children Bernard, Jr., Wanda, and Pierre and I arrived in the Killeen-Ft. Hood area in 1966. Bernard joined the Army after graduating from high school and spent over thirty-one years in the military until his retirement at the rank of Command Sergeant Major (CSM). Bernard provided leadership for the many soldiers he served and I addressed the needs of these wives whose husbands' first allegiance was to their country. After retirement from the Army, Bernard worked for the State of Texas as a counselor at the Gatesville, Texas State School for Boys. He also worked as the manager of the Parrie Haynes Youth Ranch and as a military dispatcher. We had government quarters in Pershing Park waiting for us when we arrived at Ft. Hood and I had promised myself that at Fort Hood, I would not make any friends here because it hurt too much to leave the friends I made in Germany. However, when my husband asked me to meet the wife of one of his soldiers who lived in our same duplex apartment, in that instant, I knew that to support my husband I had to make new friends. I had the wives of the 47th Medical

Battalion looking to me for leadership, and I continued the work I had done in Germany.

My first priority was to find a place to worship and a neighbor asked me to attend worship service with her at the 37th Street Chapel. I gladly accepted the invitation. This became my place of worship and I sang in the choir. I lived a full life taking care of my family and maintaining the social leadership which was expected of me. Then, in 1968 my husband got orders for Vietnam. He said to me, "You go and find a house for us to buy." For weeks I searched for a house and found one on Kimberly Lane in the Sugar Loaf Addition. We moved to our new home on May 19, 1968, and my husband left in June for Vietnam. There was only one man on my street, Major Finke, who lived next door, because all the husbands were in Vietnam. Those were hard times for wives and children because this was the first war fought that was shown on TV. There was only one other Black family on our street, and in Killeen segregation off post was still an issue. I had garbage dumped on my lawn more than once, flowers delivered to my house twice that I did not order, and the fire truck was sent to my house three times. Finally, I got fed up, and as I picked up the trash from my yard, I was looking for someone's address on a letter or magazine, but I didn't find any. I also announced very loudly, "You will never run me out of this neighborhood, and if you are looking for trouble, you just found it." Then, that was the end of that kind of problem, and ironically, I became an activist in the neighborhood.

When a construction company wanted to build apartments in our new neighborhood of single-family homes, I rallied the neighborhood and we raised enough money to hire a lawyer to stop them. As an active member of the Sugar Loaf Elementary School PTA, I helped raise money to erect a fence for the playground area. In addition, I became a den mother for Cub Scout Troop and worked with other neighbors to start a Girl Scout Troop. I also became very involved in Little League Baseball and was an active booster. I served as a chaperone for the football players and marching band for out of town activities, such as the football games and battle of the bands in many cities, including Corpus Christi, Port Aransas and Galveston. I would not have been able to do these things if it was not for the support of my husband, and I thank him for allowing me do something I really enjoyed.

Some positive changes resulted from my leadership and service to my community just by being responsible. I am grateful that my community service made a difference in my community, in the school for children and for others outside my community. This service included:

- Initiating and therefore becoming one of the first Neighborhood Watch Captains in my area to bring the neighbors together. My involvement included assisting in raising money, purchasing the signs, and having them placed on different street corners and then later acquiring permission from the Killeen Independent School District to hold our neighborhood watch meetings in Sugar Loaf Elementary School. *One person can help bring cohesiveness to a community.*

- Pursuing the city with persistence for the installation of a traffic signal light at Willow Springs Road to give residents of the Pershing Park community better traffic access at a very heavily traveled intersection. This made it a safer place in the community. *Some people will complain about a situation, but I believe in talking to someone who can change things.*

- Petitioning for a fair allocation of Block Grant Funds for "Help Centers" which were managed for Blacks or owned by Blacks, after speaking to the City Council on behalf of "Care, Inc.", a homeless shelter. I sent letters and received responses from our state representatives and the state senator in the U.S. Congress about this inequity. Then during the next year when requests were submitted, Block Grant Funds were given to the "Help Center", the "Mission House" and to "Care, Inc." *One person speaking out can make a difference.*

- Demonstrating compassion to those less fortunate in our community and encouraging others to do likewise. I assisted Mrs. Bertha Evans with the homeless shelter by helping with fundraisers and collecting clothes, by soliciting monthly donations from my church, and by serving on the Board of Directors. I also helped Mrs. Bessie Thomas with the Mission Soup Kitchen by providing food, clothing and getting other people to support this much needed ministry. *Great or small, everyone can make a difference.*

- Rallying support when Hurricane Hugo devastated Homestead, Florida. I got neighborhoods together all over Killeen/Ft Hood and Belton to send a truckload of food, clothes and toys to the survivors. I am grateful to the many people who contributed to this cause. *If you have faith in God, He will make a way for you to do what seems to man impossible.*

- Organizing a successful neighborhood gathering on the "First Night Out" celebration to meet/greet old and new neighbors; the gathering was held at our house and our neighbors came and enjoyed the evening. Over the years many other "Night Out" gatherings were held at our house. *This was my neighborhood and we are here to stay.*

Community involvement and service to humanity have always given me much satisfaction. I was honored to be a nominee for both the Jefferson Award and the Mayborn Award. While I was not the successful recipient, I attribute my good works to this old saying: "I am a nobody just trying to tell everybody about somebody who can save everybody." My faith leads me to use every opportunity I am given to be a witness for my Lord. It is the Christ in me that keeps me striving for a better home, a better community, a better city, a better nation and a better world. *Christ said, "I come to save those which are lost."*

My husband and I became members of Anderson Chapel African Methodist Episcopal (AME) Church, where I have served in the various ministries of the church as a member and sometimes as leader. The mission work and mission outreach activities in which I am involved have made a difference in my life and the lives of others in this community. My husband, who served his country with honor and loved his family unconditionally, is now deceased. Our adult children have their own families and are responsible citizens in the communities in which each of them live. *Community building requires that each one assume responsibility to get involved in the process. "Just Do it."*

Roy Jean McDaniel Lee
A Dedicated Educator Retires
Susan Smith

I am a reporter for the *Austin American Statesman Newspaper* of Austin, Texas and the daughter of the late Colonel (Retired) Junious W. and Eula M. Smith. On Wednesday, June 20, 2001, I wrote about my second grade teacher Mrs. Roy Jean McDaniel Lee. This heartwarming story about a relationship between a former elementary school student and her former teacher brings back memories of the nurturing influence of educators in the lives of those whom they teach.

"It's hard to catch a whipping when you're the teacher's pet, but I once took my licks from Mrs. Roy Jean Lee, whom I adore." Mrs. Lee was my second-grade teacher at Marlboro Heights Elementary School in Killeen, Texas. In 1965 teachers could spank students. Daddy had gone from Ft. Hood to Vietnam. Mom was the school's secretary and "Baby Love" by the Supremes was the favorite song. But if Diana Ross was my idol, Mrs. Lee was my mentor. Because I was a migratory military brat, there are hundreds of people from my childhood that I'll never see again. Bonds unraveled as quickly as I could unpack a suitcase. But the bonds with Mrs. Lee, the woman who first brought me to Austin, didn't unravel through time or travel. I knew her as the fair-skinned woman with freckles whose sternness in the classroom hid a sentimental heart. But I knew little about her teaching career before this Monday night interview with her.

Mrs. Lee graduated from Tillotson College in 1953, now Huston-Tillotson College. Her first public teaching position was in Florence, Texas in a one-room school for children of three black families. Her mother was convinced she would be a teacher when Roy Jean played rock school as a child. In rock school, a student would hold a rock in a closed hand. If the student selected the hand with the rock, the student was promoted. If the student selected the empty hand, the student was demoted. But "real" teaching is a little more complicated. Mrs. Lee went from the Florence School District to the Killeen School District. She drove from Killeen to Austin on Friday evening to spend the weekend with her four children who stayed with her parents during the week. A fifth child was born later. She said, "On weekend visits I played with my children under the abundant trees that surrounded the house on a hill on East Ninth Street."

In those days, it seemed like a long drive from Killeen to Austin on Interstate 35 because there was little to look at but grass. Mrs. Lee and I would talk non-stop, just as we did Monday night. She reminded me that when I was seven years old, I liked to write stories. I reminded her that I had a crush on Mr. Lee, who also taught at Marlboro Elementary, but I got over that when they got married. She laughed and listened to me, as she always did on those weekend rides from Killeen to Austin and back. Now she was approaching retirement the following week in June 2001, after forty-four years as a teacher in Florence, Killeen and Austin. Her statements to me at the close of my interview still rings clearly in my mind as to what an honorable profession teaching is. The philosophy for her life as a teacher was summed up in her kind and compassionate words. *"I've taught long enough to see that my teaching made a difference in a lot of people's lives,"* she said, adding that *"the reward is in student's progress, not in teacher's pay."* Developing students is community building. Roy Jean Daniels Lee is indeed a community builder.

Ira, Sr. and Mary McNeil
Serving Family and Country
Mary McNeil

SFC Ira McNeil and our family came to Fort Hood from Germany in 1964. Finding housing was one of our first challenges therefore we lived in Temple, Texas for seven months before getting housing on Post. We remained on Post until 1966 when Ira. Sr. was assigned to Fort Bliss. Our family moved to the Marlboro Heights community and I continued to work on Fort Hood. Living in this community where children were respectful at home, at school and in the community made the community a desirable place to live and rear a family. I decided to stay in the Killeen area so that the children could finish high school. The boys were doing well in their school studies and were also participating in several kinds of sports at that time. When the boys finished high school, each had established an outstanding record in sports, especially in football. We remained in Marlboro Heights after my retirement until 1988. I had worked on Post at Fort Hood for twenty-four years. My family became community builders. We supported the schools and community activities. We had good neighbors, and were neighborly in return. Ira, Sr. served our country loyally and with honor. We moved to the Houston, Texas area. Ira, Sr. and I now reside in Katy, Texas. Both Patrick and Gerald attended Baylor University in Waco, Texas, and each played football there for four years. After graduation from college, Patrick and Gerald then went on to play professional football. Three of our sons still reside in Texas. Ira is in Sugarland; Patrick is in Dallas, Texas; and Gerald is in Richmond. Danny, our fourth son, is deceased. Looking back over the years, we realized that many youths who grew up in the Marlboro Heights community are now experiencing productive lives. Many of them have families of their own. Their accomplishments have made their parents, neighbors and former teachers very proud of their successes.

Reverend Aubrey F. Pickens
Servant of God, Servant to Family and Servant to Country
Rev. Velma Hayden

Aubrey F. Pickens was a native son of Onalaska, Texas. His military assignment brought him and his family to the Fort Hood and Killeen Area in 1965. Together with his wife, Bessie; daughter, Aubrena; and son, Keith, the family became active in the Fort Hood community and later moved to the Marlboro Heights community where they became community builders. The family joined Anderson Chapel A.M.E. Church where Aubrey Pickens gave extensive service in the ministry of the church as a member of the Steward Board, the Board of Trustees, the Men's Ministry and the adult choir. Bessie Pickens contributed her time, talents and resources to the work of the Women's Missionary Society; adult usher ministry; and working with the youth of the church by making comfort items for those in the nursing home. Prior to moving to the Marlboro Community, she also worked with the Fort Hood Girl Scouts. Their children participated in the youth ministries and activities. He was an active member of the New Light Masonic Lodge No. 242.

SGT Major Aubrey Pickens retired from the military with twenty-nine years of service in the United States Army. He was a veteran of three wars: World War II, the Korean War and the Vietnam War. The last twelve years of his military career were spent serving as the sergeant major of the Personnel Service Company. After retirement from active duty, he gave ten additional years of service as a federal service employee in the position of supervisor in the Patient Administration Section at Darnall Army Community Hospital at Fort Hood, Texas.

When Rev. Pickens accepted his call to preach, his ministry was supported by his family. He served as pastor to several AME Churches in the Central Texas Annual Conference which included: Thomas Chapel and Ninth Hour, both in Copperas Cove; St. Stephens in Bartlett; St. Matthew in Burnett; and Liberty Chapel in Liberty Hill. After the demise of his wife, he was remarried to Essie Mae Houston, who also worked along beside him in his ministry. Rev. Aubrey Frank Pickens shared years of service with the military, with the community, with the church and with the family. As a family, they were also involved in community building.

Chester and Lois Fields
Compassion, Faith, Strength, and Inspiration
Lois Fields

Chester enlisted in the Army immediately after graduating from high school and began twenty years and twenty days of active duty service. We are both from Crockett, Texas and after Chester's tour of duty in Vietnam we moved to Killeen in October 1968. We were pleased with this assignment because it was close to our Texas roots of East Texas and near our parents who were getting older. It also allowed our son, Arthur, to get to know his grandparents. When we arrived in the area, we stayed in Ft. Hood guest housing until we found rental property in Harker Heights. Then later we moved to the Marlboro Heights area in Killeen on January 29, 1969. That same day we were called for government housing at Fort Hood's Pershing Park, which we did not accept.

Thinking back to our arrival, jobs were also hard to find, even for spouses in the teaching profession. I had Texas and Colorado teaching certificates but only found substitute work in the school district. I taught art to children with Kim Kerr during the summer for the Killeen Parks and Recreation Department in 1971-72. Arthur worked at Mid-Town Mall at "Chucky Cheese." There was no large shopping center in the entire area. However, we did have the Montgomery Ward and the Sears catalogue sales stores in Killeen. Later, Mid-Town Mall opened with Woolworth as the anchor store and a limited selection of other stores. Killeen High school was the only high school and U.S. Hwy 190 (now Veterans Memorial Boulevard) was only two lanes. An old wooden-frame building just off of the railhead at Fort Hood housed the commissary and young children were not allowed in the commissary. Parents had to take them to the nursery which was in a building near the commissary while we shopped.

Darnall Army Hospital had not long been completed when we arrived in the area. It was a period of *faith building and thanksgiving* for me. Our daughter, Mona, was born at Fort Hood on June 4, 1970. Within three months after her birth, Chester received orders for a second tour in Vietnam and I remained in the area. In the meantime, Mona contracted meningitis and was seriously ill. Chester had been wounded and was sent to Walter Reed Army Hospital for several weeks. When he was well enough to travel he was assigned at Brooke Army Base in San Antonio, for a short time until he could return to the medical holding company at Ft. Hood. Mona's cerebral palsy required two major surgeries: a hip surgery and a scoliosis surgery that utilized a new procedure involving inserting a Harrington L Rod to support the spine. Mona tolerated both surgeries well. Doctors had said that she would never live past her third birthday. However, she lived a full life and died just two days shy of her nineteenth birthday.

God helped us overcome all of the obstacles we encountered throughout those years. He gave us the strength, faith and knowledge that were needed, and He even provided others sources (family, friends, medical provider and school) to see us through every situation. Our family, friends and church were great sources of support for us through the years that Mona was alive. Mona even attended school with her cerebral palsy. Ft. Hood had a great support system for disabled children within the local school district. Mona touched the lives of three of my first cousins and a college roommate, and they entered the field of special education as a career. Anderson Chapel AME Church's youth center was named the *"Mona Fields Christian Education Youth Center"* in Mona's memory. Our family has been blessed and for that we are very grateful.

Much of my community service has been as a volunteer. I supervised children in painting fire plugs as a community project during the Bi-Centennial Celebration. Some of my volunteer service has been with disabled children and their families. I volunteered with Army Community Services, assisting the special needs children and with families who had to cope with disabled family members. I also assisted with special needs Scout and Brownie troops. During the Gulf War, I offered to care for children with disabilities to allow their parents needed time to shop or just to get away on weekends. I serve on Anderson Chapel's Richard Allen Community Development Corporation Board and am a founding member of the graduate chapter of Delta Zeta Chapter of Zeta Phi Beta Sorority, a public service organization of college women. I was an instructor in CPR and First Aid for the American Red Cross from 1985-2006 and now I am a volunteer church photographer and missionary ministry's historiographer. I enjoy doing outreach service for those in need.

Eventually, I found full-time work teaching young military dependents and as principal of a school. I joined the teaching staff of the Fort Hood Child Development Center in 1985 and retired from this employment in 2004. Education, citizenship, social, spiritual and moral commitments are important values in Chester's and my lives. These values were instilled in us from our parents and grandparents. Obtaining an education has also been a family focus. After retirement, Chester attended Central Texas College under the GI Bill and was certified in the building trades. Our son Arthur, a college graduate, studied photography and digital media, and has had many successful experiences in this area, which includes being a professional photographer, photography teacher and advertising editor. He has won several awards for his work in the Texas Visual Arts Coalition of Dallas.

Chester, a Purple Heart recipient, retired from the Army with over twenty years of service. Following his retirement he worked civil service for twenty-four more years until his retirement in January 2005. He was a member of the Veterans of Foreign Wars and a life member of Disabled Veterans of America. Chester Fields is now deceased. Over the years this family has been involved in community building.

Willie and Eva Jefferson
Military, Community, Civic and Federal Leadership
The Task Force

Willie and Eva Jefferson were longtime residents of the Marlboro Heights Community. Willie was a native of Richmond, Virginia, and Eva was a native of New Orleans, Louisiana. He attended Howard Payne College and St. Paul University. After retirement from the U. S. Army with twenty-six years of service, he became actively involved in many aspects of the city by contributing his leadership to civic and community organizations. He served as first vice president of the Killeen Branch NAACP and when the president, Clyde Williams, tendered his resignation in January 1972, Willie Jefferson took over the helm. His tenure as president was recognized as very fruitful and the membership including renewals grew to over three hundred by the end of the first year. Two significant accomplishments were made by the NAACP under his leadership. First, the organization's successful intervention on behalf of servicemen at Fort Hood resulted in servicemen having the right to join the NAACP. Secondly, the segregated faculty at Marlboro Elementary School was integrated into the faculties on several elementary school campuses in the school district during the 1969 school year. This created a first in Killeen Independent School District of having the largest number of integrated elementary school faculties during the 1969 school year than ever before.

Willie Jefferson was also a past president and life member of the Killeen Evening Lions Club and became the first black district governor in the State of Texas as a Lions member. In addition, he was a Fellow of Texas Lions Foundation and a Melvin Jones Fellow of the International Association of Lions Clubs.

After military retirement, he joined the federal service workforce in employment with the U. S. Postal service in Killeen and later served as postmaster at Crawford, Texas, from 1978-1979, and as postmaster in Nolanville in 1980. He remained in this position until his retirement from federal service in 1995. With both appointments, Willie Jefferson, Sr. became the first black postmaster for these two cities. The family moved to New Orleans, Louisiana, after his retirement from the postal service.

Willie and Eva Jefferson are the parents of three adult children: Carla, their daughter; and two sons, Lance and Darwin. This family made a significant contribution to community building at a time when it was greatly needed. They were community builders.

Dallas and Lillie Owens
New Experiences and New Friendships
Lillie Owens

Arriving in Killeen, Texas, during the summer of 1964 gave new meaning to the word *hot.* We had never experienced such extremely hot temperatures, such as 103, 104 and 106 degrees. When my husband received orders for the Fort Hood-Killeen area, friends were quick to inform us about the climate. They also informed us of much more about the area, which included the nature of the social climate of the town and about the possibility of encountering racial prejudice and discrimination in housing and business. As a result, we were naturally anxious to get housing on Fort Hood. Unfortunately, housing on the Post was at capacity, so we stayed in the Guest House far beyond the usual staying limits for guests. Two weeks passed and still we could not find any available housing for a family of six with a little one on the way. Finally, we sought housing in the Marlboro Heights community. It was one of two places available for Blacks to live. The other location was in Simmonsville, which was north of the highway from the Marlboro Heights community.

The search worked out in our favor this time, and we did find housing in Marlboro Heights. Fortunately, there was a vacancy on Longview Drive. This location was close to Marlboro Missionary Baptist Church and Marlboro Elementary School. The high school students in the community were bussed to Killeen High School, which was located across the highway and on 38th Street. After reluctantly moving in, we found that we liked the neighborhood very much. We found the people of the community very kind and helpful. By the time that we moved away, we had established many friendships that remain even to this day. As a result of living among our neighbors, we also became involved in programs and projects in the school, the church and the community. We began working together developing our families and practicing good citizenship, supporting the school and church, maintaining our property and improving our surroundings, making our neighborhood a safe place to live. Yes, we, too, became community builders. There were restrictions for Blacks in the community. However we found the Marlboro Heights community a friendly place to live.

CHAPTER 4

1970-1979:
The Beginning of
Community Involvement

—w—

The decade of the seventies can be described as a transitional period for both the city and its citizens. It was the decade when opportunities for community involvement by African Americans increased not only for newcomers, but also for many of the arrivals of earlier decades. The social climate of the city in this decade had become more accepting of its African American residents than in previous decades and leadership opportunities began opening for them..Among the newcomers that arrived during the decade of the seventies were: Horace Grace, Fannie Flood, LTC (Retired) Henderson and Bernice Garrett, Ecolia and Louise Dunn, Marcus Batts, and Edmond Jones. They, like many others before them, became community builders rendering service and assuming leadership roles in the community. It is important to know that there are many other African Americans who also contributed to community building and achieved important accomplishments, but are not included in this book of journals as a *TAPESTRY* project participant. As you read the journals of those sharing them, you will learn that their contributions were of significant in the process of community building in Killeen and Central Texas and many African Americans chose to establish the area as "home".

The decade of the seventies also offered leadership opportunities to residents of the earlier decades. Doors were opened and opportunities were accepted to serve. They approached their assignments with courage and seriousness in fulfilling leadership responsibilities in city government, community administration and in education. For example:

Ozell Wilkerson, a newcomer in 1967, became KISD's first African American junior high school assistant principal in 1973, and the first African American senor high school assistant principal in 1976.

Willie Gibson, a newcomer in 1955, became Killeen's first African American to be elected to the Killeen City Council in 1974, and served three consecutive two-year terms in this position.

Alice Douse, a newcomer in 1962, became KISD's first African American female principal in 1977, and KISD's second African American principal since 1955.

Wadella Heath, a newcomer in 1959, became the first African American to be appointed as KISD Assistant Director of Food Service (1973-76) and Director of Food Service for the entire Killeen Independent School District in 1976.

Marcus and Penny Batts: The Hamilton Story
"One Person Can Make a Difference"
Marcus Batts

My wife, Penny Walker Batts, and I are residents of Killeen, Texas. I came to Killeen in 1973 with military orders to report to Ft Hood. I am a native of Jacksonville, North Carolina. Penny and I are parents of a son, Marcel and daughter, Melanie. Both are Ellison High School graduates. I have served my country with honor and courage;

served my community as a spiritual leader; and have proven to be a role model in faith and trust and forgiveness. Penny touches the lives of the youth of this community daily in her role as principal of an elementary school in the Killeen Independent School District. She also touches the lives of teachers and the parents of these students. Her love for teaching and her compassion for all children were evident early in her teaching career as she taught students with special needs. The Batts family values education. Penny earned her Bachelor of Science Degree with Mental Retardation (MR) endorsement, and a Master of Education Degree and Mid-management certification. My Bachelor's Degree is in General Studies. Both of our adult children have completed postgraduate studies. Melanie is certified in education and is now a sixth-grade teacher at one of the middle schools in Killeen Independent School District. SFC Marcel Batts, a Patient Administration Specialist, has applied for OCS admission and plans to go right into a Master's program in Hospital Administration. As a family, we are proud of my military service record, college degree, high school track record, music recognition and more than twenty-five years employment with United Parcel Services (UPS); also Penny's educational accomplishments; Melanie's teaching in her former school system; and Marcel's three meritorious service medals and military and educational achievements. However, life sometimes brings obstacles that must be overcome.

In 1990 I faced an obstacle that I was determined to overcome. It was an experience now known as the "Hamilton Story." It is about racial prejudices that I encountered in my work assignment for eighteen months, and how a community's attitude changed. The Hamilton experience wasn't the first time I had encountered racial prejudice. I was raised through segregation and the integration of schools. The Hamilton Story has been in essays, sermons and in a screenplay written by actor and playwright, Mark Harelick. I have shared this experience with many groups as a Black History speaker.

The Hamilton Story

Having previously worked for UPS for seven years in Temple, I recalled my experience from 1990-1994 when I was a United Parcel Services (UPS) delivery man. I ignored the warning from my white supervisors and former customers that I should reconsider taking the Hamilton route, based on their knowledge and experiences of racial prejudices against blacks in Hamilton County at that time. When I got there, I found out it was exactly like they said. Hamilton was a predominantly white town, with a population of approximately 2,700 at that time. Initially, the people there stared at me; crossed the street to keep from making contact with me; and whispered among themselves whenever I was around. I was on my new assignment for two days when my supervisor received a call from a Hamilton resident saying he didn't want my kind down there. I was given the option to go somewhere else, but I was determined to stay and work things out. I had been the eighth UPS man in the Hamilton district for only four years.

My patience was always put to the test as I was doing my job about the town. Whenever I entered a store to make a delivery, men would huddle around and would barely give me space to get in. I felt that if I had accidentally bumped them, there would have been a problem. Then there was this woman who lived on the far south side of Hamilton County who was kind when I made a delivery. She would offer me a soda or a snack to eat. One day, I went there to make a delivery when a friend was visiting, and the friend expressed a negative comment about me in my presence. The kind woman challenged her friend's negative comment and expressed her trust in me as a friend who would come in and help her if she had fallen out on the floor.

Then, at one point while at home in Killeen, I thought that things had come to a head when I heard my seventeen-year-old son screaming to someone on the phone, "Don't talk about my dad like that!" Someone from Hamilton had called our home and had threatened to kill me if I returned to work there. Having been brought up in Killeen, my son had never encountered racism like this before. During Christmas time in 1991, my family was in downtown

Hamilton for the first time to shop. The children did not enjoy the shopping trip. They felt that the shop workers did not trust them and had followed them throughout the store. However, we continued to return as a family.

It was a very prejudiced atmosphere for me when one resident told me that there had not been a black person living in Hamilton for the past one hundred years. But after listening to seventy-seven-year-old Milton Harelick, who was born, raised and had always lived in Hamilton, I learned that blacks had been living in Hamilton, but not many lived within the town. Harelick pointed out that he can't remember any more than three black families ever living in the county, and about six or seven black children attending Hamilton School system. He also told me that if Hamiltonians are not acquainted with people, there is a tendency to be a little apprehensive around them. Therefore, it was his belief that when I (Marcus) first came to Hamilton, most of the people here were very apprehensive. But then he ended with this statement: "But it was your (Marcus') demeanor that changed all that."

I believe that the break first occurred in the perception of the town's people and the racial wall started coming down when I volunteered to bring a black gospel group from Waco and put on a concert at the theater there to raise money for the library. Until then, nobody in town wanted to have any type of contact with me. The concert raised over $1500. I then became more involved in many other community activities in Hamilton. This included hospital and nursing home visits; checking on the sick on weekends; singing at weddings and attending and supporting football and basketball games. For me, this was an opportunity for community building within the city of Hamilton. Eventually, I was also asked to preach at several all-white churches. During a Ku Klux Klan rally in Hamilton in 1993, I stood on the courthouse steps with white residents on both sides assuring me that no one would harm me. On an occasion when an inquiry was made of me, Harelick responded, "He is very well known throughout Hamilton County." I knew through my faith in God that I would overcome the racial prejudices of my customers; and after eighteen months it happened. "I claim no credit to myself." I proclaimed boldly, "My greatest gain from this experience was knowing God can open doors. It was the power of God, and it was a door he wanted to be opened." I was transferred to the Gatesville area in 1994 and when the town learned about the intended transfer, the Hamilton Community planned and observed Marcus Batts Day on March 6, 1994. God had blessed as I knew he would. Community building in Hamilton was accomplished and racial prejudices had subsided.

- I became the first African American to preach from the pulpit of the First Baptist Church in Hamilton during the Sunday Worship service on March 6, 1994. My family and I were honored at a community-wide reception following the worship service on Marcus Batts Day, and when I left, the whole town had signs put up stating they hated to see Marcus go.
- Newspapers throughout Central Texas carried the Marcus Batts' Hamilton story and my recognition extended far beyond Central Texas when I was honored by the Equal Opportunity/ Employment Opportunity Offices and the United States Army MEDDAC at the National Training Center, Fort Irwin, California, with an invitation to be the 2003 Dr. Martin Luther King, Jr. Birthday Celebration guest speaker. My story found its way into the Fort Irwin Tiefort Telegraph Newspaper.
- The Coin of Excellence #0230 and certificate signed the 9th day of January, 2003, was awarded to me for my participation as guest speaker at the 2003 Dr. Martin Luther King Jr. Celebration at Fort Irwin, California.

What do others say? Reverend Georgia Adamson, pastor of First United Methodist Church in Hamilton, urged others, if you get a chance, tell someone about how Marcus won the hearts of the people of Hamilton. "Contrary to some thinking, ONE person can be a powerful instrument for change," said Rev. Adamson, "Marcus followed the best example when he met opposition with love, the love of the living Christ."

Now for my final statement on this matter: "I claim no credit to myself. I proclaim boldly, my greatest gain from this experience is in knowing God can open doors. It was the power of God, and it was a door he wanted opened."

Ecolia and Louise Dunn
Love of Family, Country and Humanity
Louise Dunn

Ecolia and I are natives of North Carolina. We moved to Killeen in November 1971 because of Ecolia's assignment to Ft. Hood. Military housing at Fort Hood was very limited. Therefore, we rented a trailer in Harker Heights and resided there from January -April, 1972. Our family first moved into government quarters at Venable Village on Fort Hood in 1972. Two years later we moved into Comanche Village, a new housing area, and resided there until February, 1978. We purchased our home in Killeen in February 1978 and are still residing there. When we arrived in 1971, the Killeen Mall was not open and there were just a few retailers in downtown Killeen. Because of this, families traveled to Temple, Texas and neighboring cities in Bell County and neighboring counties to do our shopping. The seventies was also a time when areas of downtown Killeen were not a family friendly shopping environment because Avenue D, one of the major business streets downtown, had acquired a bad reputation.

Ecolia's tour of duty at Ft. Hood lasted from 1971-1974 before receiving orders for Korea. He served his tour of duty in Korea from 1974-1976, and our family remained in the Killeen-Fort Hood area. When his tour of duty ended in Korea, he retired from the U. S. Army and enjoyed a period of retirement from his military career from January 1976 - August 1979. In September of 1979, Ecolia received the Purple Heart, Bronze Star for Valor and Commendation Ribbons earned during his military service. He had already earned his Bachelor of Science Degree from A and T College in North Carolina, and his Master's Degree in Counseling from Prairie View A & M University in Texas, and was now ready to pursue a civilian career in the field of education. He was employed by the Killeen

Independent School District (KISD). He taught at Fairway Middle School for more than 10 years, and retired from KISD in May 1991.

His community involvement included memberships in the Lion's Club; Kappa Sigma Lambda Chapter of the Alpha Phi Alpha Fraternity, Inc.; Veterans of Foreign Wars (VFW) and Disabled American Veterans (DAV). He helped start the Corbell Leo Club with the intention that community work would help the youth develop a community relationship. Ecolia believed, as the club sponsor, that in order to be a leader you have to be responsible for the people in the community. The program was active in Killeen and during spring of 2005, youth from the Corbell Leo Club and a local church partnered and provided community service to the Home and Hope Shelter. This shelter is a United Way Agency that offers housing for homeless people and provides services to help them get back on their feet. The youth painted, mowed, performed general cleanup tasks, and cataloged books in the shelter's library.

Prior to moving to Fort Hood and the Killeen area, I had been employed for forty years as a registered nurse at various military installations in the U. S., Germany and in civilian hospitals. My desire to again utilize my nursing skills and experiences led me in the fall of 1986 to seek employment as a school nurse in the Killeen Independent School District. I was employed and became the first African American registered nurse employed in the Killeen Independent School District. This employment also established another historical fact in the history of the school district. I remained in this position until my retirement in 1994. My desire to continue rendering service was fulfilled through my community involvement. This included membership and service in the Killeen Chamber of Commerce as a Chamber Ambassador. I have been recognized for dedicated service, and was elected "Ambassador of the Quarter" and "Runner up" at three different times. My membership in the Lion's Club and the Disabled American Veterans (DAV) Auxiliary has given me other opportunities to be involved in community service. I enjoy gardening as a hobby. I love music and have been blessed with the talent to sing. Twenty-Fifth Street Chapel at Fort Hood was our church of worship, and I enjoyed singing in the chapel choir.

We are the parents to six adult children: Haskell, Michael, Melba Dunn Harris, Cheryl Dunn Partee, Kimberly and Traci. Our grandchildren are Aaron, Alecia, Jannelle, Tamara and Demetrius. The development of a strong work ethic in the Dunn children began early in their lives, and helped to mold the character of six responsible citizens who are now giving back to the communities in which they reside. At the time of this writing:

- **Haskell** attended Southern University, served in the U. S. Navy and is an electrical engineer with his own business in California.
- **Michael** began working during high school at the Fort Hood Commissary (1973) and later at Woolworth; served in the U. S. Army; earned his B. S. degree in Information System Management. He and his wife reside in Texas, where he is employed as a System Analyst.
- **Melba Harris** began working at Ft. Hood's Mess Hall in 1975; later employed with Scott and & White Hospital in Temple and Killeen; worked as a KISD substitute teacher; earned an A. S. in Office Management and Legal Assistant Technology; and is a certified legal assistant.
- **Cheryl Partee** began working during high school at McDonald's. Worked as a KISD Secretary; served in the U. S. Army; earned her B. S. in Accounting; earned two Master's Degrees in Business Administration, and is employed as a Finance Analyst.
- **Kimberly** began working during high school at Weiners Department Store. She served in the U. S. Navy, and retired with twenty (20) years of honorable service. Her B. S. degree is in Business Management. She is employed by a security company in Washington, D.C.
- **Traci's** work experiences began during high school. Her work experiences include UPS; Hyatt Hotel in Dallas; Four Seasons in Irving, Texas; Four Seasons Resort and Hotel in Atlanta, Georgia, Employment as Manager. She earned a B. S. in Hotel and Restaurant Management; now pursuing a Master's Degree in Human Resources Management.

Resides in Ohio and employed as Director of Inclusion for the Templin Company.

The Dunns consider family loyalty and support important and valuable. This has helped the family overcome individual obstacles such as family illnesses, family separations due to military assignments, work or educational pursuits. One of the happiest moments for our family was when all the children surprised us and returned to Killeen during the Christmas of 1993. We all were saddest when Ecolia and Haskell left on a tour to Vietnam. They both returned to the family following a tour of honorable service to the country, and Ecolia continued his involvement in community service until his death in May, 2008. The impact of his involvement and service as a soldier, as a teacher and in the community touched the lives of many youth and adult citizens in Killeen. Indeed, our family was involved in the process of community building.

LTC (Ret) Henderson and Bernice Garrett
A Winning Team: Healthcare and Education
LTC (Ret) Henderson Garrett

My wife, Bernice Garrett, and I are native Texans. I am from Fairfield, and she is from Riverside. I received my Bachelor of Science Degree, and was commissioned as a Second Lieutenant in the U. S. Army from Prairie View A & M University in 1952. During my 20 years of military service, my assignments abroad included Germany, Lebanon, Vietnam and two tours to Korea. I served my country in varied capacities of command such as: Special and General Staff responsibilities in the United States Army and in the Department of Defense in Washington D. C. I also served in the Defense Intelligence Agency. Among my awards during my tenure of military service are the Legion of Merit, Bronze Star Medal, Army Commendation Medal, the Combat Infantryman Badge and numerous service medals.

I retired from military service as a Lieutenant Colonel in 1972. Upon receipt of the Master of Science degree in Management Science from the University of Central Texas (formerly the American Technological University) in 1973, I entered the healthcare industry as Business Office Manager and Assistant Administrator of Metroplex Hospital (formerly Hillandale Memorial Hospital, a 35-bed hospital) in Killeen.

During the period from October 1993 through December 1995, I was an integral participant in the growth of the Metroplex Health System and served as Vice President of Operations. Among the accomplishments of this progressive institution was the increase in bed capacity from 35 to 213 beds; medical staff from six (6) physicians to in excess of 80 physicians; hospital staff from 125 to in excess of 800 employees; and the expansion of healthcare services and facilities to meet the healthcare needs in the face of rising healthcare costs throughout the hospital's service area. These facilities include Metroplex Hospital, Metroplex Urgent Care Center, Metroplex Pavilion and Rollins Brooks Community Hospital in Lampasas. Among my executive and operational duties was my direct responsibility for the management of the hospital's several professional buildings. This included the Professional Plaza in Copperas Cove; Metroplex Medical Plaza on the hospital campus; Medical Arts Center; and the Metroplex Urgent Care Center in Killeen; also the Heights Medical Plaza in Harker Heights; and North Key Medical Plaza in Lampasas.

In addition to my dedication to meeting health-care needs demanded by the community, I served the community on the City of Killeen Land Use Committee (1975-1976); Nolan Community Education Advisory Council (1984-1985); Copperas Cove Chamber of Commerce Board of Directors (1990-1994); and Vice Chairman of Copperas Cove Chamber of Commerce Board of Directors (1995). On October 3, 1993, after twenty successful years with Metroplex Health System, I retired as Vice President of Operations; however I continued to serve as Assistant to the President to manage the $4.8 million hospital expansion program until it was completed in 1995. However, my relationship continued with Metroplex Health System, where I served as Secretary of the Board of directors for Metroplex

Hospital, Inc., and as Chairman of the Board for Metroplex Management, Inc., the Corporation which oversees the operations of Metroplex Urgent Care. On August 6, 1999, LTC Garrett was elected to represent District VII on the Executive Committee of the Texas Healthcare Trustees (THT).

My wife Bernice Garrett, a Prairie View A & M University graduate, devoted many years to teaching and positively affecting the lives of the youth in Killeen and other communities. She began teaching in Trinity, Texas in the Mid-50s and worked there for six years.Her break in service as a teacher was filled with traveling with me, rearing our children and substitute teaching. She was employed by the Killeen Independent School District (KISD) in 1976. Since then she taught, mentored, nurtured and encouraged students through their educational challenges by providing instruction in remedial subjects in the elementary schools and at one of the middle schools. During her tenure in the district, she taught at Marlboro Elementary, Bellaire Elementary, East Ward Elementary, Clear Creek Elementary and Rancier Middle Schools.

In 1996, she retired from teaching in the Killeen independent School District (KISD) after giving twenty years of committed service to the youth of the Killeen communities, plus the six years of service teaching the youth in Trinity, Texas. She then shifted her time and interest to providing assistance through her volunteer service to persons who either have health challenges or to those who serve persons with health challenges. She has been equally supported and devoted to helping others through volunteer service in the Metroplex Hospital. For more than ten years, she established and maintained a close association with the Metroplex Health System through her numerous hours of service as a volunteer.

We are the parents of two adult daughters, Cheryl and Carla. In addition to family values that our daughters share, they are both products of the Killeen Independent School District educational system. Cheryl is a graduate of Killeen High School. Carla was a member of the first graduating class of Ellison High School. They are productive responsible citizens who are giving back to their communities. Cheryl serves in the position of Customer Service Supervisor with U.S. Foods Service, Dallas Division; and Carla serves in a CPA position with a Pharmaceutical Company in Fort Worth, Texas.

We worship at Pershing Park Baptist Church. and are among the many African American residents who have made noteworthy contributions to community building and in making the larger community of Killeen a better place in which to live, work and raise a family. Bernice Garrett is now deceased, but she has left a legacy of dedicated service to this community.

Horace R. Grace
Dedicated Community Service
Horace Grace and the Task Force

My military assignment to Ft. Hood, Texas, brought me to the Killeen area in April, 1979. Now retired from military service, I have stayed active in both the public and private sectors. I am a native of Timpson, Texas; a Vietnam Veteran; graduate of Prairie View A and M University and Virginia State University. I have a daughter, April M. Grace, a graduate of Blue Ridge College, Harrisonburg, Virginia. My broad leadership experiences have touched on many areas both in civilian and military settings, to include areas related to the military, government, business, finance, management and education. As a former Army officer who earned the rank of Major in the United State Army, and as a logistics instructor and operations officer (S3), I served in various procurement positions, writing and lecturing extensively on the federal government's acquisition process. I'm one of approximately 1,500 Certified Associate Contract Managers in the United States, having received certification nationally in government contracting by the National Contract Management Association. During the course of years of progressive responsibility and achievement in private industry and government, I earned an impeccable portfolio of the qualifications of an outstanding executive, with broad experience as director, consultant, writer and speaker in both business and government; and in cost-efficient management, fiscal analysis, marketing, innovative approaches to management review and strategic planning."

I am a dedicated and willing community builder who has given of my time, expertise and resources to public service in education, industry, business and human services and in matters that have benefited the community and can help many citizens locally, as well as in the state, the region and the nation. I have also influenced industry and government in positive ways through my service at the local, county, state and national levels of government. The community has benefited from my extensive service concerning matters that can help many citizens locally, as well as in the state, the region and the nation.

Locally, since 1982 I served as President and Chief Consultant of the Federal Acquisition Consultants in Killeen, Texas. This service specializes in the procurement, implementation and monitoring of government contacts. It also provides technical expertise to small business in key areas of local, state and federal government contracting. In addition, I have executive experience in managing small privately held businesses and have served as President and Chief Executive Officer of the AMG Enterprises, Inc. dba The Lawn Barber, Killeen, Texas. This service has been recognized as one of the largest privately held commercial and residential lawn maintenance businesses in the Greater Killeen Area. I accredit my success to having been blessed with the ability to be self-starting, and a goal-oriented strategist whose confidence, perseverance and vision promote success, and that my accomplishments in the public sector have resulted from this ability, attitude and manner of approaching a task.

"The focus of my local community service and affiliations below has been about community building and I am pleased to be a community builder giving service as:

- The visionary initiator and chairperson for the Center for African-American Studies and Research that officially opened on February 20, 2002.

- Past President of the Greater Ft. Hood Area United Way, and first African- American to hold this position.
- President and Director of the Clearwater Underground Water Conservation District, and first African-American to be elected county-wide in Bell County as a Director.
- President of the Board of Trustees at Cornerstone Baptist Church.
- Founding President of the Ft. Hood Chapter National Contracts Management Association.
- Founding Director of the Central Texas Alliance of Black Businesses.
- Lifetime member of NAACP.
- Director of Central Texas Better Business Bureau; and Director of Central Texas Workforce Development Board.
- Board of Directors of Extraco Bank, Killeen, Texas.
- Board Member, Brazos G Regional Water Planning Group Board, Waco, Texas; and Clear Water Underground Water Conservation District, Bell County.
- Director and Member, Central Texas Private Industry Task Force Board in Killeen which provides policy guidance and oversight for JTPA programs funding in seven counties.
- Board Member, SPRINT Incorporated Customer Advisor Board.
- Board Member of the Central Texas College Joint Institutional Task Force which was organized for the purpose of studying the possibility of the conversion of this 2-year community college to a 4-year university in Killeen, Texas, as directed by the Texas Legislature.
- Member of Killeen Independent School District H.O.S.T. Program that involved tutoring and mentoring students in their academic studies.

For many years, I had a vision to set-up a center dedicated to black studies and research. I believe that "The key to bringing racial harmony in the community is education." Therefore, communicating the culture to the community-at-large can be done through educational opportunities that will be available at this center. On February 20,

2002, the Center of African-American Studies and Research was officially opened in the Oveta Culp Hobby Memorial Library on the Central Texas College Campus in Killeen, Texas. The citizens and students in the Killeen/Fort Hood and Central Texas region have received a valuable community resource. At the time of its opening, the Center had purchased more than 100 books. This purchase was made possible through my personal donations and the Center Contributors and Partners. Center Partners are those individuals or organizations who have committed financial resources to this project. The objective for the Center is that it would achieve these broad goals: 1) Educate the community on racial sensitivity; 2) Educate the community on the African American contributions in history; and 3) Ultimately bring racial harmony to this diverse community.

As committee chairperson I championed this noteworthy project on black heritage for the Central Texas College Library, assisted by my committee members and by Central Texas College and Tarleton State University. The Killeen/Fort Hood Area is one of the more racially diverse communities of its size in the country; it is my belief that the Center's mission can be fulfilled through activities, projects and sources that recognize the current and past contribution of blacks; donate books and scholarly publications to higher institutes; offer scholarships to black students for their pursuit of higher education; and to bring speakers to address black issues. The fulfillment of these more specific goals are in progress in the Center for African-American Studies and Research. The Central Texas College Foundation continues to accept gifts and donations from the community in support of the Center for African-American Studies and Research. As a public servant and as a private citizen, I have given back to the community locally. I have strongly advocated cultural respect and racial harmony for our community. I have promoted the acquisition of educational resources and experiences as a basis for stronger appreciation for the total heritage of our community and nation.

The national, state, district, county and local levels of government and the community have afforded me many opportunities to serve; and service has brought awards, honors and positive recognition for which I am grateful. Some of my recognition include:

- Recipient of the Tarleton State University-Central Texas 2002 Outstanding Community Service Award as Chairman of the newly-established Center for African-American Studies and Research.
- Honored in 1999 by friends who sponsored "A Salute to Horace Grace Appreciation Day" for service rendered at the local, state, county and national levels.
- Recipient of the 1977 United States Jaycees Outstanding Young Men of America Award.

My public service to the State of Texas and to our nation has also benefited our local government decisions and needs. My involvement at these levels from 1965-1995 include:

o   Gubernatorial appointments by three governors;
o   A Presidential administration appointment; and
o   Many other positions of service.

Community building for me has been a desirable way of giving back service that will make a positive difference.

Fannie Flood Lewis
Building a Business while Building a Community
Fannie Flood Lewis

As a military family, my husband Leo Flood and I arrived in the Ft Hood-Killeen Area in January, 1979. Leo's military change of station orders were to Fort Hood, Texas. We first resided at Fort Hood, and then moved to Killeen in 1982. Being native Texans, we were no stranger to this part of the state of Texas. When we arrived, our early impression of the area was that an expansion of real estate was beginning. We quickly learned that jobs were hard to find. One of the largest projects that was happening at that time was the construction of the

Killeen Mall. Our duty station before coming to Killeen was in Germany and during the nine years that we were there I received a degree in Business Administration from the University of Maryland-European Division. I had also been employed in Germany with the military in the area of finance. Therefore, when we arrived in the Killeen/Fort Hood Area, I wanted a job, but I couldn't find one. I think that the entrepreneur spirit had always been there in us, because when we were in Beaumont, my husband and I had invested in real estate. Then while in Germany, we made plans about entering the world of real estate as a part of our retirement. Unable to find a job, I stayed home six months after our arrival, and then went to work for Jackson's Real Estate and Insurance Company which was owned by William "Bill" Jackson. This job did not last long and after a month at home I began exploring the possibilities of opening a real estate business.

This then became my goal. As I pursued it, doors began to open for me; in addition to the Lord speaking to me to go ahead. Business leaders in the city, whom I did not even know and whom did not know me, trusted my creditability as a tenant in locating rental space and as a customer in setting up my office with the furnishings and supplies to get started. A friend volunteered to cover the office for a few hours during the week so that I could go door to door in the neighborhood, meeting the people and delivering flyers announcing the opening of my business. The reception I received was encouraging. Yes, it was hard work. It was expected to be hard work, and I'm grateful I was able to do it. My God guided me through the entire process. He went ahead of me to those whom he directed me to approach so that they were prepared to receive me.

Flood Real Estate was organized on June 4, 1980. Our first business was located on Second Street. We rented from Mr. Hollis. When our office opened we were established as a Real Estate Sales, Service and Property Management Office. Very soon we expanded to offer life insurance, and then Flood's Auto delivery and processing service. The purpose of our auto delivery service was to move cars from the military and military affiliates to the ports of New Orleans for shipment. As a result of the untiring efforts of our staff, all of these services soon began to prosper and grow. Two years after our opening we moved our offices to business Highway 190 (now Veterans Memorial Blvd.) and Conder. We operated out of these offices for fourteen years. At this location, Income Tax Preparation service was added. I obtained my Broker/owner CRB status, and the Real Estate office had several licensed realtors to service clients.

On September 15, 1996, Flood Real Estate moved to its present location at 701 West Central Texas Expressway. This building was built for the business and is owned by me. It is the home of Flood Real Estate, which is also part of a conglomerate including: year round tax preparation; a full-service property management department; Western Union; and Briscoe Mortgage and Financial Services. Briscoe Mortgage and Financial Services is a mortgage loan department named in memory of my mother, Emma Briscoe Wallace. It is the part of the business that allows us the opportunity to help people realize the dream of home ownership. It is managed by my son, Leo. The experience of being in the military environment has enabled us to understand our customers and we are able to relate to their experiences. We use this knowledge to offer help and support in all areas in which we work. It is our goal to provide the best services available. We think of our company as "small enough to care, large enough to serve needs." This is not just a slogan for us; it is a way of life. Our plan is to be here for the customer. The establishment of the Real Estate Sales, Service and Property Management Company was a family accomplishment that is still growing and experiencing success. Flood Real Estate has been serving the Killeen/Fort Hood Area's Real Estate needs for over twenty-five years.

My immediate and extended family during those years of building a business also included our two children, Ericka and Leo III; my parents, William Wallace and Emma Briscoe Wallace, who are both deceased; and my three brothers. I am the youngest and only girl of four siblings. I was born in Port Arthur but reared in Beaumont, Texas. I graduated from Hebert High School in Beaumont, and attended Lamar University. I continued my post-graduate studies by attending the University of Maryland, Central Texas College and American Technological University. I hold an associate degree in Business Management.

As a family, we value each other, our love and the relationship that we share. At family gatherings we enjoy barbecuing, good food, playing games and good conversation. We also value the many friendships that we have made. Some of my happiest memories were at the birth of our two babies, Leo III and Ericka. Then in 2006 my happiness was sparked by the birth of my first grandchild, Sydney Alanah, who lives in Desoto, Texas with her parents, and is the "apple of my eye." It also brings me happiness knowing that I have two successful and productive adult children. Both Leo and Ericka are graduates of Killeen High School. Leo works in the family real estate business with me. He also manages the Briscoe Mortgage Loan Department within the business. Ericka lives in the Dallas/Desoto area. She is the coordinator for the Dallas Symphony Orchestra. Both Leo and Ericka have families of their own. My saddest memories were of the death of my mom.

For many years my talent for sewing gave me a feeling of accomplishment. This is also a hobby that has brought me much pleasure. I have been pleased with the family accomplishment and the individual achievement in our family. Then in 1990, I was appointed to the Killeen Independent School District Board of Trustees to complete the unexpired term of Board Trustee Kay Young. I have accepted this as an honor and as an individual achievement that pleased my community, my family and me. It generated much pride even though the length of the unexpired term was short. I did run as a candidate for this vacancy on the school board in the following year's election, but was not successful in being elected. However, because of this appointment I became Killeen Independent School District's School Board's first African American school board member.

Since we opened our doors for business in 1980, we have seen a lot of growth in this area. We watched the completion of the Killeen Mall, and we have seen the number of KISD schools grow tremendously. With the turn of the century, we are enjoying "Restaurant Row;" a regional airport; an abundance of hotel facilities; a civic and conference center; also a center that focuses on the theater arts. All of these changes have been exciting, and the most important part of it all is that we have been a part of it. Killeen is now home for me, and it is a very good place to live and work. We have also discovered the value of giving back to the community through service and by sharing other resources. Some of my involvement in the community, church and organizations include: serving as a planning and zoning commissioner; Chamber of Commerce Board Director; KISD School Board Trustee; Armed Forces YMCA Board Director; Community in Schools Director; Fort Hood Area Board of Realtors; and Rotary Club member. I am a member of Marlboro Missionary Baptist Church, and serve in the ministries of the church.

I don't see retirement anytime in the near future, but I would like to travel again when that day comes. Right now I would like to spend more time with Sydney. Our more than twenty-two years in the Army provided us many opportunities to travel. We have seen places and things that a lot of people only dreamed about. However, we still cherish the ideals of being Texans—Killeen, Texans. Over the years my experience as a businesswoman has given me greater faith. It has given me greater trust in my faith. I would advise anyone who is starting out in any vocation to:

- Investigate your options. Find out what that thing is that you really enjoy doing. Pursue your dream and never give up no matter what the obstacles. You will have snags. If you are following your passion, just hang in there; it will be worth it.
- Don't be afraid to make a "midcourse correction" if you made a mistake in your judgments. Only you can make that call. There is always room for correction. It is your life, and only you know what your true passion is.
- Visualize and see yourself "living your dream".

Edmond D. and Pamela Jones
Service to God, Country, and Community
Edmond Jones

I arrived in Killeen in October of 1972. Five years later I left for Korea and served a tour in Italy and Germany until 1991. I was reassigned to Fort Hood and returned to Killeen, Texas. My wife, Pamela Jones, and I are retired veterans of the U. S. Army. She joined the Army in 1979; served in the Regular Army until 1991; and in the National Guard from 1991-1999. She is a graduate of Excelsior University in New York and of Central Texas College in Killeen, Texas. Our son, William Jones, is a graduate of Harker Heights High School in Harker Heights, Texas. I joined Anderson Chapel AME Church in December, 1972 and as a long time faithful worker in the church I have served over the years as a Steward, Trustee, former first vice president of the Layman Ministry and former president of the Richard Allen Men's Ministry (formerly the Sons of Allen in the African Methodist Episcopal Church). My family also joined Anderson Chapel. Pamela serves as a Sunday school teacher and a Stewardess; she also serves in the Prayer and Mission Ministries of the church.

Our civic involvement in the community includes membership in K-COP. I give my service as a Killeen Citizens on Patrol (K-COP) within the community. Pam and I are graduates of the Killeen Citizen Police Academy. We give service to the community as members of the Killeen Citizen Alert Committee where I serve as president. We are also members of the Disabled American Veterans (DAV), and I serve as the chapter's Chaplain. Our active involvement in community organizations as life members includes the Veterans of Foreign Wars; membership in the American Legion; and life membership in the National Association for the Advancement of Colored People (NAACP), which is the oldest Black civil rights organization in the United States.

I have received recognition for community service which includes: A Certificate of Special Recognition for service to Hurricanes Katrina and Rita Victims. It was presented to me by Congressman J. Carter. I have also received the Legion of Honor Certificate Induction from Shriners, Inc., and the Certificate of Appreciation for Outstanding Service from Consistory #306. Former Mayor Maureen Jouett of the city of Killeen also honored me with a Certificate of Appreciation for service in the community.

My wife is a member of the Eastern Stars, the Daughters of Isis and the Golden Circle. My involvement as a member of the Masonic Family has been extensive and continuous. It includes:

- Past Patron of Star Light Chapter O.E.S. # 455 in Killeen, Texas
- Past Patron of Gladys Lee Court # 96 (charter member)
- Past Joshua of Leatha Hardeman Court #535 in Killeen, Texas (charter member)
- Presently serving as a member and chaplain of the New Light Lodge #242 in Killeen, Texas.
- Member of the 40th/8

Our community service, our church service and our organizational service are all focused on helping others have a better quality of life. We consider ourselves to be community builders.

CHAPTER 5

1980-1989:
Expanding Leadership Opportunities

—ᴍ—

Progress continued to be made in Killeen during this decade, and its population continued to grow. New arrivals, as well as some earlier arrivals, were prepared and willing to assume roles of responsibilities in community building and community leadership as opportunities opened. The 1980s newcomers included Charles and Jessie Bishop; Timothy and Maxine Hancock; Dr. Edward and Veronica Wagner; Colonel (Ret.) Otis and Rosalind Evans; James and Barbara Swift; Lloyd and Brenda Coley. This group of newcomers of the eighties became actively involved in the community's activities and emerged as leaders in responsible roles. They did not hesitate to make significant contributions to community building in the interest of the city and its citizens in areas of education, entrepreneurship, health services, public service in city government, and community service.

Jessie Bishop voluntarily gives community service in the non-profit organization of Habitat for Humanity in which she continues to serve as a member of the Board of Directors. She expanded her commitment to community service first within the local chapter of her sorority, serving as Killeen Alumnae Chapter of Delta Sigma Theta's president for two consecutive two-year terms.

Timothy Hancock was elected to the Killeen City Council and completed three two-year terms of service. His council members4 elected him Mayor Pro tem. He also later became Killeen's first African American Mayor. In addition, he is an entrepreneur and owner of a bus company: Arrow Trailways of Texas Bus Line.

James Swift took over the leadership of Killeen Independent School District's Compensatory Education Department, which included the Title I, Bilingual, and English as a Second Language Programs in 1987, and steadily guided the Chapter I Program improvements over several years to receiving State and Federal recognition.

Colonel (Ret.) Otis Evans was successful in providing committed community service in several leadership roles: His election to the council; appointment to the council as a Charter Revision Committee member; NAACP 1st Vice President and President; Senior <u>Vice Commander of VFW 9191, as an appointed council member filling an unexpired</u> City Council term; and CTC instructor at the Texas Department of Correction at Gatesville.

Dr. Edward Wagner became an adjunct faculty at the University of Central Texas teaching graduate and undergraduate courses in mathematics and statistics. He was a member of Simmonsville Baptist in 1987 and led his father to Christ in 1989 and was the first African American elected a school board trustee in 1992.

Brenda Coley began her service in the community as the Human Resource Director at Sallie Mae, a loan service organization; then moved on to the position of Human Resource Executive Director for Metroplex Health System. Later, became the first African American school board President.

Rosa Hereford, a newcomer to Killeen in 1966 and an educator in the Killeen School District explored an interest in the political arena of public service in city government and became the first woman elected to the Killeen City Council in 1984. She served three consecutive two-year terms until 1990.

Dr. Bernice Moland, a newcomer to Killeen in the early sixties (1961or1962) as an educator. She was appointed Principal of West Ward Elementary School in 1988.She was the third African American Elementary school principal appointed in KISD. She later served as the Assistant to the Superintendent of KISD.

Charles and Jessie Bishop
Community Service that Makes a Difference
Jessie Bishop

My husband, Charles Bishop, our son Kevin and I are originally from Lake Providence, Louisiana. We arrived in the Killeen area in July, 1983 and acquired housing on Fort Hood where we lived for one year until my husband's retirement. Being assigned at Fort Hood provided opportunities for which our family is grateful. The central Texas area was nearer to home than any other duty station to which we had been assigned. From central Texas, we enjoyed many quick trips home to visit our family.

The quality of the Killeen School System influenced us to remain in the area and when our son Kevin graduated from Killeen High School, he attended and graduated from Texas A & M University. After graduation, Kevin lived and worked in Fort Worth Texas for three years. He now resides in Atlanta, Georgia with his wife and family giving back to his community. The Killeen area has also afforded our family the opportunity to be a part of a diverse community and experience a wonderful quality of life. After my husband retired from the military in 1984, we continued our affiliation with the military community as we were both employed on Ft. Hood and attended Protestant Chapel services at the 4ID Memorial Chapel. I have been a member of the choir at the chapel for many years.

I have personally been involved with the Ft. Hood Area Habitat for Humanity since its inception. I served on the Board of Directors and as chair for the Selection Committee of Habitat for Humanity.

I am a member of the Killeen Alumnae Chapter of Delta Sigma Theta Sorority, Inc., and served two consecutive two-year terms as president of the chapter. Delta Sigma Theta Sorority, Inc. is a public service organization of college women. Since 1974 Killeen Alumnae Chapter of Delta Sigma Theta Sorority, Inc. has provided service within the Killeen, Harker Heights, and Copperas Cove communities by annually awarding scholarships to graduating seniors, conducting health symposiums, sponsoring political forums, donating to crisis and food centers, supporting service activities sponsored by the city, providing entertainment to nursing home, mentoring girls through our Youth Initiatives of Delta Academy and Delta GEMS. A third youth initiative sponsored by the chapter is the Debutante Cotillion program which targets high school senior girls whom we mentor and present them to society as debutantes. There have also been other service projects the sorority performed within the community. My husband, an avid golfer, routinely played in charitable tournaments in the area. The central Texas area is a good place to live and work.

Timothy and Maxine Hancock
Military, Entrepreneur, Political and Selfless Service
Timothy Hancock

We moved to the Killeen-Fort Area in 1982 because of military orders which assigned us to Fort Hood, Texas. My wife, Maxine, and I are natives of Mineola, Texas. Our immediate and extended family includes our sons: Michael, Craig and Ronald; grand-daughters: Brittany and Vanessa; and grandsons: Xavier, Joshua and Blair. Our family members are natives of Texas, Okinawa, California and North Carolina. Michael was born in California, Craig in Okinawa and Ronald in Mineola, Texas. Michael has a son and daughter; Craig, a son and daughter; and Ronald, a son.

When we arrived in the area in 1982, Killeen was celebrating its one hundredth birthday. The military exercise, Reforger, was in the news; the city's growth and the beginning of its expansion were taking place; and the population of the city was increasing. The area was also experiencing economic and social conditions at that time. There existed a housing shortage; downtown Avenue D was not very well thought of as a family environment for shopping; the crime rate and DWI rate appeared high. Nolanville's traffic ticketing was a concern, and the interest rates were high.

My employment opportunities were limited to my active military duty when we arrived in the Killeen area. My wife, the former Maxine McDowell, did not work, but took care of the family and the home. Later, after retirement, my employment opportunities expanded and moved toward a career in transportation. It included my employment with Southwest Transit Bus Company and with Killeen Independent School District (KISD), as well as, with my ownership of the Temple and Belton bus stations, and my ownership of Arrow Trailways of Texas bus line. I was familiar with some facets of transportation. In the forties, my father owned and operated several trucks. My brothers and I worked with my father. He contracted to buy trees, cut them down and then sold them. We worked cutting and hauling pulpwood. The trees were converted into an assortment of wood products for building and others purposes. We sold blocks of wood for housing and logs for industry to make cross ties for railroad tracks, to cut telephone poles and light poles.

My involvement in bus transportation came about in an unexpected way. In 1982 when I was assigned to Fort Hood I attended an AUSA meeting and met a Colonel whom I had met earlier during my military career. Eleven months later, he called me for an interview to which I attended. I was interviewed by Stan Lohse and was hired in October, 1983 to work there for Southwest Transit Bus Company. I worked there from 1983-1988. Southwest Transit Bus Company was sold in 1986 and a new owner came in. The company had been placed in bankruptcy and under its new ownership became American Arrow Bus Company. The new owner began its reorganization within the company, which was still under bankruptcy, and brought in their own management team. I worked for American Arrow from 1986-1988.

In 1988, I left the company as reorganization was in progress; purchased two bus stations; and began running bus stations in Belton and Temple, Texas. This left the American Arrow owners to run their own company. As time went on, the company began experiencing problems and I was rehired to run the company. However, even as I returned as an employee of American Arrow, I retained my two bus stations in Belton and Temple. The company did not come out of bankruptcy until 1990. The workers were concerned about their jobs as the ownership began to change or separate; and they said to me, "Why don't you buy the company?" After some thought about the question, I did not go to the new owners of the company, but I went to the owner of the assets of the company. I purchased the bus company that was then operating under the name of Southwestern Coaches dba Arrow Trailways of Texas. I became the owner of the company in 1992. The Arrow Bus line is the original Kerrville Bus line that was operating in 1944. It is the bus line that refused to let Jackie Robinson, a U.S. Army officer, ride. No one would have imagined the change that would come about in future years. Now, a black man owns that bus line.

I consider myself to be a lifelong learner. I have attended Prairie View A and M University, Joliet College, El Paso Community College and Purdue University. I have received specialized training related to business and transportation in a program out of Purdue, and earned my certification through this program. I am a certified Transportation Industry Specialist.

Our family's involvement in church, organizations and the community includes participation in the Fort Hood Military Chapels; the NAACP; the VFW; the Killeen Chamber of Commerce Board of Directors; the AUSA Board of Directors; and my political and public service involvement as a Killeen City Councilman and as Mayor of the city of Killeen.

As a family, we are grateful for the achievements that we have experienced in the Killeen-Fort Hood area. Our family shares my honorable service in the military; our ownership of a transportation company; my election as a Killeen City Councilman; and the opportunity to have served as Killeen City Council Mayor Pro tem. They also share my election as the Mayor of the city of Killeen, and the honor of being

Killeen's first black Mayor. They share my selection as a Fort Hood Good Neighbor, and the many community honors and recognition that I received from various organizations and agencies. The support of my wife, Maxine Hancock, who is a co-honoree in these achievements, has been exceptional in our realizing our many accomplishments.

As a family, we are also grateful for the accomplishments we have made in locations beyond the Killeen-Fort Hood Area. In our hometown of Mineola, Texas we have, as a family, successfully completed projects and are currently pursuing projects for the welfare of that community. Three goals that are very important and dear to us have been achieved for this small community. The first goal was the establishment of the "Addie E. McFarland Foundation," honoring the principal of our school when Maxine and I were students. The Foundation has as one of its purposes to award a scholarship every year to help a student in the community to attend college. The second goal was the renovation of the junior high school in the South Side community of Mineola, Texas, for use as a community center. Our third goal was the conversion of the gym of our former community school (which sits on seven acres of land that we purchased and gave back to the Foundation), into the "L. C. Gregory Recreation Center," honoring our school coach in our hometown community of Mineola, Texas, and providing recreational opportunities for the families there. It's about giving back to a community and remembering our roots.

Some of our family's happiest memories are being able to serve this community in many small ways: helping citizens toward the accomplishment of some of their goals, assisting young people with opportunities to continue their education and achieve other personal goals. The continuation of post-high school education is a focused commitment of Timothy Hancock and my wife, the former Maxine McDowell. Many high school graduates in the Killeen Independent School Districts have been recipients of scholarship assistance from us. Organizations and agencies have also been the recipients of our generosity. Our personal welfare and the welfare of people are important and valued by our family. We consider our desire to help families and our youth to be a special calling or gift in our lives. It brings us much pleasure.

Our sons are responsible and productive adults, and have made us very proud. Maxine, as a nurturing mother in our home, made a desirable and positive difference in the lives of our sons. Michael's interest was in aviation. He aspired to become a pilot. He is a Tarleton University graduate; at this writing, he is now on active duty, has the rank of Major and is a helicopter pilot. Our son Craig is also a Tarleton University graduate and served on active duty in Iraq. He has the rank of Warrant Officer. Ronald, our youngest son, is an Ellison High School graduate, and received a full scholarship in track at the University of Texas in Arlington. He ran track with Michael Johnson, the "All American" of Baylor University. He is now in Management and Retail Services and is currently manager of a Walmart Super Center. After entering a manager's training program at Walmart, within three years he had gotten his store. We are grateful for his career success in his managerial venture. First he became a Walmart co-manager in Ft. Worth; then became a manager of a Walmart store in Kansas that was experiencing difficulties, and he turned that store around. Next, he managed a store in Cedar Park, near Austin, Texas. This store was also experiencing difficulties, and he turned that store around. A third opportunity was presented to him to manage a store in Indiana that was also having its difficulties. Again, Michael turned that store around. He then became the manager of a new store, a Walmart Super Center.

We have experienced extensive travel throughout the United States via air, bus, train and automobile. Our overseas travel includes Korea, Okinawa, Japan, Guam, Wake Island, Europe and South America. Killeen, Texas, is now our home, and we have been blessed with the opportunity to give back to the community through our service and resources. Giving back service as community builders has been a fullfilling experience.

James T. Swift, Jr.
An Educator who is committed to the Education of Students
James Swift, Jr.

I am a Dallas native who arrived in the Killeen-Harker Heights area in the fall of 1987 and was employed by the Killeen Independent School District (KISD) as the Director of the Federal Compensatory Programs: Title I (now changed to Chapter I), Bilingual, and English as a Second Language. As a student at St. Anthony Catholic School, James Madison High School and later, college, I had no thought of becoming a part of a school district as unique, as diverse and as mobile as KISD. Because of the preparation that I received while at St. Anthony Catholic School, James Madison High School, Huston-Tilliston College, Prairie View A and M University, University of Texas, Baylor University and the Texas Education Agency; together, the Federal Compensatory Programs, department staff under my supervision, and the support of principals and teachers at the campuses brought recognition to the Killeen Independent School District. It also brought knowledge, success and pride to the students; and satisfaction to the staff for a job well done. Prior to joining the Killeen Independent School District, I had been a school teacher and an administrator in the Austin Independent School District. I had also served as an administrator with the Texas Education Agency (TEA) in Austin, Texas. Three of the many things that impressed me upon my arrival in the Killeen area were: the growth of the city of Killeen, the school district and Fort Hood. I was also impressed by the concern of minorities in the community about the number of Blacks employed in the Killeen Independent District, especially at the administrative levels. I also thought that Killeen was an interesting military town.

My family includes my wife, Barbara Sue; two sons, James T. Swift, III and David K Swift; and our grandchildren. My wife, Sue Swift, is a graduate of the University of Texas at Austin, and employed as an administrator with the Texas Rehabilitation Commission. James, III and David are both KISD high school graduates. James T. Swift, III is also a graduate of Southwest Texas University, and David K. Swift is a graduate of Southern Methodist University. Both of whom are responsible citizens giving back to the respective communities in ways that make us proud as parents. My father was a businessman in Dallas, and his mother and grandmother were housewives. One of my grandfathers was a Methodist minister in Marshall, Texas and my other grandfather was a farmer. My aspiration was to be a priest. During our stay in Killeen the family became members of Anderson Chapel AME Church in Killeen and the Cornerstone Baptist Church in Harker Heights. Our faith is very important to us. In addition to our faith which we greatly value, the Swift family also values strong family love and support, friends and education.

My community involvement included membership in the NAACP; Omega Psi Phi Fraternity, a fraternity dedicated to public service; and the Killeen Chamber of Commerce. In addition to the Compensatory Program activities, my involvement included participating in the Communities in Schools (CIS) Program and the Families in Crisis Program. My commitment to the education of students and the support given to community earned recognition for me as Man of the Year, Educator of the Year and Boss of the Year. In 1992, the Central Texas Annual Conference of the African Methodist Episcopal (AME) Church honored me as Man of the Year for my yearly outstanding contributions in assistance throughout the local communities. During that same period in 1992, our department was putting together tutorial programs for young adults and helping to obtain scholarships for deserving minority youth. Three former compensatory education students in KISD had then been awarded college scholarships. A summer program had been approved to be used with computers at kindergarten and first-grade levels. My personal giving back to the community in other ways includes volunteering for many years to coach a little league organization in the Austin and the Killeen areas, and I continue to help those in need whichever way I can.

My experience with the Killeen Independent School District has been a rewarding one. During the time that I served, the program's name changed from "Title I" to "Chapter I," and the Director's title changed to "Director for Compensatory and Federal Programs." However, the name change from Title 1 to Chapter it did not change the mission, goals and objectives of the programs. Therefore, our staff and the classroom teachers kept the emphasis on improving student academic performance, and bringing boys and girls up to grade level. (Title I is part of the Federal Elementary and Secondary Education Act, which was a program started by the late President Lyndon B. Johnson as part of his Great Society Program.)

In 1991, the Chapter I Program, conducted through the Killeen Independent School District, earned high marks for the high standards and quality of the program. KISD Chapter 1 was recognized as one of four programs in the state of Texas, and one of 105 programs in the United States to earn recognition by the U.S. Department of Education as an outstanding Chapter I Program. Dr. Charles Patterson, Killeen Independent School District Superintendent, as well as U.S. and State Officials, all recognized me for the leadership I provided toward KISD's accomplishment of receiving both state and national recognition for excellence with a successful Chapter I Program. Superintendent Charles Patterson and I also attribute much of the success of the Killeen programs to parental involvement and to an enthusiastic staff. Therefore, the parents also deserve congratulations.

In announcing the Chapter I Program recognition, commendations were received from local, state and national officials. Texas Education Agency included Killeen Independent School District in the permanent records of the State Board of Education; selected KISD to participate in a Leadership Special Program and selected Chapter 1 to participate in a six-year study of an outstanding Compensatory program.

Commendations were extended to me, personally, for providing invaluable service of counseling, tutoring and summer experiences that were positive reinforcement and a big motivational incentive for the students. However, I must acknowledge that the experience and achievement that I had received from the Texas Education Agency had provided me with the expertise to put into motion special programs designed to meet the needs of all children of the district.

In 1997, The Chapter I Program again received recognition. Commissioner Mike Moses of the Texas Education Commissioner in congratulating the programs for achieving these high levels of performance among the students served in the Title programs stated that, "They are outstanding examples of the many schools across the state that are providing those students in high poverty schools with the knowledge and skills they need to improve their lives and become successful adults." I enjoy athletics and have a very competitive nature as a person. I strongly believe and am convinced that the importance of a positive Black role model cannot be overemphasized in the home, in schools, in church or in the community.

During my employment in KISD I suffered a personal event of sadness. Obstacles have challenged many families, and my family and I faced a personal challenge to overcome. October 16, 1991, as a result of the Luby's Cafeteria tragedy, became our saddest memory. My recovery later became our happiest memory. It was "Boss's Day and some of my co-workers had taken me to lunch at Luby's Cafeteria in Killeen, Texas. While dining there a gunman rammed his pickup truck into a crowded Luby's Cafeteria during the lunch hour and opened fire indiscriminately on the patrons. I was among the victims of that tragedy. I was shot by the assailant and required hospitalization for several months. Two co-workers died in the tragedy along with more than twenty other persons who were dining at Luby's that day. There were also mass injuries in this tragedy. I am a grateful survivor of this horrendous tragedy and this is an event that I will always remember. My motto has often been "Success is a testament of Hope." Helping students succeed is what community builders do. I am a community builder.

Dr. Edward L. and Veronica Wagner
Family, Educator, Mentor and Ministry
Dr. Edward L. Wagner

 I am a native of Monroe, Louisiana; a 1967 high school graduate; and a graduate of Southern University, where I met and married my wife, the former Veronica Vernice Williams. My wife, Veronica was a "stay-at-home" mom until all our children left home. Then she returned to college, received her degree from the University of Mary Harden Baylor in 1997, and joined the workforce. We are proud parents of three outstanding children, Voranique, Lee and Vania. Voranique Wagner Simon, our oldest daughter, a 1993 Texas A&M graduate, is a Registered Professional Engineer with the Engineering firm of HMTB, Corp. of Dallas, Texas. Lee, our only son, also a Texas A&M graduate is a Mechanical Engineer. Our youngest daughter, Vania Wagner Walker, a Baylor University graduate, chose college preparation in the field of social work. These adult siblings now have families of their own. Blake and Voranique Simon are the parents of sons, Brandon and Andrew; Roderick and Vania Walker are the parents of sons, Jaylen and Jackson. And there is Edward Lee Wagner II and Jennifer Wagner. Veronica and I hold the prestigious position of being proud parents and grandparents who cherish the memorable events and experiences we share with our family. We are a very close family. One of my many memories of happiness in our family is when the children were young and we would gather around the fireplace and I would share with them how I grew up. They would listen patiently, ask questions and would genuinely be interested in those stories, even though I would tell them over and over. Sometimes, our oldest daughter would even ask me to tell those stories.

We value the importance of family and unity! This is when a family is working hard, staying together, giving to our community and trying to make things better for the next generation. Most of our travel has been going home to Louisiana and visiting family each year so that our children would know their extended family. Our family also values the importance of education. My wife and I, all of our children and their spouses are college graduates. We will encourage all of the grandchildren to do the same. The greatest aspiration that we have for our family is to have five generations of two-parent homes. This aspiration started with me and my wife. Each of our children has families with two-parent homes; now it is left up to our grandchildren and their children's children to aspire for the same. Growing up, my grandparents' home became my two-parent home with two people to guide and provide for, me and my brother, as best they could.

You see, I was born in Rayville, Louisiana and as a child did not enjoy the privilege of living in a two-parent home. Instead, I lived in a two-grandparent home. My parents were living together, but not married when I was born. My father left shortly after I was born and my mother left shortly after his departure, thus leaving my brother and me to be raised by our maternal grandparents. My grandfather had a fourth grade education, and my grandmother never went to school a day of her life. We grew up in a poor, segregated environment with sub-standard schools, limited jobs for blacks and the sting of prejudice throughout the community. All of which were obstacles I had to overcome.

My grandparents knew the value of education; therefore, they ensured that I went to school every day and did my best. Despite being a poor family that could not afford to send me to college, I was able to attend college on a scholarship. My school teachers took an interest in me and always encouraged me to do my best. God always had a *"ram in the bush"* for me in every endeavor. I stand on the shoulders of many black men and women that not only encouraged me, but took an interest in me to point me in the right direction. Mrs. Mansfield, my high school math teacher, made sure that I took every math course the school had to offer. Mrs. Draper (my fourth grade teacher) and Mrs. Minor (my high school English teacher) made me develop a love for reading. Mr. Calvin (my eighth grade teacher) made sure that I learned to think about the consequences of all my actions. All these people and more inspired me to want a college education, and made sure that I was ready to achieve when the door of opportunity swung open. Thanks for wonderful teachers and other community leaders, I was able to overcome: poverty, poor male role models, segregation, limited education opportunities, a broken home and much more.

I was sixteen years old when I met my father and I have seen my mother less than a dozen times in my life (usually when there was death in the family). When I met my father I was a Christian; therefore, I was able to receive him into my life and have no need to ask any "why" questions. My father and I developed a wonderful relationship and visited often. He was the proudest man in all of Louisiana when I received my Ph.D. I became the happiest man in all of Louisiana when I was able to lead my father to Christ in 1989. This experience was also another one of my happiness memories in my life. My father died in 1996. I was very proud that God gave me the opportunity to lead him to salvation before he died.

Obtaining an education made a great difference in my life. My educational preparation included obtaining a Bachelor of Science Degree in Mathematics; a Bachelor of Science Degree in Civil Engineering; a Master of Science Degree in Civil Engineering; a Master of Arts in Management; and the Doctor of Philosophy Degree in Philosophy of Religion from Southwest Baptist Theological Seminary. My military experience includes a career as an officer, which spanned over twenty years where I was branched in the Corps of Engineers. I have management experience in a variety of top-level positions involving decision making, problem solving and people-oriented leadership. One of my most rewarding assignments was as Associate Professor in the Department of Engineering at the United States Military Academy, West Point, New York. During this assignment, I taught structural steel design to the senior class.

When we arrived in the area we purchased a home, and after getting the family situated, I was assigned to Korea. So I left my family here and spent the next year in Korea. Upon returning in April 1987, I was assigned to the Combined Arms Operation Research Activity at West Fort Hood. I spent the next four years there and after a rewarding career I retired December 1, 1991. When I returned to the area in 1987 I was not active within the community; my military duties had kept me extremely busy. However, having three children in school I did notice that there were very few black teachers, and almost no black administrators within the schools that my children attended. After my retirement I became involved in the community. During this time I was an Adjunct Faculty with the University of Central Texas, teaching graduate and undergraduate courses in mathematics and statistics. Some of my community activities included serving as a member of the Governmental Affairs Committee of the Greater Killeen Chamber of Commerce in 1996-1998; president of the Killeen Branch NAACP in 1992; and member of the Killeen Independent School District (KISD) Board of Trustees in 1992-1997. During 1996-1997 school years, I served as vice president of The Board. My election to KISD's Board of Trustees holds historical significance. I hold the distinction of being the first Black elected to the Killeen Independent School District Board of Trustees. After serving six years on the board of trustees, my support of the KISD mission continued in at least two unique ways:

1) As a member of the "KISD Bond Election Campaign Task Force" and the citizen's approval made available funding for the construction and expansion of school facilities to accommodate a growing student population.
2) As a member of the "KISD Foundation" which provides funding of Teachers' grants for the implementation of curriculum projects which expand students thinking, their knowledge, and their love for learning.

I am the founder and senior pastor of Cornerstone Baptist Church (a church that I founded in September 1995). The church is a vision from God through me. Its purpose is: (1) to bring people to Jesus and membership in His family; (2) to develop them to Christ-like maturity; and (3) to equip them for their ministry in the church and their mission in the world in order to magnify God's name. The vision of Cornerstone Baptist Church is to model God's message of hope, power and love in the community we serve and beyond. I have more than 31 years in the Gospel Ministry, serving a diverse spectrum of Christian ministries. A number of awards and honors have been bestowed on Cornerstone Baptist Church. The noted honors include the "Salt and Light Award;" the "Pacesetter Award;" Recognition as "the #1 Church in Cooperative Program Contributions;" and Recognition with honors by achieving for three years being one of the "Top Ten Churches in Cooperative Program Contributions." The "Charles H. Spurgeon Outstanding Church Award" also honored Cornerstone Baptist Church for being one of the Top 200 Healthy Churches in the State of Texas.

Prior to the founding of Cornerstone Baptist Church, my church involvement included service in the ministry: 1992-1994 Associate Pastor, Comanche Chapel at Fort Hood, Texas; 1990-1991 Associate Pastor, Providence Missionary Baptist Church, Marlin, Texas; and 1987-1990 Member at Simmonsville Missionary Baptist Church, Killeen, Texas.

In addition to being actively involved in the activities of our local community and our neighboring communities by giving back to them in positive ways, I had many other opportunities to give of my service to other causes and groups. These included:

- 1993-1996: Served on the Central Texas University Task Force. The group that was formed to bring a four-year state-supported university to Killeen.
- 1993-1995: Served as a member of the Central Texas Council of Government.
- 1993-Present: Serve as mentor and advisor to a group of minority professionals that is making a career transition into the teaching field.
- 1992-1995: Served in the Comanche Chapel Mentor and Tutoring Program, working one day each week with young people to tutor them in math and mentor them in life skills.
- 1991- Present: Serve as mentor for a host of young black boys, ages 12-18.
- 1992-Present: I have been a motivational speaker for secondary and post-secondary student events, and keynote speaker for community and state professional organizations, among which are the: Baptist General Convention of Texas African-American Fellowship Conference; Central Texas

College Graduation Commencement and Student Services, Heart of Texas Boy Scouts Council Annual Breakfast; and others.

I have received local and state honors, awards and recognition for which I am grateful:

- April 23, 1999—Appointed by Governor George W. Bush to the Protective and Regulatory Board of the State of Texas. This board regulates all Child Protective services and adult protective services within the state of Texas.
- 1998—Honored by Central Texas College Family by receiving the Central Texas College (CTC) Public Service Award for my contribution to the community.
- 1998—Selected the Omega Psi Phi Man of the Year; I am also the recipient of the Alpha Kappa Alpha Community Service Award.
- I have been honored with a nomination for the Jefferson Award.

My Public service has made a positive difference in the community.

Colonel (Ret.) Otis and Rosalind Evans
Committed Leadership and Community Service
Colonel (Ret.) Otis Evan

I am a native of Brenham, Texas, and Rosalind is a native of Decatur, Georgia. We are parents of a daughter and two sons. Our immediate family includes: daughter, Donna Allseitz, and husband Evan; son, Russell Evans, and wife Tanisha; son, Anthony; grandsons Dante and Brandin; and a great-granddaughter, Kailyn. Donna and husband live in Woodbridge, Virginia and are employed by the U.S. Central

Intelligence Agency. Her husband is employed in the Pentagon (he was present in the facility during the 9/11 attacks). Russell is a graduate of Prairie View and works with the agency that provides computer technical support for the Texas Lottery. Anthony is an active duty soldier. He is stationed at Fort Hood, and has completed two deployments to Iraq. On his last deployment, he was awarded the Bronze Star Medal. Patches is our Calico cat. She is currently unemployed and generally mooches off the family. Even though we left Killeen on occasions due to my military assignment, we kept returning to the area.

After graduation from Pickard High School in Brenham, Texas, I attended Prairie View A & M College and received a B.S. Degree in Agricultural Education. I also received my M.A. Degree in Management and Public Administration from Webster University in St. Louis, Missouri. During my military career, I received a wide variety of training in the U.S. Army, ranging from field medical operations, helicopter pilot certification and hospital administration, to culminate as a graduate of U.S. Army War College. I earned a number of Army medals while on active duty. They range from the Army Achievement Medal to the Distinguished Flying Cross, the Legion of Merit and the Silver Star Medal.

Rosalind is a graduate of Trinity High School, Decatur, Georgia. She maintains a current cosmetologist license. Currently, Rosalind has become very creative in making a variety of handcrafted home decorative items which she has turned into a small business. The uniqueness of the products has been well received and has brought requests from many sources.

In 1971, after a tour in Vietnam as a helicopter ambulance pilot, I returned to Fort Hood to command the Post's first Medical Helicopter Evacuation Unit. The military installation and Killeen had not changed much. The social atmosphere was essentially the same except there was increasing unrest from the Vietnam anti-war activists. Of special note was the visit from Jane Fonda and her anti-war entourage. Desegregation was well underway, as was the case in most Texas cities.

Our residency as a family in Killeen began in 1983 when we purchased our home here and resided here from 1984-1987. However,

I had previously come to the Killeen/Fort Hood area as early as 1967 as a recent graduate from Prairie View A&M and newly commissioned 2nd Lieutenant. Fort Hood was my first duty station. Fort Hood was the Army of the sixties and was primarily engaged in supporting the war effort in Vietnam. Killeen was the typical Army town that catered to the demands of soldiers. There were numerous car dealers, laundry/dry cleaning establishments, barbershops, local finance companies, pawnshops, nightclubs and stores that sold military-unique items. Socially, Killeen mirrored most Texas towns of the sixties. The races and ethnic groups tolerated each other, but kept to their separate social/traditional practices. The cost of living in Killeen was very reasonable for the prudent person.

In 1984, as a newly promoted Lieutenant Colonel, I returned to Fort Hood/Killeen for a third tour to discover phenomenal growth on the installation. All vestiges of the Vietnam era anti-war sentiments were gone as the Post focused heavily on training and readiness. I witnessed similar strides in the city. There was now an expressway through the city; a shopping mall; and two high schools. At that time, we purchased our current residence in the Turtle Bend sub-division. The cost of living in Killeen was very reasonable. However, the interest rates on home mortgages were exorbitant. Killeen was chosen the site of retirement because our youngest son wanted to complete high school in Killeen, Texas.

Upon retirement from the Army in 1994 and having attained the rank of Colonel, Rosalind and I returned to Killeen. Significant growth had occurred in the scant ten years that we had been gone. We moved back into our home in Turtle Bend. Rosalind began to work as a Library Assistant at Ellison High School. I took a part-time job with Central Texas College as instructor at the Texas Department of Corrections in Gatesville, Texas. I subsequently found employment in long-term health care at Wesleyan Homes in Georgetown, Texas. I have been employed at Wesleyan as Facilities Manager since 1997. Of interest, it was very difficult for me to readily find a job compatible with my professional training and experience in the Killeen area. It's not that the jobs weren't here; they were all taken.

I have been involved in community service since 2001. I have served on the City of Killeen Charter Revision Committee; first Vice

President and President of the Killeen Branch NAACP; Senior Vice Commander of VFW 9191; and in May 2006 was elected to serve my first term (a two-year term) as Councilmember, City of Killeen Municipal Government. In May 2008, I was appointed to serve out the unexpired term of a former councilwoman after my unsuccessful race for re-election. Rosalind participates in numerous city-sponsored events, including opening festivities for the Killeen Civic and Conference Center, opening festivities for the regional airport and the 125th birthday celebration for the city.

We have predominantly kept our worship to the Protestant non-denominational churches on Fort Hood and have not sought or maintained membership in any local church. I maintain an association with my hometown church in Brenham, Texas.

Typical to most military families is the periodic movement from one geographical locale to another. There is always the stress of moving children from one school environment to another and the stress that a spouse endures related to frequent employment changes. Frequent moves, especially overseas, often bring financial stress, as well as separation from familiar friends and family. To lessen the impact of frequent relocation of the family, we have always sought military assignments that would accommodate relocation of the family unit versus relocation of only the military sponsor (active duty soldier).

By the very nature of the service in the U.S. Armed Forces, military families travel all over the contiguous United States, as well as abroad. Except for combat duty, my family traveled as much as possible with me. Each assignment brought opportunities to visit places that the average family could only see via special vacation events. We have visited Niagara falls, the Grand Canyon, Gettysburg, Tombstone, Pikes Peak, Death Valley and Diamond Head, to name a few. We have traveled to Germany, Korea, Panama, Italy, France, Holland, Great Britain and Canada, to name a few.

Killeen has become a great place to live and work. The demographics are truly diverse. There is opportunity for both personal and professional growth. These opportunities do not just jump out and grab you. You must put some effort in finding them. We have found them, and we are quite happy. Civic responsibility and service for a better community are what community builders do.

Lloyd and Brenda Coley
Exemplary Leadership and Service
Brenda Coley

Service is an intricate part of our family's life. Service rendered in the military and service in the community. My husband, Lloyd Coley, Retired Command Sergeant Major, and I came to the Killeen-Fort Hood area as a career military family. Lloyd is a native of Virginia and I am a native of Florida. We have been blessed with over thirty-one wonderful years of marriage. We are the parents of two adult children, Ebonie and Justin. Ebonie is a 1998 graduate of Killeen High School. Justin is a 2004 graduate of Harker Heights High School. The Coleys believe that "family" is important, and they value the family relationship that they share. They also value the friendships that they have experienced, both as a family and as individuals.

Lloyd's military career spans over thirty years in the United States Army where he bravely and with honor served our country protecting the freedoms we all enjoy. In addition to his assignment to Fort Hood, his military tours of duty included Fort Bliss; Korea; Mainz, Germany; Mannheim, Germany; and Iraq. He retired in 2004 from a rewarding career of military service. He and the family are now engaged in the community.

My service in this area began while Lloyd was on active duty when I began working with Sallie Mae, a loan service organization, as their first Human Resource Director. From this position other opportunities with even greater responsibilities opened up for me and I became the Metroplex Health System Human Resource Executive Director. I am a graduate of Florida State University and have also earned a degree from The University of Central Texas (Tarleton University) in Killeen.

In 1996, I became the first Black woman elected to serve as a school board trustee for the Killeen Independent School District.

My election as a school board trustee began an eleven year tenure of service to the children, teachers, parents and all citizens of Killeen, Harker Height, Nolanville and Fort Hood in the interest of education in our community. During the last three years of my eleven year tenure on the board I served as president of the School Board. Now I hold the distinction of being the first Black ever to hold the position of president of the Killeen Independent School District Board of Trustees. At the end of my eleventh year in office I did not seek re-election to the board and submitted my resignation effective at the end of May, 2007. I was honored on May 9, 2007 by the KISD Community and the citizens of Killeen, Harker Heights, Fort Hood and Nolanville for the service I had contributed to this community.

Over the years, my membership on several organizational boards in the community also provided me opportunities for service within the community. I served as a member of: the Board of Directors for Families in Crisis; the Greater Killeen Chamber of Commerce; the Board of Regents of the University of Central Texas; the Executive Board of Communities in Schools; the Board of Directors for the YWCA; and the Killeen Evening Rotary.

Our family's church membership is at Cornerstone Baptist Church, and we have been actively involved in the ministries of the church. I am one of the founding members of Cornerstone; Lloyd is a deacon of the church; Ebonie was the church's first pianist; and Justin assisted with the audio/visual ministry.

I am the recipient of the "Mu Theta Omega Award" presented by Alpha Kappa Alpha Sorority, Inc. in recognition of my service to Education.

Upon Lloyd's retirement, the family chose to remain in the Killeen area where we were given the opportunity to make a significant contribution to the community. Killeen is the first community in which we've lived that felt like home.

CHAPTER 6

1990-1999:
Witnessing Prolific
Leadership Opportunities

—ɷ—

K illeen's population had reached 64,200 residents by the 1990s, and Killeen continued to experience a steady population growth. During these ten years, opportunities continued to emerge and events continued to occur that left the community with a bright and hopeful outlook. Opportunities for African American leadership increased. Plans for opening an upper-level university program and beginning construction of a larger and modern airport were being made. These projects were expected to provide a better quality of life for all residents therefore, there was much excitement. The 1990s also became the decade for giving recognition to a national African American leader, a local African American leader and an African American Military unit with street namesakes in their honor. Approval for the recognition was given by the Killeen City Council. May 13, 1990 marked the date of the naming of Dr. Martin Luther King Jr. Boulevard in Killeen; March 23, 1992, marked the date of the naming of Rev. R. A. Abercrombie Drive in Killeen; and August 2, 1996, marked the date of the naming of 761 Tank Battalion Avenue in Killeen.

The decade of the 90s brought five African Americans civic leaders to the forefront: Connie Green, Dr. Edward Wagner, Alexander Vernon, Darryl Holmes and Brenda Coley for their contributions to community building and service. The decade continued receiving newcomers to the city. Among the community's newcomers of this decade were Ernest Wilkerson; Bernard "BaBatunde" Jones and his wife Johnnie; also Leon Chisholm and his wife Terry. They also participated in the *TAPESTRY* project.

Connie Green accepted the appointment from the Killeen City Council as Director of Finance of the City of Killeen in May 1990 and became a part of Killeen's developing history as the first African American to serve in this position. He was appointed City Manager in July, 2005 and became Killeen's first African American City Manager.

Dr. Edward Wagner was elected to the Killeen School Board in 1992 and served until 1997. He was the first African American to be elected as trustee to the Killeen Independent School District School Board. He also served as Vice President of the School Board during his last year on the board and He became the founding pastor of Cornerstone Baptist Church in Harker Heights, Texas in 1995. *Fannie Flood Lewis, also an African American, served earlier as the first appointed trustee to the school board to fill an unexpired vacancy that existed. Her bid for election was not successful.*

Alexander Vernon, an arrival of the sixties became the first African American to be named to the position of State Commander for the Veterans of Foreign Wars Department of Texas for 1996-97. He was also selected by Governor George Bush in 1996 to serve as a member of the Texas Veterans Commission for a six-year term; and in 1998 was selected by the Jewish War Veterans as the Texas Representative to be part of a delegation of prominent non- Jewish veterans to tour Israel and meet with political leaders.

Darryl Holmes was elected to the Killeen City Council on May 3, 1997 and became Killeen's third African American city councilman. At the close of his first two-year term, he ran a strong campaign for re-election to the city council but lost his bid for re-election by 4 points. Darryl Holmes, the incumbent candidate, received 743 votes and his opponent received 747 votes.

Brenda Coley was elected to the Killeen Independent School District School Board in 1997 and served until 2007. She was the second African American elected to this position. Her eleven year tenure of service ended in 2007 and during her last three years she became the first African American to serve in this position.

During the decade of the nineties leadership opportunities were occurring in the areas of administration and supervision within the Killeen Independent School District and we witnessed the prolific advancements by African Americans in education during this period.

Prior to the decade of the 1990s, during the 1986-87 school year, Dr. Bernice Moland became a KISD Assistant principal at Willow Spring Elementary School. During the 1988-89 school year she appointed Principal of West Ward Elementary and became KISD's third African American principal in the school district. She remained in that position through the 1992-93 school year. In the meantime beginning:

1990-91: Jerry Broughton became KISD's fourth African American principal with his appointment as Principal of Marlboro Elementary School. Gloria Breaux McNeal was appointed a KISD's Classified Personnel Officer and Brenda Alexander became the first African American educator to serve on the school district's teacher appraisal team for secondary teachers.

1991-92: Brenda Perry Alexander completed her second year as an appraiser of secondary school teachers.

1992-93: Eartha Bason was appointed Assistant Principal at East Ward Elementary. She was later appointed Director of Employee Relations. She was the first African American to serve in this position. Sandra Brown was appointed Principal of Manor Middle

School; Brenda Perry Alexander was appointed Assistant Principal of Rancier Middle School; Fannie Kay Assistant Principal of Willow Springs Elementary school; and Laurice McCellan Assistant Principal of Killeen High School. During this same school year, Gloria Breaux McNeal became the first African American to serve in the position of Coordinator of Auxiliary personnel and Linda Pelton became the first African American to serve as KISD Parent/ Community Volunteer Coordinator

1993-94: Dr. Bernice Moland was appointed Special Assistant to the Superintendent, Dr. Charles Patterson, at the KISD's Central Office. The school district also added its fifth African American elementary school principal with the appointment of Jerry Jones as principal of Brookhaven Intermediate School. Annie McMullen was appointed Assistant Principal at Nolan Middle School and Sandra Forsythe Assistant Principals at Ellison High School.

In **1994-95:** Brenda Perry Alexander was appointed Principal of Nolan Middle School. Penny Batts was appointed Assistant Principal at Peebles Elementary; Floristine Gray was appointed Assistant Principal at Eastern Hills Middle School and Ronald Gray appointed Assistant Principal at Fairway Middle School. He remained at Fairway until 1997. Linda Pelton continued to serve as the KISD Parent/Community Volunteers Coordinator.

1997-98: Linda Pelton was appointed Principal of Haynes Elementary School on Zephyr Road and Patrick Bingham, also African American, was appointed assistant principal at Haynes. Ronald Gray was appointed Assistant Principal at Rancier Middle School for the 97-98 school year and remained there until 1999.

1998-99: Sandra Forsythe was appointed Principal of Smith Middle School; while Anna King became Ellison High School's Director of High School Curriculum; and Betty Barr appointed Assistant Principal at Killeen High School. Thomas Jones was appointed Assistant Principal at Montague Village Elementary School and Doris Wilkerson-Ellis was appointed Assistant P:rincipal at Meadows Elementary School.

1999-2000: Ronald Gray was appointed Principal of Fairway Middle School and remained in this position until 2004. Penny Batts was appointed Principal of Trimmer Elementary School. Leadership opportunities for African Americans continued to open into the following decade.

In 2001 Floristine Gray was appointed Principal of Manor Middle School and served in that position until 2007. After achieving her doctorate degree she joined the administrative staff at Ellison High School.

In **2004** Ronald was appointed Principal of Union Grove Middle School in Harker Heights. Then **In 2006,** Ronald Gray was appointed principal of Robert Shoemaker High School and became KISD's first African American High School Principal. These leadership roles and others provided opportunities for African Americans to make significant contributions within the community, and indeed they did.

Connie Green
Killeen's First African American City Manager
Research Team and Connie Green

Connie Green graduated from C. H. Yoe High School in Cameron, Texas, where he excelled in academics and sports. He is listed in the 1979 publication of "Who's Who among High School Students." He is a 1981 honor graduate of Temple Junior College in Temple, Texas, and a 1983 honor graduate of the University of Central Texas in Killeen, Texas. He received his CPA registration in March, 1985. In May 1990, his acceptance of the appointment from the

Killeen City Council as Director of Finance for the City of Killeen marked a historical event. With this appointment, Connie Green became the first African American to serve the city in this capacity. Prior to this appointment, he held the position of Director of Finance for the City of Belton, Texas. He had also been employed as senior accountant/auditor of a private firm in Killeen, Texas. In September 1996, his certified government finance manager designation was confirmed. In 2001, he was promoted to the position of Assistant City Manager of Administrative Services for the City of Killeen.

In March 2005, upon the departure of former City Manager Blackburn, the Council voted to appoint Connie Green, who was then serving as the Assistant City Manager of Administrative Service, to the position of Acting City Manager for the City. The vote from the council members was unanimous. Council members expressed their confidence in his proven ability to fill the position, as they had observed the quality of his past performance. At the time of accepting the position of acting City Manager, he had been in the employment of the City of Killeen for 15 years.

He experienced a successful outcome in each position. His progression through the levels of positions resulted from the hard work, effort, dedication and commitment that he was willing to give to all assignments and responsibilities. In July 2005, the Killeen Council members voted to approve him as the new City Manager of Killeen, Texas and another historical mark was made. Killeen had its first African American City Manager and the business of the city continued to move forward.

The mission of the City Manager is to provide overall management throughout the city organization and staff. The City Manager is also responsible to provide recommendations of various guidelines, procedures and processes for City Council to utilize, thus providing effective municipal services to the citizens of Killeen. Connie Green's community and professional affiliations and involvement included membership in the American Institute of Certified Public Accountants; the Texas Society of Certified Public Accountants; and the Government Finance Officers Association of Texas (TGFOA). He served on the TGFOA Professional Development Committee; served as Public Relations Chairperson within the Central Texas

Society of Certified Public Accountants (CTSCPA); and member of the Greater Killeen Chamber of Commerce."

The tenure of his service as city manager was approximately six years. He retired as city manager in 2011 after having already given over twenty years of dedicated service in city government at that time. He returned to his private practice in the city of Killeen after leaving City employment. He was a committed and competent public leader and a valued community builder.

Ernest and Angenet Wilkerson
Service: Military and Community
Ernest Wilkerson

I met my wife, Angenet, during the summer of 1992 while stationed at Fort Hood, Texas. Angenet's family had resided in Killeen since the summer of 1977, when they were first stationed at Fort Hood. In 1994, we were married and after the wedding moved to Huntsville, Texas. In 2000, we returned to Killeen. Initially we both were in the Killeen area because of our military connections; but when we returned to Killeen in 2000, it was to be "home," and closer to family. Since returning our residence has been at Fort Hood and now it is in Killeen. I am a native of Reidsville, North Carolina and a 1990 graduate of Reidville High School. I earned a Bachelor degree from Central Texas and Tarleton State University in 2001; and I began working toward an MBA from Tarleton State University. Angenet is a native of Lawton, Oklahoma and a 1987 graduate of Killeen High School. She received her Bachelor Degree from Texas State University in 1993; and is now working toward the Master's Degree in Education. We are the parents of two daughters, Surena Nicole and Kaylynn Genet

My dad and mom, Solis and Roylene Wilkerson and my brother, David reside in North Carolina. My brother Paul is deceased. Angenet's family includes her dad and mom, Ronald and Ethel

Ellis; sisters, Dora and Delena and her brother, O'Dillard. She has traveled with her parents within the USA and overseas and I traveled a lot less in Texas and Fort Polk, Louisiana.

When I arrived in Killeen, I observed economic and social issues existing in the city. In 1992 many soldiers were gone to Desert Storm, leaving Killeen struggling economically. In 1993 the city of Killeen was working towards becoming a City of Promise under the leadership of Mayor Raul Villaronga. During the late nineties there was economic growth in the city which included: retail development; expansion of Skylark Field; and new schools in the Killeen Independent School District (KISD). Our impression of the area at that time was that Killeen was a city rich in diversity. Although a large majority of the citizens arrived to Killeen via the military, Killeen has a "small town" way of life that causes her people to come together. When I ended my term in the Army in 1994 and was hired to work for the Texas Department of Criminal Justice at Ellis Unit in Huntsville and then returned in 2000, we observed economic growth. There was more shopping, and there was more dining out.

Our community involvement has been focused in areas that provide us the opportunity to make a positive difference in the lives of individuals and in the life of the community. Our family believes in being participants in the life of the community, the church and the organizations in the areas in which we reside. I grew up at Garrett's Grove United Church in Reidsville, North Carolina and was involved. When we moved to Huntsville in 1996 I got involved and was ordained a deacon at Greater Zion Missionary Baptist Church in Huntsville, Texas. My involvement in Killeen area organizations include membership in the Killeen Branch NAACP; Fidelity Lodge #221; Alpha Phi Alpha Fraternity, Inc.; Armed Services YMCA Board member; First Tee Board member and Killeen Educational Foundation. I also had membership during different years. In 2000-2007 as a Development District of Central Texas Founding Board member; in Texas Economic Development Council; Killeen Economic Development Corp. in (2000-2006); Texas Municipal league Board member (2006-2007); Regional President (2005-2006).

We were former members of 19th Street Chapel, Fort Hood, TX and Westside Baptist Church, Killeen. We are now are members of Christian House of Prayer of Killeen. I have served in the ministries there as a Deacon and drill team leader. Angenet has served in the choir, Praise Team, Youth and Young Women Ministries, also as a Sunday school teacher and a deaconess. Her community involvement includes the Killeen Branch NAACP where she has served on its Education Committee and its Youth Council. She is also a member of Alpha Kappa Alpha Sorority, Inc. and an educator. Angenet possesses leadership, organization and motivation skills that she utilizes well in her church, school and community endeavors. She is an encourager and a doer.

Our individual achievements include my election as a Killeen City Council Member and the success that I experienced as a councilman. My fellow council members elected me to serve as Mayor Pro Tem for the City of Killeen. Angenet was recognized as "Elementary Teacher of the Year" for Willis Independent School District in Willis, Texas with four years of classroom teaching experience. She was also the recipient of the Killeen Branch NAACP 2007 Torch Bearer Award.

In 1998, our daughters and I were in a horrific automobile accident involving an 18-wheeler. Because of the amount of blood that I lost, I was not expected to live. The girls and I are alive, healthy and using all of our limbs. We are thankful to God for His blessings in overcoming this great obstacle that we encountered in our lives. Life leaves us with memories of happiness, sadness, laughter, chuckles and fun. Some memories that bring me happiness are remembering the purchase of our first home, and the family's visit to Disney World. However, as a family we have been blessed to experience some form of happiness daily. When the memory of the loss of our second child comes to mind, it causes sadness; as does the loss of my brother Paul Anthony Wilkerson. Spending time with our daughters bring us lots of laughter and fun. They are very funny. Therefore, there are many memorable and humorous happy experiences that we have had as a family that have brought us much happiness. We consider family time, eating meals together, writing love notes to one another and praying together as valuable to our family's life style. We also believe that education is an important goal to strive for and achieve; and being respectful and independent are important attributes to cultivate and practice. Our family's interest and aspiration include service. Our family loves service. We find pleasure in helping others. Angenet and I want to be a part of growth. I want to help build strong communities. Angenet wants to help develop youth into strong, leading adults. Our daily prayer is for God to order our steps.

BaBatunde and Yetunde
Entrepreneurs Giving Back to the Community in Many Ways
BaBatunde

 I am a native of New York. I entered the U. S. Army in 1969, and retired from the military on May 31, 1993 as 1st SGT, with twenty-four years of active duty. Bernard Jones is my legal name, and BaBatunde is my Afrikan name. My wife, Johnnie, (Yetunde) and I lived in Copperas Cove, Texas, for over twenty-two years. Our daughter, Kettisha, graduated from Spelman College in Atlanta, Georgia, and is a Principal in the Houston School District. We are also grandparents to a grandson, Khan. For us, 1991 became a year of opportunities and my decisions for fulfilling my goal for a business. After returning home from the war in Kuwait, my company commander informed me that while in school at Leavenworth, Kansas, he had visited a store that was black owned and sold black art. He suggested that this was something that I could do in Killeen. However, I wanted to open something other than an art gallery. There was already an art gallery and Greek shop in Killeen, which was only ten miles from Copperas Cove, Texas, where we and a group of friends wanted to go into business. A second opportunity was presented when my daughter was accepted to Spellman College in Atlanta, Georgia. The summer before attending her freshman year at Spellman, she was sent a list of 20 books to read, each of which

was written by Afrikan-American authors. We attempted every avenue available to locate these books, to no avail. Therefore, I sent the list to my family member who was a mail-order book distributor on the east coast to have him send the books to us. We also decided that books would be our primary product in our store. However, we would not only carry books, but that we would have many other products, all "Under One Roof." The concept for "Under One Roof" was a seed planted years prior to opening our first store in Copperas Cove, Texas, on February 15, 1992. As a teen in the early sixties, I had the opportunity to work in an Afrikan-American owned and operated businesses in Harlem, New York. One of the businesses was a shoe store, and another was a grocery store. I had no idea that the seed of entrepreneurship was being planted. But throughout my twenty-four years in the military I always had the desire to be in business, and was always looking for opportunities that would lead to business. The desire to be in business was also motivated by the fact that after working for someone else for twenty-four years, I decided that I wanted to be my own boss, to be self-employed, wanted to create jobs for other Afrikan-Americans, and to become a community outlet for Afrikan-Americans.

In late 1991, I met a "Brother" by the name of Brian Joseph (Bydee Man), in the Austin Mall who sold his own designer T-shirts at a Kiosk in the mall. After conferring with him, he offered that I could carry his T-shirts if I decided to open a store. Then in 1992, a "Sister" friend who was a real estate agent found a location for us to open a market place that was about 3600 sq. ft., and we rented one third of the space. This 1200 sq. ft. that we rented we called "The Cobweb" with mostly antique items for sale. At the beginning, there were eight difference businesses in the Cobweb, including "Under One Roof." Yetunde and I chose the name "Under One Roof" after doing demographics of Central Texas and realizing there were many things missing for the Afrikan-American Culture in Central Texas. With our entire savings of $5,000— which we had to pay for the inventory, the renovation of the building, as well as all other expenses—we decided to become entrepreneurs. We started out on a part-time schedule because both my wife and I were still employed full-time. I was in the military, and she was a contractor on Ft. Hood.

In 1992, the grand opening of the Cobweb was held. "The Under One Roof Afrikan American Bookstore" was a sub-leaser, and had taken the earlier offer from "The Bydee Man" to carry his T-shirts. On the day of the Grand Opening, we only had T-shirts because the books that we ordered did not arrive on time, and on our first day in business our total sale for that day was $5.00. I identified the problem as not enough advertising and sought out what local media was available. My first real advertising was free advertising of a story about the business in the local newspaper. My next most important thing that I did was to be a vendor in the local area at different events. The PX (Military Post Exchange shopping center) approached me about displaying our cultural items for Christmas and Black History Month, which we did. During that three month period, we were exposed to many Afrikan-American people who did not know about Under One Roof. We were able to start building a customer base from that experience. Because I was still in the military and receiving a monthly paycheck, we were able to re-invest all monies back into the business that was made in the business. We next began advertising with television commercials and then on radio, and within two months, I knew the difference that advertising had made.

I got involved in local Afrikan-American business organizations to better network our business and to get involved in local community activities. In 1993, I founded the Afrikan-American Chamber of Commerce to bring the local Afrikan-American businesses together and have a safety net of support. I was founder and past president of the Afrikan-American Chamber of Commerce in Killeen, Texas (which is inactive at this time) from 1993-1997. Dr. James Love, Mrs. Benita Love, Dr. Aubrey Jolley, Dr. Joyce Wilson and Misters Elzie Ellis and Howard Bagwell were also founding members. In the same time frame, we became independent of the Cobweb Complex in Copperas Cove when it was sold to another owner. In 1994 "Under One Roof" opened under an online program at the Killeen Mall for one year. After that year you could become a permanent store. We started and were successful with the Kiosk, then moved into a temporary online store for one year. However, after that year, we decided that it was not in our best interest to continue the business in the Killeen Mall. The lessons learned were: (1) never go into a mall without the finances to cover the high cost of maintaining business overhead, which was exceptionally high and (2) when you are in a mall, you truly do not own your business. Your business becomes a part of the mall.

When we opened our first store, *Under One Roof Afrikan American Bookstore and Cultural Shop* in Copperas Cove, Texas, and became known in Killeen and by surrounding communities, including Fort Hood, Texas, our entrepreneurial spirit provided a service and a resource of great significance which was overwhelmingly beneficial to the Killeen area communities. We made available volumes of information of interest specifically for and about the African-American culture; and enlightenment in general to the diverse population of the Killeen and the central Texas area. The concept caught on quickly in the Killeen Community, and Johnnie and I opened our second store, Under One Roof #2, in Killeen on June 12, 1995. Almost three years later, in October 1998, we closed the Copperas Cove store and consolidated both stores in Killeen. But the service and resources of the Killeen Bookstore and Cultural Shop remained available to all surrounding communities. Yetunde and I are entrepreneurs of a cultural center of enlightenment that allows you to shop in one location and select from a variety of resources of various mediums. You can also select from items of knowledge, such as History, Philosophy, Religion, Music, Art and many symbolic products intended for the preservation of the rich heritage of the Afrikan-American's history. For all the years that we have been in business, we have consistently promoted the preservation of Afrikan-American history; have encouraged self-empowerment, self-sufficiency, economic empowerment and cultural enrichment in the community.

In 1994, we organized and promoted the first annual Afrikan-American Expo which continued until 1997. In 1995, our Scholarship Fund, *"Under One Roof's To Whom You Give Your Money is to Whom You give Your Power Scholarship,"* was organized, and continued through 2009 when we closed our Killeen store. Through this scholarship fund from 1995-2009, we had donated thousands of dollars to assist Afrikan-American students with scholarships, preferably those attending a Historically Black College.

In 1995, Under One Roof also started the only Afrikan-American newspaper in Killeen, Texas, the "Afrikan Posta" Newspaper. Since then, The Afrikan Posta Newspaper has serviced this central Texas area with FREE valuable sources of Afrikan-American history, information, opportunities, presentations, art forms, and display artwork. In May 2007, during the celebration of Killeen's 125th birthday, Yetunde and I made a significant contribution to Killeen, Fort Hood and surrounding areas. We compiled and published Issue #5, volume II, dated May 2007 of the Afrikan-American Posta Newspaper. This special issue The Afrikan-American Posta Newspaper dedicated a 14 page color edition on the Afrikan-American history in Killeen. It is an historical literary work that will become a legacy that Yetunde (Mrs. Johnnie) and I have given to this community. Afrikan-Americans and all citizens, regardless of race, ethnicity or other identities, will recognize its value to Killeen, one of the most diverse cities in Texas. It was a phenomenal production, and exceeded all other issues in content and layout. This special issue of the Afrikan-American Posta addressed the "First Accomplishments" in the areas of the military, education, religion, politics, sports, entertainment, civic and fraternal organizations. It also included the mentoring activities in the area of Black History that are sponsored by the Under One Roof organization throughout the year in the Killeen and Fort-Hood communities. It also addressed the struggles of Afrikan-Americans, in the past and present, in Killeen and in the United States of America.

In 1996-97, we started the first effective Poet's Night in Killeen, Texas. It provided a forum for Poets, as well as Rap Artists, to have a safe environment to come and show their talent. We also sponsored a quarterly statewide Poetry Slam, which extended opportunities to even more participants.

I gave presentations for schools, churches and organizations' activities, and provided artifacts and books for display, especially during Black History Month. I had many opportunities to provide cultural enrichment presentations to students. Programs were presented each year to teach about Kwanzaa to many of the elementary schools in the area. In addition, through my speaking presentations, Afrikan-American heritage and the history of Black History Month was shared with many organizations in the area. The newspaper publication, "Afrikan Posta," served as a great resource of enlightenment for the community.

Annually during the month of February I taught "The 28 Days of Black History" and "The Key to Learning All about Me." The purpose of this program is to remember the past and shape the future (our children). The goal is "To plant the seeds of Black history in our children for knowledge, growth and empowerment; and to preserve our future through education." A study-group mentoring program for Afrikan American males was also organized by Johnnie and me. This program, *"Building Children Instead of Repairing Men and Women,"* promoted and supported academic achievement; personal and social development; and African-American heritage and cultural enrichment. I created BaBatunde's Creed to encourage the children and males I taught or mentored to pursue economic and intellectual empowerment; personal development; social development; and knowledge of African-American heritage and culture. BaBatunde's Creed states: "If no one will teach me, I will teach myself, and teach someone else. If no one will help me, I will help myself, and then I will help someone else. If no one will save me, I will save myself, and then I will save someone else. If no one will give me a job, I will make a job for myself, and then I will make a job for someone else. If no one will recognize me, I will recognize myself, and then I will recognize someone else."

My family, through our vision for Under One Roof; our tried and proven business knowledge and skills; and our resourceful and determined ability succeeded in accomplishing positive goals through opportunities provided for African-Americans and other races and ethnicities to learn of the Afrikan-American culture. We were successful through our sincere desire to give back to the community of Afrikan-Americans and to inspire within them a greater appreciation of our rich heritage. We are grateful to have had the opportunity to give back to the community and be a supporter of the activities, benefit efforts and humanitarian causes of non-profit organizations.

We take pride in our work as community builders who would not be distracted from the honorable mission that we are pursuing: Educating the Afrikan-American child and adults to the rich history of Afrikan-Americans to ensure that the history of their heritage is preserved. Our work as community builders in Killeen has been significant, enlightening and rewarding

Black Cultural Centers Past and Present
Research Team

Three important cultural centers were established by Blacks to provide cultural enlightenment to the community. They are Carol's Art Gallery and African American Museum founded by Colonel (Retired) Carl and Carol Settles; Under One Roof founded by Babatunde and Yetunde (Bernard and Johnnie Jones) that you read about in the previous journal and the Center for African American Studies and Research, a long awaited community resource envisioned and accomplished through the leadership of Horace Grace. Two of these cultural centers have closed however; their service to the entire community was of great value. The Center for African American Studies and Research is active and available now as a priceless and valuable source that focuses on knowledge and contributions of Blacks to the diverse world in which we live. Each of these local centers provided an opportunity for residents of all races and ethnicity to learn, understand, appreciate and respect the culture of its Black citizenry in this diverse community in Central Texas.

Carol's Art Gallery and African American Museum opened on Dr. Martin Luther King, Jr.'s birthday during the 1990s and was Killeen's first museum of Black culture. It provided opportunities to explore art for its educational value and to obtain art for its decorative value. The quality and variety of art items available at the gallery were beautiful, enlightening and sparked a feeling of awe and a desire to learn more about Black history. The museum also included a meeting area, *Inside the Soul,* which was available for literary, cultural and social gathering; for performances, lectures and forums; and for organization and group meetings. The gallery and museum closed in 2003.

The Center for African American Studies and Research is a centrally located collection of resources available through books and events such as lectures and symposiums. Its mission is to educate the diverse communities within the central Texas area on past and current contributions of Blacks in history and in central Texas; to raise self-esteem among Blacks; to provide easy access to obtaining information for cultural enlightenment; to raise racial awareness and sensitivity among all races and ethnic groups and ultimately to bring racial harmony to the diverse communities in Central Texas. Through assistance by Central Texas College and Tarleton University; the generous initial donation from Horace Grace; and the donations that were pledged and given by citizens in the community; Horace Grace's vision was realized. The Oveta Culp Library on Central Texas College now houses this dedicated center of Black history studies. The resources in this center are available to college students, high school students, all students and the public citizens in Killeen and the central Texas communities. Contributions to the center are welcomed.

The cultural center, **Under One Roof,** closed in 2009. It had been valuable in providing cultural enlightenment in Black History within our community and the central Texas area. The center's founders and owners were BaBatunde (Bernard Jones) and Yetunde (Johnnie Jones) and their journal is included in this *Tapestry* collection.

Leon and Terry Chisolm
"A Ministry to the Grieving"
Leon Chisolm, Jr.

I am a 1980 graduate of Ridgeland High School in South Carolina, and a U. S. Army veteran. Terry Chisolm, my wife is a 1984 graduate of West Hardeeville High in Hardeeville, South Carolina. Now, we see the fulfillment of my life-long dream and our "calling" to be a Ministry to the Grieving. I remember the first funeral I attended when my cousin died due to a motorcycle accident in Ridgeland. I sent the family home to rest and I stayed all night in the hospital beside my comatose cousin's bed. The next morning, my cousin was pronounced dead, and I had to pass the word to the rest of the family. "The preparations for the funeral were hectic and difficult, and it gave me the greatest desire to help families in tragedies and hard times. Memories of two other experiences in my life kept the fires of my desire to be helpful to others smoldering. When I was twelve years old my relationship with an older gentleman in my community contributed to the development of a stronger desire to help others during their bereavement. While helping this older gentleman in a wheelchair to get around town, the two of us often visited the city cemetery in Sumter, South Carolina. This man told me about the lives of those buried there. "I became fascinated with it." Then Mrs. Helen Goodman, the town florist, would take me along with her two sons when she delivered flowers to the local funeral homes. The caskets, hearses and service intrigued me, and because of this exposure, I yearned to be involved in every funeral procession I saw and having my own funeral home became my lifelong dream. Unfortunately, family hardships caused me to join the Army. I stayed in for thirteen years, but the smoldering dream was still alive. After Desert Storm and the military draw down, I saw an opportunity to pursue my dream. The first opportunity came while still stationed at Fort Hood, when I began working at Darnall Army Community Hospital morgue. Then I accepted my second opportunity as a path toward achieving my strong desire to make my lifelong dream come true. After the Luby's cafeteria incident in September 1991, when twenty-six people were shot and killed, I started volunteering in 1992 at Crawford-Bowers Funeral Home. I believed that learning more about a field of work in which I was interested, and working as a volunteer, were of great value to me. Therefore, I was willing to give my service in this manner. In that same year, 1992, I was honorably discharged from the Army and worked for two and a half years as a full-time employee right along with the regular employees of Crawford-Bowers. "God placed a spirit of excellence in me, and as a result, all tasks that I undertook were accomplished with a high standard. This resulted in my being offered a full-time position prior to attending mortuary school."

My preparation and experience of ten and a half years of employment in the Central Texas Community with Crawford-Bowers

Funeral Homes in Killeen and Copperas Cove, Texas and my managerial experience at the Killeen Memorial Park Funeral Home in Killeen, Texas from May 2002 to May 2003 have contributed to my successful service to the community. My resume reflects my skill and performance in training, as well as my integrity in service. It also reflects my desire to provide the best service to families in the communities that I served. Therefore, I prepared myself to do just that, and my preparation reads:

- Graduate of Dallas Institute of Funeral Service with an Associate of Applied Science Degree.
- Received National Funeral Directors Examination Board Certificate.
- Holds Texas State Funeral Directors and Embalmers License.
- Holds a Texas Insurance License and Texas Notary Public License.
- Received the Professional Funeral Association Commendation for Excellence Award for providing premier service and outstanding contribution to mending-client-family loyalty
- Received the Scholastic Achievement Award.
- Graduate of Minnesota Graduate School of Theology of Brooklyn Center.
- Employed ten and a half years in the Central Texas Community with Crawford-Bowers Funeral Homes in Killeen and Copperas, Texas;
- Manager for Killeen Memorial Park Funeral Home, Killeen, Texas, 2002-2003.
- I am a twelve year veteran in U. S. Army, serving in the Gulf War.

Upon completion of mortuary school, I was hired as maintenance personnel instead of being hired as an Apprentice Funeral Director/Embalmer with provisional license. However, I did not become discouraged by this. I was also required to sign a statement that I would volunteer to do provisional licensee responsibilities. About a year after I received my license, I began meeting with families alone.

I remained as an employee at Crawford Bowers until May 2002. During my ten and one half years' employment at Crawford-Bowers, I served the families in Central Texas in a dignified, sincere, caring, sensitive, reverent and supportive manner that was remembered long after the funeral was over. I was an outstanding representative of the quality service expressed and provided by my former employer. I received the Professional Association Commendation for Excellence Award. This award recognizes those who provide premier service and outstanding contributions to mending-client-family loyalty. I am also a graduate of Minnesota Graduate School of Theology of Brooklyn Center.

In May 2002, I became Manager at Killeen Memorial Park Funeral Home in Killeen, and remained in that position until May 2003, which was a few months prior to opening my family's own funeral home and florist, The Chisolm Family Funeral Home and Florist. It is the first and only Black owned Funeral Home in the Copperas Cove/Killeen/Fort Hood area. It provides a service to the Central Texas Families in a manner that *Every Memory Is Cherished*. When the Chisholm Family Funeral Home and Florist opened on July 5, 2003, at 813 M. L. King, Jr. Drive in Copperas Cove, Texas, my smoldering dream of owning a funeral home as a Ministry to the Grieving was fulfilled. The dreams of my wife, the former Terry Fuller of Hardeville, South Carolina, along with our son, Leon Chisolm III were also fulfilled.

Our first funeral home facility shared its 2,000 square-feet of floor space among two viewing rooms with seating areas outside each room, a reception area, an administrative office, work area and casket showroom. The decor of the funeral home arranged by Terry Chisolm was designed to make customers feel comfortable even in their discomfort. The funeral home staff then consisted of me, the Funeral Director; Terry Chisolm, Administrator; Marvin Williams, Business Manager who has been with the company since its inception, consulting regarding the business aspect of the company's operations, and a team of loyal staff members. In addition, other full-time employees and part-time drivers and counselors joined the staff after its opening. A 2004 update after the first year of operation indicated that Chisolm's Family Funeral Home was voted the 2nd best funeral home in the area, As owner and Funeral Director, I responded in this manner, "The staff is most appreciative of this honor and wants to extend a heartfelt thanks to the community and the families they were privileged to serve. The business was established to provide customer service that is highly personalized, and a quality product at affordable prices. The professional staff at the funeral home understands that the passing of a loved one is a very sensitive time, and they strive to provide friendly, personal service which makes the final arrangements of loved ones easier. We make every effort to understand and accommodate the particular needs and concerns of our families. We strive to exceed their expectations while building lasting relationships."

With a desire to provide service for the communities of Killeen and Copperas Cove, Texas, we partnered with a 100-150 seat chapel in Copperas Cove, and with several churches in Killeen that allow customers without home churches to hold funerals. These communities and families embraced the funeral services that were available to them, and the Chisolm's Family Funeral Home embraced these communities and families. In November 2005, we welcomed Joe Decroce, our newest funeral director, on staff.

From the renting of caskets for those being cremated or shipped out of state; to the selling of wooden and metal caskets; or caskets with special lock box features for keepsakes; or decorations that detach for mementos; not one tiny detail is overlooked. It's the last time to do something special for a loved one. I want it to be right because they can't go back and do it again. Therefore, I meticulously endeavor to restore the deceased's features and to help give the families closure. Every family is important to me. I never want to be apathetic about my work. These families actually become a part of your family. A local elder of a church, Dr. Jerry O'Donnell has known Terry and me for more than eleven years. Having attended several funerals conducted by me, he described them as family-oriented, dignified and spiritual. O'Donnell said sensitivity is important because people react differently to death.

"Groundbreaking for a funeral home facility in Killeen, Texas was held in August 2011, at 3100 S. Old F.M. 440 Road, in Killeen, Texas. The Grand Opening and Ribbon Cutting were held August

25, 2012. Our own funeral home "Where Every Memory is cherished" now has relocated to Killeen, Texas. The Killeen facility has a spacious chapel with seating for 150 persons, and is equipped with a pull-down screen that hosts DVD presentations. Its spacious reception area is beautifully decorated; has a comforting environment; and the company has an expanded staff to meet the service needs.

Dreams are sometimes inspired in the oddest places. For me, son of Mary Simmons of Ridgeland, South Carolina; and Terry Chisolm, daughter of Minnie Jones of Hardeville, South Carolina; it was an unnamed gentleman in a wheelchair who endeared the lives of those in the graveyard to the heart of a young man who would later care for both the deceased and their families. A seed planted in Sumter,

South Carolina in the mind and heart of a twelve-year-old boy with a sincere desire to help others, germinated over the years. By overcoming rough places and hard times as it grew; becoming stronger in faith and determined hard work with each victory; acknowledging the source of ALL possessions of this world; seeking guidance, listening for an answer, responding to the message, believing in the promise, I received my inheritance from the Lord: *Chisolm's Family Funeral Home*, "Where Every Memory is Cherished". It is now location in Killeen, Texas. We are grateful for the opportunity to provide a *"Ministry to the Grieving"* for the families in Central Texas. Our service has contributed to community building and we are thankful that we can be a part of the process.

CHAPTER 7

2000-2010:
The New Millennium
Opens New Horizons

—ⱲⱲ—

The first decade of the New Millennium, 2000-2010, ushered in new opportunities for African American leadership in city government. It also opened new horizons for service in community building. Killeen citizens chose three African Americans as leaders by election, appointment or selection for first-time positions of leadership in this decade. They were Killeen's first African American Mayor, Timothy Hancock; Killeen's First African American City Manager, Connie Green; and the first African American Chief of Police of Killeen, Robert L. Jackson, Jr. Police Chief Jackson's selection on December 19, 2000 was a significant and memorable milestone for the city and its citizens. Although Chief Jackson's tenure of public service in this position was very brief, he was welcomed by the citizens of Killeen during his short stay. This was especially significant to the African American community that this very diverse community of Killeen had again selected and welcomed diverse leadership to be involved in the governing and management of city government in this decade. Five Black council members had also been elected to serve on the Municipal Council during this decade, however not all served during the same terms of office. Each of these elected officials demonstrated interest and willingness to serve as representatives for community progress. They also embraced diversity as strength for the community because that is what community builders do.

Among the newcomers to Killeen during this decade is Dr. Claudia L. Brown, a Tapestry project participant. Like so many of the earlier newcomers she also became a community builder. Let us meet Dr. Claudia L. Brown, a 2005 newcomer to Killeen.

Claudia L. Brown, Ph.D.,
An Advocate for Education and Public Service
Dr. Claudia L. Brown

When I first arrived in the city on May 10, 2005, my son and youngest grandson were with me. We lived first on Post and later off Post in Harker Heights until my house was built. I moved in my newly built house, located in District Four of Killeen, on October 25, 2005. I was born and raised in Baltimore, Maryland (the only place that I have ever lived), as were my two children and some family members. We were impressed with the contrast of a growing small city to established large city life in Baltimore. There was a warm intimacy in business dealings in Killeen, as opposed to the cold anonymity in Baltimore. It was exciting and refreshing to live in a much smaller city with a country feel. To me, Killeen is a budding metropolis with cows on one side, and comfortable homes on the other side. Reflecting on daily life in Killeen revealed a contrast in economic opportunity; the cost of living; price differences for goods and services; and educational opportunities as compared to Baltimore, Maryland. I moved here to help my son to serve as "Mr. Mom" to my grandson while his wife served as a soldier on Fort Hood, with Iraq as her destination. My immediate family consists of my son, two daughters and three grandchildren. My son is an entrepreneur: a former owner of a hair salon business and corporate cleaning business. My daughter is an animal groomer, and lives and works in Atlanta, Georgia.

As I read the Killeen Daily Herald as a new arrival, I learned about our local NAACP Chapter meeting and met wonderful and helpful people who helped me explore the political scene in the city. Killeen's warmth was extended through Mayor Jouett's luncheon forums. There, I learned more about Killeen's political structure, its history, successes, challenges and needs and *where I can serve*. At the Mayor's forum, I also learned about the Killeen Sister Cities program, and joined its Board as secretary. Later, I decided to campaign for a seat on the Killeen City Council, and was unopposed in my race. I was sworn in as a Killeen City Council member on May 12, 2007, serving District Four and enjoying my service as a city council member. I hoped to be a positive agent for change in my role as city council member.

I resigned my seat on the Killeen City Council during my first year of a two-year term when it became necessary to have knee surgery performed. I was later employed by the City of Killeen in another capacity at City Hall. I am very excited about the future for Killeen. I enjoy the diversity of the people, and my affiliation with my new friends in the African-American, Caucasian, Hawaiian, Korean communities and cultures. Many military people have settled here. Prior to being elected to the City Council, I worked as a substitute teacher in Killeen's school district. I leaned that Texas Education Agency (TEA) guidelines do not allow me to even tutor without certification. Therefore, I had my credentials evaluated by the Texas Education Agency and was advised that I qualified to take the examinations for certification in early childhood through grade 12, and the principal's examination. I also felt comfortable inquiring at Tarleton State University for a position, to no avail. Therefore, to provide more opportunities for myself, in 2006 I started an education consultation business, and received a notary public commission for the State of Texas. A future prospect for employment, should the opportunity occur, is to teach two continuing education courses at a college in the community. The first course would be on identifying the exemplary middle school, as this is what I wrote about in my dissertation, which is published; and the second course is on cultural diversity. The first client in my new business was a private all-white

Christian school in Fort Worth, Texas, which required me to research and present training on this subject.

My professional experience includes serving as an elementary school principal; ten years of experience in social work; six years' experience as a planner; and eight years of experience as a license commissioner. My Bachelor's Degree is in elementary education; Master's Degree is in planning and administration; and Doctorate held in interdisciplinary studies, with a concentration in urban education. I retired after serving as teacher, curriculum coordinator, assistant principal and principal for thirty years. My organization and leadership service include:

- Chairman of the Board of Directors and the Co-Director of the Social Work Department in a neighborhood comprehensive Health Center.
- Founder and President of the Baltimore, Maryland, Neighborhood Association.
- Member of a Community Corporation Board comprised of 44 neighborhood presidents.
- Notary public for the State of Maryland for 34 years.
- Recipient of the Service Key for service on the Board of the John Hopkins University Phi Delta Kappa Fraternity organization (for educators). The Mayor of the city of Baltimore, Maryland, awarded me a two-year women's commission.
- Two Governors (one Republican and the other Democrat) and the Maryland General Assembly awarded me 4 two-year commissions to serve on the Board of Licenses for the State of Maryland.

My family has always valued education. While I chose to impact the changing of the public education system as an administrator, my sister chose to do the same as an extraordinary high school classroom teacher; one student at a time. We have many professionals in our family. Also, an uncle who served as the first Black customs worker for the United States; and an aunt, the first black person to be placed on the Board of the Association for Supervision and Curriculum Development (ASCD), who was instrumental in the integration of the two segregated organizations. At age sixty-two, I pursued a doctoral degree because of a promise made to my granddaughter and as an accomplishment to honor my aunt. I graduated in 2004 with a Ph.D. We are a musical family and a family of faith. My maternal grandfather was an African Methodist Episcopal minister. My mother served as the church organist and pianist. We accepted Jesus Christ as our Lord and Savior and follow the teachings of the Holy Bible. After marriage, I attended a Baptist church, where I became president of my church circle. My husband and I were selected "Man and Woman of the Year."

Travel experiences have been educational and memorable to us. As a child, we also enjoyed trips to Atlantic City, New Jersey, and Arlington, Virginia; and as an adult, we continued our yearly fall visit to Harpers Ferry, West Virginia. From slavery, my family owned land in Harpers Ferry, West Virginia, on which they built the famous Hill Top House. Many presidents, great statesmen and generals frequented and continue to patronize Hill Top House for boarding and meals. My service in the community in which I reside has always been to help its citizens and make the city a better place in which to work and live. Now that I am a resident of Killeen, Texas, I will also be a community builder here through my service.

Killeen Elects an African American Mayor
Service to Country and to Community
Alice Douse

About one hundred years after the establishment of Killeen, Texas on May 15, 1882 a newcomer, Timothy L. Hancock, and his family arrived in the Fort Hood/Killeen Community with no idea of the role he will attain in the history of this unique, very diverse and fast growing community. His integrity and that of his wife, the former Maxine McDowell and their service as community leaders and community builders resulted in his election as the first African American Mayor of the city of Killeen, Texas in 2007. By this time they had been residents of the Killeen/Fort Hood Community for more than twenty years. Obtaining the position of Mayor had many people very proud of his success. You read about this family earlier in Chapter five. The Honorable Timothy Hancock was born in Tyler, Texas. His parents, both deceased, were Chester and Adie Hancock. He was educated in the public schools in his community and graduated from McFarland High School in Mincola, Texas. He began his college studies at Prairie View A & M University in Prairie View, Texas, but interrupted that endeavor to join the United States Army. His leadership and service had been demonstrated in several venues. He served his country as a soldier in the United States Army retiring at the rank of Command Sergeant Major with thirty years of honorable service. After his military retirement he pursued a career as a successful businessman in transportation. He provides service to Killeen and neighboring communities while maintaining his own business and managing that of his employer.

The Honorable Timothy Hancock also experienced a successful political career as a six-year municipal councilman and a productive six-year administration in the position of Mayor. His official political career began in the city of Killeen with his election to the Killeen City Council in May of 2000 and he served three two-year terms that ended 2006. Due to time limits he was not eligible to be re-elected for another term as councilman. Therefore he then entered the campaign for Mayor of the city. He was elected in 2006 and served three two-year terms as Mayor that ended in 2012. He was not eligible to be re-elected for another term as Mayor.

As Mayor, he serves as the head of the City of Killeen's government for all ceremonial purposes, and for the purposes of military law. Along with the council members, the Mayor is responsible for soliciting citizen's views in forming policies and interpreting them to the public. He presides at the council meetings; facilitates communication and understanding between elected and appointed officials; assists the council in setting goals and in advocating policy decisions; and serves as a promoter and defender of the community.

In addition, the Mayor serves as a key representative in intergovernmental relations

He and his wife, the former Maxine McDowell, are the proud parents of three adult sons, Michael, Craig and Ronald; and grandparents of granddaughters Brittany and Vanessa, and grandsons Xavier, Joshua and Blair. The Honorable Mayor and Mrs. Hancock leave a legacy of service and support of educational opportunities, youth endeavors and support of community causes. The senior residents and many other residents of this city have been the benefactors of the family's generosity and service. Mrs. Hancock shares the honors Mayor Hancock received for service during his mayoral administration; as a municipal councilmember and in business endeavors. As a former "First Family" and citizen of the city they continue to serve in various capacities in the interest and support of the city of Killeen and its citizens.

Among Honorable Mayor Hancock's community involvement over the years are service on the Greater Killeen Chamber of Commerce Board of Directors, the Central Texas Chapter AUSA Board of Governors, Trailways Transportation System Board of Directors in Washington, D.C., and community civic organizations He and Mrs. Hancock are also founding board members of the Addie E. McFarland Foundation of Mineola, Texas. He and Mrs. Hancock also share many honors from organizations in the community. His willing and loyal service to our country for the protection of the citizens of the United States of America and America's allies; also his service to the city of Killeen, Fort Hood and neighboring communities are positive milestones that will be remembered by many.

CHAPTER 8

Community Churches:
Essential to Community Building

—ɱ—

Alice Douse

F our priorities were important to Killeen's African American
residents as they began settling in their new community. They
were to fulfill their employment responsibilities; to establish a nurturing home life for the family; to establish places of worship; and
to ensure the availability and accessibility of an education for the
youth in the community. The family journals presented in Chapters
one through seven of *TAPESTRY* captured history about the family
and the home life of these community builders. Chapters eight and
nine of *TAPESTRY* provides a brief history of the establishment
of churches from 1951 through 1997. The role of the church has
had a significant influence on community life for many years and
persons of faith know the importance of having a place of worship
and prayer, a refuge in times of crisis and a place to assemble in the
community. Traditionally, the institutional church not only minis-
tered to the spiritual and physical needs of the families, but also to
their social, emotional and some economic needs.

The brief histories of the churches in Chapter eight are enlightening. Early churches, in some instances, were organized by a small
group of Christians assembling with a spiritual leader. Other early
churches began through a joint missionary effort of church sponsors
or established religious associations, church workers and spiritual

leaders. As the Black population in the city increased other churches were established independent of this direct assistance. During 1950-1960, six churches were founded by African American spiritual leaders and African America worshipers in the area. Simmonsville Missionary Baptist Church and God's Holy Tabernacle Church of God in Christ were established in the Simmonsville community. Marlboro Missionary Baptist Church, The Servicemen Church (which no longer exists) and Anderson Chapel African Methodist Episcopal Church were established in the Marlboro Heights community. The sixth church was established in the Harker Heights community. It was first known as Zion Temple Church of God in Christ in the early years. The name was changed in January 2004 under its new administration, to Deliverance and Praise Temple Church of God in Christ. Initiatively, all six early churches were founded and administered by its founding pastor. A brief history of five of these earliest churches and five others that were founded from 1983 to 1997 are also included in *TAPESTRY*. Each of their beginnings is credited to an African American spiritual leader who with the support of the worshippers nurtured the growth and sustainability. In addition, a brief history of the First Church of God in Christ; Westside Baptist Church; Greater Peace Missionary Baptist Church; Cornerstone Baptist Church; and Greater Vision Community Church are also presented in this chapter of TAPESTRY. All ten churches presented are now serving diverse congregations in the worship services. When we consider the mission of each of these spiritual institutions and the leadership of these spiritual leaders, we recognize the positive and significant impact their contribution in service has had within the communities of this area.

There is also a list of other established churches at the end of Chapter 8, but these are without details of their beginnings and service. However their contribution and that of neighboring churches to community building were also essential and significant to community progress in this city. As you read the histories you will find that this list of churches or ministries were also organized by African American spiritual leaders and are viable institutions in the community.

Simmonsville Missionary Baptist Church
Reverend John Wiley Bosier, Founding Pastor
Melba Olean Davis

In the 1940s, there was no place for Blacks to worship in the city of Killeen; but because of a desire to have a place of worship, Rosie Ellison, Osia Maze, Melba Olean Stacy Davis, Gladys Locke, Othella Flakes, a woman known to the group as Grandma, a minister and William (Bill) Simmons gathered at a small building owned by Mrs. Rosie Lee Hamilton for a special meeting about establishing a church. In time, the erection of the church was started. It began on the land donated by William (Bill) Simmons, a white man for whom the city of Simmonsville was named. He had once been a Baptist preacher. The land was designed to be used only for a church. The group was overjoyed, thinking that finally they would have a church for worship services, only to learn in a few months that the building will be delayed, when the minister announced his plans to leave and stated that it was because of the lack of help and enough finances. Before leaving, however, the minister did leave the group with the building framework that he had begun. As time passed, the frame work for the church became somewhat worn and weather-beaten.

The Temple Sub-District Board of the St. John's District sent its Missionary, Reverend A. R. D. Hubbard, into this field to assist and oversee the project of starting a church. Several meetings were held at Mrs. Ellison's house, under the leadership of Missionary Hubbard and other ministers on the Temple Sub-District Board of the St. John's District. The name, Lone Star Community Baptist Church, was chosen for the new church. This was not only the first church in Simmonsville, but is the first Black Church in Killeen.

Early in 1951, Reverend John Wiley Bosier, a Baptist minister, came to the Killeen area and stated that he was sent by God. He and his family resided in Taylor, Texas, and it was from there that he was commuting to Killeen to work, helping to build Camp Hood. Reverend Bosier reconstructed the old, worn, weather-beaten frame that had been started, and built the first edifice for worship service. He was the builder and first pastor of the Lone Star Community Baptist Church. He also began the organization of the church in 1951 with its first elected officers. The congregation met for worship in the building known as the Cadillac Inn on the corner of Business 190 and 38th Street until the church was ready for use. Reverend Bosier was a friend to the pastor of Bethel Church on E. Veterans Memorial Boulevard, and was allowed to baptize there for the Lone Star Community Baptist Church. His tenure as pastor was from 1951-1954. The year 1951 commemorates both the anniversary of the official naming of the church under a Baptist minister and the anniversary of the official edifice in which to worship.

The Reverend A. R. D. Hubbard became pastor in 1954. Bill Simmons once again met with the group. He requested that the church be named Simmonsville Baptist Church in honor of his family tree. However, his request was not granted immediately. Later during Reverend Hubbard's administration (1954-1971), Mr. Simmons' request to rename the church Simmonsville Baptist Church was granted and the church was given the name Simmonsville Missionary Baptist Church. When there was a need for a better constructed building, a Fort Hood barrack was purchased and renovated. Enough finance was raised to pay cash for the barrack and to have it moved to the church's land. Reverend Hubbard's health began to fail, and he required assistance in the ministry. An honorary pastor position for him was recommended which he did not accept. Therefore, considering his failing health, the members declared the pulpit vacant by a majority vote. It was a sad day indeed for all.

From August 1972 to February 1973, Reverend Hubert E. Debose Sr. served as the church's interim pastor, and a major renovation project was initiated. The first service in the newly renovated Simmonsville Missionary Baptist Church was held in January 1973. The church was pleased with Reverend Debose's leadership and offered him the first "call" to pastor the Simmonsville Missionary Baptist Church in 1972. However, he declined that "call," expressing as his reason that he was so young in the ministry at that time. The church then called Reverend Eddie B. Coppage, Jr. as Pastor of Simmonsville Missionary Baptist Church in March 1973. There were many accomplishments. His administration lasted until his death in October 1982. After months of praying and seeking God's guidance, Reverend Hubert Edward Debose, Sr. accepted the "call" in February 1983 as Simmonsville Missionary Baptist Church's fourth pastor. He became the active pastor in March 1983. The membership quickly exceeded the capacity of the Todd Street sanctuary, which held only 180 people. A new sanctuary was completed on July 28, 1984, at 509 S. 42nd Street. By March 2001, the membership had grown to 1,100. The future site for a new church has been designated. Reverend Debose's administration has continued to the present time as Senior Pastor of Simmonsville Missionary Baptist Church.

Note: Portions of this information were taken from written copies of the church history; special occasions' church programs; the Killeen Daily Herald, March 12, 2001; Sarah Sewell, the daughter of Reverend John Wiley Bosier; and Melva Olean Davis, a founding member of the church.

Marlboro Heights Missionary Baptist Church
Reverend Dr. Roscoe A. Abercrombie, Founding Pastor
Wadella Heath

Marlboro Heights Baptist Church had its beginning as a Mission in the Marlboro Heights community. There was a need for a place where families could meet and worship together. Before the mission was established, some families living in the Marlboro Heights community traveled as far as Belton, Temple and Waco to worship. Marlboro Heights Mission held its first worship service in the Marlboro Heights Elementary School. It was conducted by Reverend Hartwell, a missionary carpenter for the southern Baptist Convention. After conducting Sunday school and worship services for several months in the school, the people saw that they could better provide religious education activities for their children and promote religious work in the community if there was a local church in the area. A census taken in June 1955 of all citizens of the Marlboro Heights community received positive responses for a local church.

In June 1955, after the survey, a joint missionary effort by a part of the Bell County Baptist Association; two local churches (First Baptist and East Side Baptist); along with the state workers of the Southern Baptist Convention and many well-wishers set in motion to secure building grounds, materials and volunteer labor for the construction of a church building. These people, all determined to see religious work progressing in the Marlboro Heights community, devoted their time, talent and finances to this effort. While the building was still under construction, an invitation was extended to a young, dedicated, ambitious minister, Reverend Roscoe Abercrombie, to conduct a meeting for one week. During this week of service the Lord added to the church as he saw fit, and the following charter members joined: Nathaniel Anderson, Elnora Banks, Mary Bowens, Napolcon Bowens, Carmille Greene, Elnora Griffin, Ruth Jackson, Ella Johnson, Geoffrey G. Langrum, Nonie Langrum, Ruth O'Neal, R. Pasley, Rosie Pope, Willie Sedberry, Estelle Story, Mary E. Williams, Julia F. Williams and Milton Williams.

These members were then called together by Reverend Abercrombie for an organizational meeting on June 19, 1955. This group was guided to organize a church that would be named after a preacher was called. The body of charter members extended a call to Reverend Abercrombie as Pastor. He accepted the call as pastor, and the Mission had its first pastor. Reverend Roscoe A. Abercrombie remained to help finish the work of building the church that was in progress. The church was completed in July, 1955, and named Marlboro Heights Baptist Church. At the second business meeting under Reverend Abercrombie's leadership, fourteen auxiliaries were organized. As the church grew in numbers and strength, twenty-two auxiliaries were added. The membership continued to grow. The church records showed that several Brothers had accepted the call to preach the gospel. Over many years, the church's growth was continual. A second sanctuary was built to accommodate this growth. Even with this expansion, the space of both the original facility and the new sanctuary were used in carrying out the church's worship and Christian education programs. There were four singing choirs, and they had recorded two albums. A youth service was held each Sunday, and a well-staffed nursery was available. Reverend R. A. Abercrombie served as pastor of the church until his death, in March, 1992.

In June 1994, Reverend Dr. Shaun L. Moton was installed as the pastor of Marlboro Heights Missionary Baptist Church. Reverend Dr. Moton became the second pastor to serve the church since its organization in 1955. A new sanctuary was needed to again accommodate the growth. In October 2009, the Marlboro Missionary Baptist Church began worshiping in its new beautiful sanctuary constructed on a spacious site at 2901 East Illinois Avenue in Killeen. It was constructed during the administration of the Reverend. Dr. Shaun L. Moton, Pastor of Marlboro Missionary Baptist Church.

Note: Portions of this history were obtained from community sources, newspaper articles and programs of special services.

God's Holy Tabernacle Church of God in Christ
Reverend Elder E. M. Green, Founding Pastor
Reverend Rudolph Jackson

God's Holy Tabernacle Church of God in Christ was organized in 1958 by Elder E. M. Green, an ordained Elder, and Missionary Catherine E. Green. This was the first black Pentecostal/Holiness Church in Killeen, It is the Mother Church of the Churches of God in Christ in the Killeen area. It is located at 500 South Superintendent E. M. Green Street (formerly 44th Street), Killeen, Texas. The church has been in this location for more than 43 years. The late Superintendent E. M. Green came to the Killeen-Fort Hood area by way of the military. The family lived in Temple, Texas at this time, and Elder Green had to travel back and forth to Killeen. He met Elder R. M. White who was working at the Southwest Bus Station in downtown Killeen. During the conversation that they had Elder Green asked Elder R.M. White if a person can start a church in

Killeen; to which Elder White responded, "Yes, you can." The rest is history. Seeing the need for a church, by faith Elder Green rented a building for $35.00 a month. In November of that year, he acquired another building on Highway 190. The only members of the church at that time were his wife, Catherine, and his children.

The first revival was held in December 1958, by Elder Green. Five souls were saved in that revival. The first members were Mrs. Ida Prem, Tommy Sanders and Wheeler Smith. Souls were added to the church. In 1959, Elder Green and his family moved to Killeen. They resided in the Marlboro Heights community, and Elder Green was a leader in this community. He was involved in community, and was concerned about the welfare of the people in the community. Mother Catherine Green started a prayer meeting in December 1959. She would go from house to house praying, regarding neither race nor color. She would pray wherever God would lead her to go and pray. She would pray in Killeen, Fort Hood, Harker Heights and Copperas Cove, and in homes where she could. Many were healed and saved in the prayer service. She served as the Church Mother, a prayer warrior, Sunshine Band president, Bible Band president, teacher and praise worshiper.

Elder Green later rented a building at the corner of 46th and Turner Street. The church met there until God moved Elder Green, in May of 1965, to purchase the land at 500 South 44th Street. Later, God blessed Elder Green to get a building, which is now "God's Holy Tabernacle Church of God in Christ." The first member saved in this building was Mother Sweeney. There were some hard times for Elder Green and the church. It seemed that people did not like the way they were having church. The church was Brick Batted, cherry bombs were place under the building and complaints were filed with the police department because of the "noise". None of these things moved him; neither did he count his life dear.

Under his leadership there were many outreach programs organized that were a blessing to the church. He was an advocate for street ministry and witnessing door to door. His preaching and teaching were so profound and down to earth, that anyone could understand what he was saying. The members that passed through here were blessed to have known him, for many who came here were new converts in the Lord and some were preachers, missionaries and deacons. The success of the church did not come without some heartaches and pain. There wasn't ever enough money, but God always made a way. With fasting and prayer God provided for the church and Elder Green's family. There were sickness and death of loved ones, but God was always there when the family and church needed Him.

Elder Green was elevated to the office of District Superintendent of the Killeen District. He held that office until God called him home on July 13, 1983. Superintendent Green was a pioneer, a leader, a visionary and a lover of people. Under his leadership, the church grew as he was led by the Spirit of God. At the death of Superintendent Green, I was appointed the pastor of God's Holy Tabernacle Church of God in Christ and was installed on October 25, 1983. Under my leadership the church continues to minister to the spiritual and phys- ical needs of families in Killeen and the surrounding communities. It also continues to provide opportunities for worship and a place where Christian believers can give expressions of their faith.

It has not been an easy task, but God has been there to carry me through. He has proven Himself to me in the times that we are living in. God is the leader of this church. Many of the former members are yet in the Killeen Area: Elder and Missionary Billie, Superintendent Grove, and some are yet members of the church. District Elder and Missionary Jenkins were members, also. God's Holy Tabernacle Church of God in Christ's members were primarily residents of Simmonsville, Marlboro Heights or Ft. Hood. These were the only areas where Blacks could live at that time. As Blacks settled in sur- rounding areas of Harker Heights, Nolanville and Copperas Cove, the church gained members from all of these communities. God's Holy Tabernacle Church of God in Christ was the second church organized in the Simmonsville community that served Blacks, and was the third church organized in Killeen for blacks. In 2007, the Killeen City Council voted five to two to change the name of the street from 44th Street to Superintendent E. M. Green Street. It was a blessing to have the street named in honor of the late Superintendent Green for his labor and accomplishments. It is good when you can appreciate what someone else has done. We give God all the glory for what He has done at God's Holy Tabernacle Church of God in

Christ. There is a lot of history here in Killeen and I am glad to be a part of it.

Anderson Chapel African Methodist Episcopal Church
Reverend Arthur Anderson, Founding Pastor
Alice Douse

Anderson Chapel African Methodist Episcopal Church was organized February 10, 1964, under the leadership of the founder, the Reverend Arthur Anderson. The organizational meeting was held in the home of Frederick and Velma Hayden at 3215 Longview Drive in Killeen, Texas and is now located in Marlboro Heights of the city of Killeen. Ten residents were in attendance. Rev. Arthur Anderson, Mary Anderson, his wife; Velma Hayden, his daughter; Eddie Mae Johnson, Mary Manjang, Willie and Bertie Sworn, Marion J. and Alice Douse and Mary Reed. Frederick Hayden was not present at the organizational meeting due to an overseas military assignment with the United States Army. However, he had expressed a desire to become one of the charter members of the newly founded church. Mary Reed chose not to affiliate as a church member. Reverend Aurhor Anderson presided at the meeting and held the election of the first officers. Members of the newly organized church boards and auxiliaries were:

Bro. Willie Sworn	Steward Board
Bro. Marion J. Douse	Trustee Board and Church Treasurer
Bro. Fred Hayden	Trustee Board
Sis. Mary Manjang	Stewardess President
Sis. Mary Anderson	Stewardess Board
Sis. Bertie Sworn	Secretary, Church Clerk and Junior Choir Director
Sis. Alice Douse	Sunday School Superintendent
Sis. Velma Hayden	Stewardess Board, Assistant Sunday School Superintendent, Allen Christian Endeavor (ACE) League Director
Sis. Eddie M. Johnson	Missionary President, Stewardess Board
Cathy Douse	Pianist
Founded	Rev. Arthur Anderson was pastor of Bethel African Methodist Episcopal Bethel African Methodist Episcopal Church in Lampasas, Texas at the time that Anderson Chapel was organized. The newly organized Anderson Chapel African Methodist Episcopal church became a part of the Lampasas-Killeen Circuit of the Austin Capital District and the Central Texas Conference of the Tenth Episcopal District of the African Methodist Episcopal Church. As circuit churches, Bethel at Lampasas and Anderson Chapel at Killeen would meet on alternating Sundays for worship.

The members were tasked to locate a meeting place to hold our worship services. A building at 3631 Turner Avenue and 46th Street that was formerly a jail for the Lone Star Community, now known as Simmonsville, became Anderson Chapel's first church. The first worship service was held on March 3, 1964.

On January 1, 1966, almost two years after its organization, Anderson Chapel AME Church relocated from Turner and 46th Street to its present site, 1002 Jefferies Avenue. This building was purchased from Sunset Baptist Church in Killeen and moved to the Jefferies Avenue site. On August 7, 1966, Bishop O. L. Sherman, Presiding Prelate of the Tenth Episcopal District of the African Methodist Episcopal Church presided during the Dedication Service for Anderson Chapel AME Church. In October 1966, during the 83rd Session of the Central Texas Conference, Anderson Chapel was designated a Station Church. That meant that Rev. Anderson would serve as the pastor of only one church, Anderson Chapel AME and Sunday worship services would be held each week

Rev. Arthur Anderson and his wife, Mary Anderson, commuted from Lampasas, Texas, to serve as pastor of Anderson Chapel for 10 years. On October 11, 1974, at the 91st Session of the Central Texas Annual Conference, Rev. Arthur Anderson retired. He had also spent more than 50 years as an itinerant minister of the African Methodist Episcopal Church, preaching the gospel throughout Texas. Since 1964, Anderson Chapel has served Killeen and surrounding communities as a place of worship and a refuge for prayer in the times of crisis and trouble. It has been meeting the spiritual, physical and emotional needs of families and individuals in the community locally, regionally and globally. Anderson Chapel African Methodist Church is an evangelistic and mission oriented congregation.

Its mission is to minister the saving Gospel of Jesus through worship, teaching, evangelism, mission, ministries, fellowship and discipleship. Each area of this mission statements receives its proper focus at Anderson Chapel. Under the current administration of Reverend Dr. William M. Campbell, Jr., youth ministry has an important focus within the church regarding youth training, participation in the activities of the church and their development of a sound relationship with the Lord. The vision of Anderson Chapel AME Church is to be an evangelistic, stewardship-focused, mission-oriented congregation. The church is greatly involved in its Mission ministry locally through two established mission houses that provide food, clothing and other household essentials to those in need of it in the community. Through its *Mission House One* and ***Mission House Two*** that are located at 1004 and 1102 Jefferies Avenue in Killeen many families have been served. The Mission ministry has also extended regionally as far as Galveston, Texas. The Mission Ministry has also extended globally as far as the island of Jamaica and the continent of Africa.

Under a leadership structure of itinerant pastors in the AME Church, each pastor receives a one-year appointment to a church from the Bishop each year. Since Anderson Chapel's beginning in 1964, the leadership of Anderson Chapel AME Church has been shared by eleven pastors, all of whom have been committed to ministering to members in the church and to families and individuals in this community. The appointments include Reverends Arthur Anderson 1964-74, J. A. Peterson 1974-75, Preston Edwards 1975-76, B. J. Satterwhite 1976-77, James R. Anderson 1977-80, T. J. Shepherd 1980-81, M. C. Cooper 1981-90, Dr. C. A. Jones 1991-92, Dr. Lawrence Emanuel 1992-96, Walter McDonald 1996-2002, and Dr. William M. Campbell, Jr. 2002- present. The church has experienced continuous growth through the years. As a body of believers. Our faith and trust are in God our Father; Christ our Redeemer; The Holy Spirit our Comforter. We acknowledge Mankind as our Brother.

Deliverance and Praise Temple Church of God in Christ
Reverend Edward Roy Billie, Founding Pastor
Lillian Lois Billie

Deliverance and Praise Temple Church of God in Christ, formerly Zion Temple Church of God in Christ (C.O.G.I.C.) was organized March 12, 1969. Its founders were Rev. Edward Roy Billie, Jr. and his wife, the former Lillian Lois Hodge of Corpus Christi, Texas. Elder Edward R. Billie, a native of Vallejo, California, was stationed at Ft. Hood, Texas. His wife, Lillian, was employed by the Killeen Independent School District as the music teacher at Marlboro Elementary School in Marlboro Heights. Both were former members of the God's Holy Tabernacle Church of God in Christ in the Simmonsville Community, where Elder E. M. Green was pastor. The first service of Zion Temple Church of God in Christ was a Sunday School service held at the Killeen Community Center, which is located at Veterans Memorial Boulevard (formerly Business 190) and W. S. Young Drive. They worshiped there until the church moved to the Serviceman Church, which was located on Zephyr Road. There, they held 12:00 p.m. worship services.

In August of the same year, the church found a house at 408 North Ann Boulevard in Harker Heights, Texas and made it their house of worship. Zion Temple Church of God in Christ was the first church organized by Blacks and at that time for Blacks in Harker

Heights, Texas. The congregation worshiped at this location until March 4, 1978 when the church burned down. For three months Zion Temple Church of God in Christ had no church home until Rev. Eddie Coppage, then pastor of Simmonsville Missionary Baptist Church, invited Elder Billie and his congregation to have church in Simmonsville's very first church, which was located in Simmonsville on Todd Street. Blessings continued to be showered upon this congregation of believers, and on July 4, 1978 the church returned to the Harker Heights Community to a new location at 702 Harley Drive, the church's current site. This ministry has flourished and has served many citizens throughout Harker Heights, Killeen, Fort Hood and surrounding areas.

On July 16, 1987, Bishop A. LaDell Thomas, Sr. was appointed pastor of Zion Temple Church of God in Christ and he continues to provide spiritual leadership to the congregation and to the community. The church's name was changed in January 2004, to Deliverance and Praise Temple Church of God in Christ. However, its mission remains unchanged. In 2007, the city of Harker Heights honored Bishop LaDell Thomas, Sr. by approving the naming of a section of Harley Drive, on which the church is located, as Bishop Thomas Boulevard.

The Church of God in Christ Denomination was founded by Bishop C. H. Mason in 1907.

First Church of God in Christ Church
Superintendent Dr. John C. Robinson Founding Pastor
Mabel May Robinson

The First Church of God and Christ was founded and organized by Elder John C. Robinson at 3202 Taft Street, Killeen, Texas, in October 1983. The church started with four members, consisting of the pastor's wife Mabel May Robinson and their three children. Mother Bertha Williams, who had just moved to Killeen from Chicago, Illinois, was the first member outside of the family. Mother Williams, Pastor and Bishop C. Moody had prophesied prior to her leaving that she would help start a church. The First Church of God in Christ was chartered a non-profit cooperation in Killeen, Texas on April 15, 1984. Because of the rapid growth, the church began having services at West Ward Elementary School, located on Dean and Hillcrest Streets. The membership soon climbed to over fifty-five members. In the summer of 1984, the church paid $5000.00 down and began purchasing approximately 2 acres of land in the 4100 block of Zephyr Road. This was to be the future site of First Church of God in Christ. The church began having services at Haynes Elementary School, 4100 Zephyr Road. During these times, Sunday school and morning worship services were held at the school. A weekly night service and auxiliary meetings were held at the pastor's house.

The Trustee Board consisted of eight men and women. We had a Home and Foreign Mission Department, Outreach Ministry, Sunday school with over five classes, YPWW with two classes, Bible Band and Usher Board. We also had a hospitality committee, sick committee, young adult choir, church choir, Sunshine Band with choir and a Brotherhood group with choirs.

In May 1987, the church property at East Rancier and Massey Street was purchased. Many souls accepted Christ and the work of the ministry and the membership continued to grow. A larger facility was needed. Therefore in 1998 construction began to build a new facility for worship, teaching and fellowship. On Saturday, June 13, 1999, in preparation for the move to the new church, First Church of God in Christ planned a "Power Walk," an occasion when the congregation participated in a parade, complete with banners and cheers and with a tractor driven by one of its members. It began at the intersection of Massey Street and Rancier Avenue (the location of the early Massey Street Church) to start a four-mile walk to the northeast sector of Killeen to the location of the new church at 5201 Westcliff Road. District Court 264 Judge Martha J. Trudo was invited to ride along in the parade. The Sunday edition of the Killeen Daily Herald carried the story of the Power Walk of the First Church of God in Christ. The four mile walk took approximately one hour and fifteen minutes.

The construction of the nearly 18,000-square-foot structure was expected to be completed by August 1999, but bad weather had caused a delay in construction. During the fall of 1999, the congregation witnessed the opening and dedication of a new church. Their new religious facility was equipped with a spacious sanctuary, adequate classrooms, offices and fellowship areas at 5201 Westcliff Road, Killeen, Texas. A celebration service for the accomplishment of the historical milestone in the life of the First Church of God in Christ was held. Rev. Dr. John C. Robinson, Mrs. Mabel Robinson and the congregation witnessed the opening and dedication of their new church.

Westside Baptist Church
Rev. Hallie Tolbert, Sr. Founding Pastor
Rev. Hallie Tolbert, Sr.

"Go ye therefore, and teach all nations, baptizing them in the name of the Father and of the Son, and of the Holy Ghost: Training them to observe all things whatsoever I commanded you and lo, I am with you always, even unto the end of the world. Amen" *(Matthew 28:19-20).*

An organized body of baptized believers, commonly known as "the church", is the vehicle often used by the Holy Spirit to carry out the directions of the great commission. In obedience to the Holy Spirit and in accordance with the ministry and goals of the Baptist General Convention of Texas and of the Bell Baptist Association, Rev. Dean Parmer, Interim Pastor of Pershing Park Baptist Church, proposed to the Pershing Park Church Council that the church sponsor a new Baptist work in Killeen. After considering the proposal, the council voted to present the ideas to the membership of Pershing Park Church at the June 1985 business meeting. The church voted to establish a mission in the vicinity of Old Copperas Cove Road, – acquisition of land.

The late Dr. David Cannon, Rev. Jack Medford (Church Planter), Rev. Don Warden (Field Consultant-Mission Division of the Baptist Convention of Texas) and the Pershing Park Mission Committee's selected temporary site was a mobile home located in the Angel Trailer Park on Old Copperas Cove Road. Pershing Park Mission Committee selected July as the start-up month for the mission, and named the new work, "Old Copperas Cove Road Baptist Mission." The Mission committee also called Rev. Jack Medford, a Mission Corp worker, to be the pastor, and the first worship service was held on August 18, 1985. On November 26, the Rev. Jack Medford resigned as pastor of the mission to return to his home in Azle, Texas, and the Mission Committee selected G. A. Gore as pastor. He served until his resignation in October, 1986. Under the leadership of Pastor Gore, the mission grew to approximately 25 members (7 adults and 18 children).

In January, 1987, the mission committee appointed Rev. Hallie Tolbert as interim Pastor. He immediately began to change the mission from a babysitting ministry and began to seek another site for worship which would provide room for growth. Pastor Hallie Tolbert, along with Rev. Frank Smith and Rev. Billy Rosebur, began witnessing in the surrounding area. Their work began to pay dividends and by late May the mission had outgrown its location. It was in March 1987, that Pastor Tolbert resigned his position as Assistant Pastor of Pershing Park Baptist Church and assumed the position of Pastor of Copperas Cove Road Baptist Mission. He continued his search for a place to relocate the mission to facilitate growth, and submitted a request to the Killeen independent School District Board of Trustees to use the Willow Spring Elementary School facilities. The Board granted the request and in December 1987 the mission began to worship in the Willow Spring School. It was during this same month, December 1987, that at the request of Pastor Tolbert, the membership voted to change the name of the mission to Westside Baptist Church. We consider 1987 as the birth year of the church, since that's the year the Mission changed from a babysitting ministry to an evangelistic ministry.

In December 1988, Westside Baptist Church leased a building at 1600 Old Copperas Cove Road and after extensive church renovation by the membership; the first worship service was conducted at the new location in January 1989. Initially electricity was provided by a 5KW generator and a space heater to knock the chill out of the air. The church continued to pray for a permanent location and a decade or more blessings were experienced by the church.

In October 1990, Sister Cleo Owens located a piece of property on Stagecoach Road. It contained fruit trees, a doublewide mobile home, a storage shed and a house. Westside Baptists Church's request to Pershing Park Baptist to purchase 3.2 acres was approved and submitted to the Baptist Church Loan of the Baptist General Convention of Texas. In January 1991, Pershing Park closed on the property and after extensive renovation on the house, the building became our worship center. The mobile home served as the education and fellowship building and the garage was converted to the pastor's office and administration building. In November 1992, the congregation incorporated as the Westside Baptist Church of Killeen, Texas. Then in December 1992, the church purchased an additional 1.6 acres of adjacent land, giving the mission a total of 4.8 acres.

To solve the overcrowding problem we were experiencing, two morning services were scheduled at that time. However on June 6, 1995, because the church continued to grow, the pastor and building committee began planning for a new worship facility. Construction of a new sanctuary began in 1997. The dedication of the new sanctuary was held on February 22, 1998, with over 600 people in attendance. Our theme was "We've come Far by Faith." In December 1999, God continued to be faithful as we ended a century and began a new millennium. Over 212 attended Watch Night Service on December 31, 1999. Ten individuals accepted Christ during that service. Please pray for Westside as we continue to be led by the Holy Spirit to do Kingdom work.

Greater Peace Missionary Baptist Church
Reverend J. A. Moland Founding Pastor
Wadella Heath

God, in His mercy and infinite wisdom, brought together a group of forty-seven dedicated Christian servants and on May 31, 1994, this group of servants organized the Greater Peace Missionary Baptist Church. The Rev. J. A. Moland was extended the call and accepted as Pastor of this newly formed local congregation. Under the leadership of Pastor J. A. Moland, God continued to bless us. As God continued to pour out his Spirit upon us and we began to reach out to the community; as a result, our church grew. God placed in the membership another 112 souls. Several ministries were also established: Bell County Jail Ministry, Gatesville Prison Ministry, and Nursing Home Ministry, Families in Crisis Ministry, Evangelical Ministry and Internal Ministries of Service. Many souls have been won and added to this local body of Christ and numerous lives have been blessed by these various ministries.

God has kept his promise. He has allowed us to grow spiritually and financially. Out of His graciousness, God enabled us to purchase property for our future sanctuary. The ground breaking for turning the dirt was scheduled for May 28, 1995 at 9:45 A.M., and on May

28, 1995 we held the Ground Breaking Service. Officers and members of Greater Peace Missionary Baptist Church were in attendance. City officials—to include Raul Villaronga, Mayor for the City of Killeen; Young H. Hwang, member of the Planning and Zoning Committee for the City of Killeen; Ernestine Hill Warren, Mayor of the City of Rosebud; Thomas Wood, Prince Hall Mason from the Killeen-Fort Hood Area—were also present and witnessed the Ground Breaking Ceremony. Remarks were given by the Reverend J. A. Moland, Pastor of Greater Peace Missionary Baptist Church.

Giving thanks for the ground breaking as projected and completed, Greater Peace Missionary Baptist Church continued their prayers and their work and looked forward to the completion of their building project with the assurance that if it was God's will, the near completion of the sanctuary as projected will be August 1996. On Sunday, August 4, 1996 at 10:00 A.M., Greater Peace Missionary Baptist Church held its "Entrance Service." The Dedication Service for Greater Peace Missionary Baptist Church was held at 3:30 P.M. on the same day. Greater Peace is a testimony of what God can do when we are obedient and submit ourselves to his leadership.

Greater Peace's newly constructed 12,000 square foot church was completed in August 1996. The funding source was from offerings and gifts. The sanctuary has a seating capacity for 500 persons. Cordus Jackson Jr. served as Moderator for the organization. Vivian Dishman was chosen as clerk. Evans Washington was selected as secretary for the organization's proceedings. God's blessings were and are upon us.

Cornerstone Baptist Church
Reverend Dr. Edward L. Wagner, Founding Pastor
Reverend Dr. Edward L. Wagner

Cornerstone Baptist Church was founded in 1995 and is the vision from God through me, Pastor Edward L. Wagner. This was to be a church like none other, a New Testament church dedicated to the Lord and following New Testament doctrines to model God's message of hope, power and love in the community we serve and beyond. I was led by the Holy Spirit to set in motion this vision in reaching the physical, emotional, social and spiritual needs of the people of this community. Cornerstone Baptist Church's purpose is to bring people to Jesus and to membership in His family; to develop them to Christ-like maturity; and to equip them for their ministry in the church, and their mission in the world, in order to magnify God's name.

Cornerstone Baptist Church values relationships; values the Word of God and values our community. Of these three values, building relationships is our number one goal in this area. The two other relationship goals that we value are to create a family bond that cherishes and prioritizes relationships; and to ensure the assimilation process related to building relationships occurs for our new members and visitors.

Cornerstone Baptist Church's goals, based on the Word of God, are to establish a knowledge-based teaching/preaching foundation of the Word of God. The purpose of this emphasis is to strengthen each believer in the knowledge of God's Word; and to develop a Sunday school program that gives the Word of God to everyone – the saved and the lost. Therefore the church's vision for today and for future generations of African-American youth is to educate them in the Word; grow them into the knowledge and understanding of our Lord and Savior Jesus Christ so that the Word of God will continue to be in the next generation and beyond.

Cornerstone's Community goals are to establish an outreach ministry that aggressively seeks to reach out to the lost; to develop a ministry that focuses on the building of Church-Community relationships; and to be actively involved in the building, growth and development of our community. Therefore Cornerstone Baptist Church partners with community projects and outreach missions through its Nursing Home Ministry and Prison Ministry; the Home and Hope Shelter; the Hope and Pregnancy Center; and through Habitat for Humanity.

To establish the new church, I directed the initial group of believers to organize and to form a Board of Trustees. Part of their early strategy involved seeking and receiving assistance from Bell Baptist Association and the Baptist General Convention of Texas. On August 7, 1995 a reception was held to give members of the community an opportunity to join this new endeavor, and from the reception the core membership was established. In those beginning months, many new activities created opportunities for the vision to flourish. I began a series of sermons from the First Book of Corinthians to teach the new congregation what God's expectations are for His church. Reverend James Freeman confirmed God's call to the ministry by delivering his first sermon on October 29, 1995 and a Building Fund Committee was established to begin planning for the future growth of the church. The initial building fund goal was set at thirty thousand dollars. Through prayer, we asked the Holy Spirit to direct our giving to accomplish this goal; and as more and more members pledged, the excitement began to escalate. I granted permission to start a Children's Church Ministry, and Rev. Freeman was named the Youth Minister.

In 1996, God continued to bless Cornerstone's efforts, as he had done from the beginning. The membership roll continued to grow. The first Sunday school program began January 7, 1996, and the first Bible study class was held. I appointed a church musician and on February 4, 1996 the choir delivered its first songs of praise to an enthusiastic assembly of believers. The new usher board ministry took charge of Cornerstone's support services. Three deacons were ordained to aid me in ministering to the needs of the growing church body. Also during the month of February 1996, I called the first Church Council and Church Conference. The church Council gives those in leadership positions an organized planning session to coordinate activities. The Church Conference gives the members the opportunity to address church government. During one of the early actions of these auxiliaries, the church approved the purchase of 20 acres of land on which our church now stands.

In 1996, we saw the initiation of the Outreach Ministry, ministerial staff, ladies fellowship (Virtuous Women) and the ordaining of three more deacons. We began to broadcast our worship services on KPLE television in November 1996, and these worship services have continued to be broadcasted on KPLE television every Thursday evening at 7:00 p.m.

The year 2007 brought a magnitude of blessings: the pulpit ministry had two powerful associate ministers to assist me as Pastor. The Deacon Family Ministry had a total of sixteen dedicated deacons. The church membership numbers increased to 386. The church offers nineteen ministries for members to exercise their spiritual gifts. Sunday school and Mid-week service attendance increased. The church's blessings have been many. However, there were obstacles that the church had to overcome and we thank God, who directed the purchase of the land, the approval for the funding and Cornerstone's accomplishment of paying off the church mortgage. Through prayer and sacrificial giving, the church body rallied together to pay off the mortgage on the church. Through the guidance of the Holy Spirit, it took only seven years to achieve this goal. This was a great achievement.

Our church has been the recipient of a number of notable awards and honors: The "Salt and Light Award," "Top Pacesetter Award," "Charles H. Spurgeon Outstanding Church Award." It has been "recognized as one of the top 200 healthy churches in the state of Texas," and named the #1 church in the Cooperative Program Contributions.

The members of Cornerstone Baptist Church, under my guidance as Pastor looked to "a new beginning" with the planning and building of our new edifice. The future is bright and the excitement high as we continue to seek direction from the Holy Spirit.

Greater Vision Community Church
Reverend Dr. David Glynn Reynolds, Founding Pastor
Reverend Dr. David G. Reynolds

On April 10, 1997 I, Reverend David Glynn Reynolds, then a U. S. Army Chaplain at the rank of Major, assembled with some 35 people in the first meeting held to organize a church. I became the founder and pastor of Greater Vision Community Church. This is a ministry with a vision to impact the spiritual, physical, emotional, social and economic well-being of the community. (Proverbs 29:18 and Luke 9-17) From a humble beginning in Killeen, Greater Vision Community Church became one of the fast growing congregations in the Killeen area. The first worship service was held on the First Sunday in August 1997. The Killeen Daily Herald in announcing the first public gathering of the Greater Vision Community Church, described the setting for this first worship service in this manner: "Using folding chairs and a portable wooden podium at Carol's African-American Art Gallery in downtown Killeen, the first worship service of the Greater Vision Full Gospel Community Church was held on the first Sunday in August, 1997. After many hours of meetings and planning, the church had become a reality".

We continued our services at the art gallery while plans for building a church were proceeding and established our leadership ministries. The work of the church moved forward with milestone after milestone in the life of the church being met. June 17, 2001 marked an historical event for our congregation Patricia Reynolds and this founding pastor because it was just four years earlier that we had first assembled to hold our first worship service. On this date the historical occasion was the dedication of the Greater Vision Community Church at 2001 E. Stan Schlueter Loop in Killeen, Texas. Plans to build the church had projected the date for the first worship service in their newly constructed facility to be December 15, 2000. However, several rains during the construction period caused a delay and the projection plans were extended to May 2001. In May 2001, Greater Vision Community Church's new 15,000-square-foot, non-denominational religious facility was completed and equipped with comfortable seating for 600 worshipers. At the time of the dedication, June 17, 2001, the congregation had grown to more than 300 members. In a special 4:00 P.M. service held on Sunday, June 17, 2001 I, the founding pastor, symbolically unveiled the church's cornerstone showing me as the first pastor. Also engraved on the cornerstone were the names of the other founding Reverends, the first deacons and the first trustees of the church. By the year 2008, this ministry had more than 1,500 members. The work of the church continued in worshiping and rendering selfless service and Greater Vision Community Church's historical milestones in ministry were accomplished. The following are some historical highlights and milestones in ministry during the church's first thirteen years.

1997: We established the adult ushers ministry in August; the finance committee in September and the adult choir in October. Our church Dedication Service was held in December and the dance ministry and sign language ministry were also formed.

1998: Formed the youth and children choirs and youth ushers in January; held the first youth forum and public health fair in May;

the first Deacon Ordination in June; the first Vacation Bible School in July and the Men of Vision Ministry was formed. Greater Vision also celebrated its first Church Anniversary in August; purchased its first acreage of land in November; installed its first Deaconesses and formed the Women of Vision Ministry. The year ended with a Church Dedication service in December; a Public Relations and Marketing Ministry and a Building and Design Committee formed to build the current church.

1999: Observed the first Women's Day in March; the first Pastor's Appreciation banquet in April; Deacons were ordained and deaconesses were installed in May. Published the first newsletter in June; paid the land debt in full!!! Then we formed a Youth Advisory Committee in November.

2000: Expanded the trustee board in January; held the first Gospel Explosion in February and changed the church name from Greater Vision Full Gospel Community Church to Greater Vision Community Church in May.

2001: Completed Greater Vision's new 15,000 square foot non-denominational religious facility in May equipped with comfortable seating for 600 in cushioned pews and located at 2001 E. Stan Schlueter Loop in Killeen, Texas; held church Dedication Service in May, and unveiled the church cornerstone. The "Mighty Men of Valor" also made their first Mime Ministry debut in May, 2001.

2002: Established the Institutional Ministry in March; formed the first church softball team in April, ordained six deacons and installed five deaconesses in July.

2003: Established the Men of Vision Choir in August and the Angel Tree Ministry in September. Purchased 8.12 acres of land in November. This totaled 20 acres of land purchased by the church. Began the Plans & Committee for Building Expansion in November.

2004: Began Young Adults (18-30) Dance Ministry in June and held the first youth led service in August.

2005: Licensed five ministers in January through March; established the Ministry of Construction/GVCC 20/20 in April; held the First Night of Laughter in May; a Ground Breaking Ceremony in June and "Operation Vision Assist" provided aid to Hurricane Katrina Evacuees in September.

2006: Ordained two ministers in February; held the church's First Women of Vision Retreat in March; the First Leadership Conference and First Men of Vision "Men's Night Out" Musical in April; and The Men of Vision Leadership Conference in May. Licensed one minister in July; began Phase II of Parking lot; ordained one minister in August; completed Phase II parking in October.

2007: Held its First Singles White Ball in February; the First "Youth Retreat 2007" at Buda, Texas in June; the First Marriage Enrichment Dinner and First Christmas Eve Musical in December.

2008: Held its First Seder/Passover Meal Jointly with Anderson Chapel AME Church in February; its First Good Friday Musical in March; and its First Youth-Led Prayer Service in May. Established the 18-24 (years of age) Sunday school and the 25 and over (years of age) Sunday school classes in May.

2009: Continued faithfully in the work of the Kingdom and partnered with Anderson Chapter AME Church on a global mission trip to Nakuru, Kenya, in Africa in 2010-2011.

Greater Vision Community Church has received recognition for our community and outreach program in the City of Killeen. I serve my congregation as a full time Pastor and personally dedicated countless volunteer hours and actively leads my congregation to support a number of community and non-profit organizations and efforts. For example, such causes as American Cancer Society's "Walk for Life," Sickle Cell Anemia Foundation, Hope

Pregnancy Centers; Home and Hope Shelter; American Red Cross; American Diabetes Association; NAACP; Food for Families; Care Incorporated; Rosewood Nursing Facility; Hill Country Nursing Home; and the Mission Soup Kitchen. The church, my wife and I have made a significant contribution in Community Service and Community Building.

The work of the Kingdom is alive and active at Greater Vision Community Church.

Other Area Churches and Ministries

There are many other area churches founded by or pastored by African American spiritual leaders in this community. This has greatly contributed to this city's progress. It is to our churches and spiritual leaders that we turn to for guidance, faith building and as a place of refuge and prayer in times of crisis. Some of these churches or ministries are listed below. Many serve a diverse congregation.

Cathedral of Central Texas Christian House of Prayer, (K and CC)
Garden of Gethsemane Church of God in Christ, (HH)
St. John's Faith Outreach Baptist Church, (K)
Adams Chapel African Methodist Episcopal Church, (HH)
Thomas Chapel African Methodist Episcopal Church, (CC)
New Zion Christian Fellowship, (K)
Bibleway Church of God in Christ, (K)
Rivers of Living Waters, (K)
Unity Missionary Baptist Church, (CC)
Praise and Deliverance House of Prayer, (K)
Tabernacle of Praise, (K)
Transforming Life, (K)
Bible Way Missionary Baptist Church, (CC)

*Killeen (K)
Copperas Cove (CC)
Harker Heights (HH)

CHAPTER 9

School: An Essential Part of Community Life

—⚭—

Killeen's First School for African American Students
Research Team

Marlboro School of 1954 became Marlboro Elementary School in 1961.

C hapter nine of Tapestry provides a brief history of the establishment of Killeen's first school for African American. The evolution of education for these students and educators is a part of this history. During the 1950s the importance of quality public school education in the Marlboro Heights and Simmonsville communities paralleled that of establishing nurturing homes and places of worship for African American families. School was also an issue of concern for the NAACP. This chapter re-visits the development of public school education for African Americans prior to 1954 and on through 1969. Marlboro School was built in 1954 in the Marlboro Heights Community as Killeen's first school for African Americans. Thirteen acres of land made up the school property. The original construction was three classrooms and a smaller room, which became the principal's office. When Marlboro School opened in 1954 as an "All Black" School, Mrs. Vera Lankford Nelson and Mrs. Vera Scott Wabbington were hired as the first teachers of the school. At the opening of Marlboro School's second year in 1955, Dock Jackson, Jr. joined the staff as a teaching principal. The assignment of Miss Scott and Miss Lankford to Marlboro School gave them the distinction and an historical honor of being the first two African American teachers employed in the Killeen Independent School District. Prior to 1955, schooling for the African American civilian students living in the town was nonexistent within the town of Killeen proper. Public school education for these civilian students living in Killeen was provided through an arrangement with the Killeen School System and the neighboring school system in Belton, Texas. Therefore, prior to 1954 Black students rode the bus to Belton to attend a school for African Americans.

Fort Hood had its own school system and provided for its African American military dependents of elementary school age within its own school system. A school for Negro students had been established at Ft. Hood in the early fifties. African American elementary school age students of civilian parents employed and living on the military installation could also attend Fort Hood's school system. However, the Fort Hood School for this group of students was a segregated one which was at that time the law of the land. The school had assigned African American teachers, but had no assigned principal; therefore, the Superintendent of the Ft. Hood School District, Mr. Robert E. L. Jones, was its overseer. The Fort Hood School system consolidated with the Killeen school system in 1952. African American military dependents that were elementary school-age students continued to attend school on Post until 1954 at which time Marlboro School opened in Marlboro Heights.

Issues of concern from the NAACP emerged regarding equality of educational facilities, as well as the education of junior high and high school-age students. This educational equality issue was partially addressed with the opening of Marlboro School in 1954 because the school served African Americans both civilians and military dependents, from first grade through eighth grade. However, the education equality concern was not totally addressed until 1956.

Prior to 1956 all African American students in grades nine through twelve had to ride the bus to T. B. Harris High School in Belton, while students in grades eight and below attended Marlboro School. In 1956, the Killeen Independent School District Board of Trustees voted to integrate the secondary level African American students in ninth grade through twelfth grade, who would have had to attend school in Belton, into the formerly "all white" Killeen High School. Fourteen students chose to integrate when given the choice to either continue attending school in Belton or attend Killeen High School. These students showed courage by enrolling during the first semester of integration. The group included juniors: Cecil Anderson and James Beneford; sophomores: Mary Dockery, Marjorie Jarman, Dorothy Johnson, Suzie Lloyd; and Freshmen Oscar Anderson, Prentis Clayton, Patricia Dockery, Sandra Terry, Joe Searles III, Ethel Jo Todd, Brenda Williams and Johnnie Yeager.[7] The reception by the high school students was not a totally welcoming one when these African American students departed their bus the first day of school in 1956. They encountered obstacles and unkind acts from some of the students; but "The Fourteen" were willing to face the obstacles and not allow them to prevent their pursuit for an education. One of the students, Joe Searles, was an excellent athlete and became the first African American varsity player at the high school. He excelled on the football field and in the classroom. He contributed to the winning of many games and brought honor to the school and to himself. Oscar Anderson who played with the B-football team also brought honor to the school and himself. The fourteen students can be credited with keeping the door open for other African American students to walk through and pursue their education in an integrated school environment. The decision by

---

[7]   Reference: Gra'delle Duncan, Killeen: Tale of Two Cities, pp.127, 128.

the Killeen Independent School District to integrate the upper level students in grades 9 through 12 into Killeen High School resulted in the Killeen school district becoming the first school district in Central Texas to integrate even before it was required by law.

The table below was provided through the courtesy of Betsy Hilliard, a retired school nurse. This copy was taken from her school materials she saved and was originally produced by the superintendent's office. It shows the enrollment of Marlboro School in the Killeen school district during the 1954-1955 through 1957-1958 school years.

TABLE 1
Killeen Independent School District-Membership by grades for the years
1954-55 through 1957-58

Grade	1954-55		1955-56		1956-57		1967-58	
	White	Negro	White	Negro	White	Negro	White	Negro
1	460	12	493	20	480	16	489	25
2	578	15	585	19	534	26	595	19
3	438	11	556	16	554	24	596	26
4	285	08	399	05	488	21	556	22
5	340	06	301	10	362	10	526	21
6	319	05	340	09	304	14	391	11
7	382	06	312	05	319	12	332	12
8	265	06	256	06	282	07	295	12
9	186		202	05	226	09	286	11
10	129		183	03			220	06
11	115		105		153	04	162	04
12	100		112		104	01	124	01
TOTAL	3,417	69	3,844	08	3,995	151	4,596	170

Table 1 shown above was shared through the courtesy of Betsy Hilliard retired school nurse. The data above was supplied by the superintendent's office in 1958

The road to educational inclusion of African American students at the junior high level was accomplished when forty-five seventh and eighth grade students from Marlboro School integrated Nolan Junior High School in January 1961. Marlboro School then became Marlboro Elementary School, serving grades 1-6, and later, K-6 grades. The elementary-aged student population of the Marlboro school continued to increase, and in 1961, four classrooms, an office and clinic areas, a kitchen and cafeteria were added. This addition allowed for increased student population and additional faculty and staff members. After the seventh and eighth graders enrolled at Nolan Junior high school, Principal Jackson remained in the dual role of teacher and principal until May, 1963. In the fall at the beginning of the 1963 school term, Dock Jackson, Jr. became a full-time principal of the school and served in this position for the next six years. In the meantime another expansion to the school occurred in 1966 when three additional classrooms were constructed.

Students began integrating school campuses after the law to integrate schools passed; but integrating school faculties did not keep pace in doing so. Marlboro Elementary School's faculty remained predominantly minority until its closing in June 1969. Prior to June 1969, three elementary schools had begun the integration of their faculties. Meadows Elementary School, which is located on the Fort Hood Installation, was the first elementary school to integrate its faculty with the hiring to its campus Ida Wright, a military dependent. In 1966, Alice Douse also a military dependent and a former sixth-grade teacher at Marlboro Elementary School integrated the faculty of Pershing Park Elementary School as its first African American teacher. Joe Lockhart was Principal of Pershing Park at that time. In 1969, Doris Washington and Clarence Brown, also former teachers of Marlboro Elementary, joined the faculty at Pershing Park. Hewiue Montgomery, a military dependent joined the Pershing Park faculty a few years later. Fannie Kay, a military dependent integrated the faculty of East Ward Elementary School during the late 1960s; and Marie Henderson also a military dependent became the second African American teacher to join Meadows' faculty.

During the 1968 school year, Marlboro Elementary School's student enrollment and the faculty and staff were predominantly minority. Federal representatives from the U.S. Health, Education and Welfare Department visited the school district and conducted an investigation related to integration. In January, 1969 the announcement was made that Marlboro Elementary Schools would close at the end of the school year. The decision was made that the students, faculty and staff would be assigned to other campuses. Parents voiced their concerns to the Superintendent and the School Board to include the safety of students leaving their neighborhood and having to walk to another neighborhood to attend school, but to no avail. The closing and transition of students, faculty members and staff proceeded as planned.

The 1969-70 school year began as scheduled with more integrated elementary school campuses and classrooms in the district of students, faculty and staff than ever before. The Marlboro Elementary School's former principal remained with the school district in his new role for a few years. He later found employment with administrative responsibilities in another school district. Marlboro Elementary School was later re-opened and operated as an integrated school until 2003, when in February, the entire school moved to Ira Cross Elementary, a newly constructed school within the school district. Marlboro School remained the property of the school district and was used for administrative offices. On August 24, 2008, the Killeen Independent School District Board of Trustees rededicated the Marlboro Elementary School as the *Dock Jackson, Jr. Professional Learning Center* in recognition of the school's first principal, Dock Jackson, Jr., who dedicated 17 years of service there.

CHAPTER 10

Celebrating Our Community Trailblazers

—៣—

Why Celebrate?

Alice Douse

Establishing a community for African Americans and later integrating residents within the total citizenry has added value to the population and to the progress of the city in which we now live. From 1940 to the dawning of this New Millennium, the progress of the Killeen area has shown continuous growth and the African American population has made a contribution to that growth. We shared our skills, abilities, talents, ideas, creativity, knowledge, work ethic, labor, economic resources and a rich culture with the community. We celebrate the trailblazers for their faith, vision, courage, perseverance, service, loyalty and accomplishments as they began to build a community and make a better life for their families. The residents of the forties, fifties and sixties created the path that formed an African American community and endured the challenges they encountered by helping one another.

We celebrate the community spirit that was adopted by willing and supportive African American families during each of following decade. Eventually, this resulted in African Americans becoming valuable contributors to a diverse city in its process of change. When we think about the courage of our trailblazing families and learned of the evidence of their accomplishments it created a spirit of hope for the residents who arrived after them. It encouraged newly arriving families to work together and joined the efforts that were in progress, and to siege the opportunities to serve and be involved in matters that impacted African Americans lives and the entire city. New trailblazers were produced during each decade in various endeavors by using their intellect and abilities, their gifts and talents and their ideas and skills in their service to the community. Our youth also became trailblazing students in school, at church, and in the community. Students pursued leadership position in organizations or in class elections and succeeded. There were many more than the few listed here. For examples. Raymond Pearcey, Jr. was the first African American elected president of the Killeen High School Student Council. Over the years students continue to excel academically. Eddie Jenia Wright and Brand'ee Jewel Milton earned top honors of valedictorian of each of their graduation classes and became the first African American at Ellison High School and at Shoemaker High School respectively to attain this achievement. Some students achieved athletically. Gwendolyn Wilkerson, Killeen High School first African American majorette and Tommie Harris a graduate of Ellison High School are among those who excelled athletically. Killeen High School students Adrian Hankins excelled in music and Leonard Freeman excelled in art. There have been other student achievers in different areas of giftedness.

We celebrate every person who contributed service and hope in various ways that produced a better city in which to live. Each individual and family has had a role in the legacy that we hope to leave to the community and its surrounding neighbors. Each contribution is an important part of our history and heritage as African Americans. There will continue to be trailblazers in new services, new honors and new accomplishments within this city. We also celebrate churches and schools for their essential and significant contributions to the growth and progress of the city; to the spiritual life of the families; and to the development of responsible youth by allowing them to gain the knowledge necessary to successfully achieve their aspirations. Many of the students of the forties, fifties, sixties and beyond became leaders in the communities in which they reside and are touching and impacting the lives of our next generation of youths in positive ways. such as: Dr. Christine Heath Diggs, Elise O'Neal Spears, Cathy Douse Harris, Mabel May Robinson, Linda Smith Pelton, John Campbell, Rev. Charles Maze and Charles O'Neal, Attorney Michael Nelson and others that we cannot list here.

Faith, prayers, cooperation and service have brought us to a better community. Our highest praise, honor and gratitude go to God our Father and to Jesus Christ our Lord and Savior for the guidance, protection, provisions, encouragement and wisdom given us on our journey through successes and challenges. You have read about the trailblazers and community builders presented in *TAPESTRY.* We also know that surely there are others who are not included in this book but are trailblazers indeed. For example: Dr. Altrac Ruth Tomlin, Killeen Independent School District's first African American counselor at Killeen High School. Gladys Sharkey, the district's first African American librarian at Nolan Middle School; Hazel Carter, the first African American counselor at Ellison High School and Eltra Youngblood Abernathy, the district's first African American coach are all trailblazers in their own rights. Therefore we celebrate all African Americans whose experiences, service, educational achievements, positive accomplishments and economical resources contributed to progress and a better community in which to live.

In 2007, Bernard "Babatunde" Jones and his wife, Johnnie, during the celebration of Killeen's 125th Birthday, compiled and published issue 5 vol. II of the "Afrikan Posta"[8] his Afrikan-American newspaper, with information about African American contributions and service to the Killeen and Central Texas communities and region. Having read that issue, we know and can say, "Yes, there are many others, in addition to our *TAPESTRY* Project participants, who are trailblazers and community builders.

Community involvement that results in community building is an honorable service and a rewarding contribution. Its role has been valuable in transforming our community and its neighboring communities in growth, diversity, and progress. The involvement

---

8   Bernard "Babatunda" Jones, "Afrikan Posta" Newspaper, Issue #5 Volume II, May 2007.

of families working together in community building is key to the success of this project. African-Americans proud knowing that they, too, have been making their contributions as community builders to the progress of a city which they have chosen to call home.

Index

—m—

M

N

O

P

R

S

CPSIA information can be obtained
at www.ICGtesting.com
Printed in the USA
FFOW05n0028090217